Gender and Soul
in Psychotherapy

Nathan Schwartz-Salant and Murray Stein, editors

Chiron Publications ● **Wilmette, Illinois**

The Chiron Clinical Series
ISBN 0-933029-51-9

© 1992 by Chiron Publications. All rights reserved. No part of this publication may be reproduced, stored in a retrieval system, or transmitted in any form, by any means, electronic, mechanical, photocopying, recording, or otherwise, without the prior written permission of the publisher, Chiron Publications, 400 Linden Avenue, Wilmette, Illinois 60091.

Printed in the United States of America.

Book design by Elaine Hill.

Library of Congress Cataloging-in-Publication Data

Gender and soul in psychotherapy / Nathan Schwartz-Salant and Murray Stein, editors. — (The Chiron clinical series)
  p. cm. — (The Chiron clinical series)
  Includes bibliographical references.
  ISBN 0-933029-51-9 : $19.95
  1. Anima (Psychoanalysis) 2. Animus (Psychoanalysis) 3. Jung, C. G. (Carl Gusav), 1875-1939. 4. Psychotherapy. I. Schwartz-Salant, Nathan, 1938- II. Stein, Murray, 1943- . III. Series.
  RC506.G45 1992
  150.19'54 — dc20

91-618
CIP

Contents

GENDER AND SOUL IN PSYCHOTHERAPY

Anima and Animus in Jung's Alchemical Mirror

Nathan Schwartz-Salant

Introduction

I do not find the concepts anima and animus to be clinically useful. I believe they are, in large measure, aspects of a way in which Jung tried to work out a very deep vision that was part of his descent into the unconscious after his break with Freud. He recorded parts of this vision in his "Seven Sermons to the Dead." It is a vision of life in its pleromatic fullness as contrasted to and linked with its space-time form. But to label something as anima or animus, *or even to think that way with a patient* has rarely proven useful in my clinical experience; instead, it has usually been distancing in a destructive way.

Yet I do know that I have an anima, and some of my deepest experiences concern an inner sense of linking with a feminine figure who I know as truly Other and with whom I feel enlivened, purposeful, challenged, and whole. I experience my anima as urging me to speak from experience honestly and to question the language I have introjected and face the consequences, whatever they may be. A feeling of desire has been usually associated with these inner states. I also know

Nathan Schwartz-Salant, Ph.D., is a Jungian analyst, trained in Zurich, Switzerland, and in private practice in New York City. He is the author of *Narcissism and Character Transformation, The Borderline Personality: Vision and Healing*, numerous clinical papers, and is co-editor of the Chiron Clinical Series. He is president of the Salant Foundation and director of the Center for Analytical Perspectives (CAP).

1

women who have had similar experience with an inner male figure. But I have also had the experience of at-oneness and sense of mystery, desire, and purpose from connecting to an inner male figure, also felt as Other, and there are women who have had corresponding experiences with inner female figures.

Gender differences exist, but I do not know how to codify them *as aspects of a male or female unconscious*. If I allocate a quality of continuity of experience and embodiment to the feminine figures and a more expansive sense to the masculine ones, or an impetus toward relatedness and intimacy to the female figures and an impetus toward penetration and differentiation to the male ones, I soon find these categories to be perhaps reasonable descriptions of the varying strengths of men and women, but wrong as images of their unconscious psyches. Such gendered conceptions of structure might have been more correct fifty years ago, but are far less correct today. So I have asked myself what, for me, is the real issue clothed in the gendered terms *anima* and *animus*? Is the anima/animus theory a historical anachronism, deeded to the past and Jung's *Zeitgeist*, to German Romanticism, and essentially useful to Jung as he worked out his myth in his time? If so, why can't I shake free of it? Is this only an issue of cowardice, a fear of losing these cherished objects which give a sense of kinship with Jung and certain other analysts who have been important to me?

I am deeply committed to Jung, and I know the difference between having access to my anima and having this experience degenerate into either projections or spiritualizations. My colleagues make explicit use of anima and animus in their clinical thinking, and these concepts seem not to be problematic to many. For example, John Beebe (1984) used the anima concept in a novel way to explore his notion of the father's anima. As an example of the importance these ideas hold, Ann Ulanov speaks for many Jungians when she says, "The contrasexual archetypes galvanize the deepest issues of individuation. . . . These are the archetypes that open onto the Self in the individuation journey. They touch all aspects of our human life: our past experiences and future hopes, our sexuality, our bodies, our souls, our sense of purpose or purposelessness" (1982, p. 75). There was a time when I would have said the same things. I know the importance of the inner feminine in myself, especially as it differs from my maternal experiences. I know many women who have had a similar experience of the inner masculine (and, by the way, many who have not, for whom this way of thinking makes little sense and borders on misogyny).

While the notion of a man's anima makes sense, the notion of the animus in a woman is a more jarring concept, generally something I feel is a foreign term imposed on a woman's material. The widespread dissatisfaction among Jungians with the notion that only men have an anima and only women have an animus has been the source of many hours of reflection. I have never liked this "extension" of Jung's thinking, and, given my general reserve about anima and animus as useful concepts in clinical practice, it has not been easy to sort out why I even care about it.

Is the problem, as James Hillman suggests in his book *Anima*, one of *Zeitgeist*? Is our "task now to discover what descriptions suit [the anima] in this time and how she is mythologizing today?" (Hillman 1985, p. 13). Hillman has rethought Jung's anima concept with great care and effort. He has differentiated anima from eros and from feeling and has uncovered how with "Jung's de-libidinizing of the very basis of psychoanalytic theory, the archetypal premise of the unconscious shifted from Aphrodite to Hermes-Mercurius, and the soul's fluxions were removed from the sexual eroticism and personal concretism of Aphrodite" (ibid., p. 31). He tells us that "Aphrodite still awaits recognition for the influence she has upon analytical psychology's notion of anima" (ibid., p. 29). Hillman is arguing against the long-standing identification of anima and eros, while also trying to do justice to the erotic. "If anima is defined as the eros factor, then we are always bound to assume that sexual excitation is a soul message and cannot be denied—who would deny the call of soul?" (ibid., p. 32). Yet he must recognize that "though anima is not eros, her first inclination is toward love. So she seduces in order to be turned on, set afire, illumined. So she makes advances in order to move pure reflection into connection" (ibid., p. 33).

Hillman is especially critical of the idea that only a man has an anima and a woman an animus. "The *per definitionem* absence of anima in women is a deprivation of a cosmic principle with no less consequences in the practice of analytical psychology than has been the theory of penis deprivation in the practice of psychoanalysis" (Hillman 1985, p. 63). And, "Why do we call the same behavior in one sex 'anima' and in the other 'naturally feminine' or 'shadow'? What effect does this have on the psychological differences between the sexes, if the same image in a man and a woman is in his case ennobled as a soul-image (anima) while in hers it is part of the realm of shadow?" (ibid., p. 59). Strong words indeed! How can one disagree? Yet, disagreement there is, and from no less a competent and dedicated thinker than Elie Humbert.

Humbert's statement that "contrary to what many advocate, the anima is not a model of the feminine, just as the animus is not a model of the masculine" would surely agree with Hillman's, but his conclusion—"consequently, woman does not have an anima and man does not have an animus"—could not differ more strongly (Humbert 1988, p. 127). "Those who claim otherwise," he tells us, "desexualize the mediating function" (ibid.). For Humbert, the main issue is *desire* as the mediating function between male and female, ego-consciousness and the archetypes. "Sexual identity occurs in particular as one becomes aware of desire. Even though he does not use the term 'desire,' Jung recognized the images of desire in anima and animus" (ibid., p. 59). One's sexual identity could not exist if men had an animus and women had an anima: "The anima and the animus . . . organize everything that relate to the sexual identity of the subject, in particular, oral and anal eroticism, fantasies of castration, and Oedipal relationships" (ibid., p. 56). Thus, for Humbert, to locate the animus in a man and the anima in a woman would undermine the essential function of desire and the fact (albeit not very explicit) that, for Jung, *desire* is an essence of his anima/animus theory. This may be merely a French fascination with desire, yet Hillman demonstrates an awareness of the function of desire in the anima, even though he tries to limit its signifying function. Perhaps the quandry is to be found in Hillman's apparent refusal to recognize desire as an essential element of animus, which he allocates to spirit. But things are not so simple; Hillman and Humbert are only two of many Jungian thinkers whose views could be similarly opposed. What is the conflict here? The entire anima/animus question nags at me, and I feel somewhere that Humbert is on the right track. This is reflected in Hillman's (1985) last chapter, entitled "The Anima in the Syzygy."

In a sense, this chapter reads like an afterthought that came to him as something of a shock. Here Hillman must come to terms with Jung's insistence that anima and animus are parts of a syzygy. Jung says, "Anyone, therefore, who does not know the . . . significance of the *syzygy* motif . . . can hardly claim to say anything about the concept of the anima" (1954, par. 115). Hillman comments: "The implications of this are staggering, so let us move cautiously" (1985, p. 171). His cautious approach is to think of the syzygy as an archetypal pattern that demands that we never think of anima or animus alone. "We cannot take any stand regarding anima without, *horrible dictu*, taking up an animus position. There is no *other* vantage point toward either than the other" (ibid., p. 171).

For Hillman, the syzygy means that anima and animus are always in "tandem," forming a "hermaphroditic consciousness," which

> works in the following way. . . . When we feel we have caught a glimpse of anima in an image, mood, or projection, the immediate next question is "where is the animus?" Most likely it is in the perceiving ego itself that has made the observation possible in the first place (i.e. we see the one through the other). Thus *the observation is also a projection*, part of the mutual fantasy system of the anima-animus which the ego does not recognize. (1985, p. 177)

What Hillman has done is to work the syzygy into an *implied* relationship between anima and animus and to lean toward anima as soul and animus as spirit-ego. In other words, the syzygy has become a kind of hidden parameter, running things in the background and creating "endless tandems" between anima and animus (ibid.). Others, too, have employed the syzygy in this way. For example, through such reflections on the syzygy, Katherine Bradway has brought order to a good deal of her clinical experience (1982, pp. 275).

This "tandem" approach does not answer the implications of the importance of the syzygy which *are* "staggering." It is in the syzygy, the divine image of pairing, that the true essence of Jung's anima/animus theory resides.[1] We find this essence not in the syzygy as a background ordering pattern, but as an imaginal reality whose *presence* must be sensed, felt, or seen.

Desire inheres in the field of the syzygy in which there is no next question but an imaginal simultaneity. The syzygy weaves together the factors called anima and animus in Jung's theory. The soul lives in the syzygy and is made or discovered there. For me, the central significance of the syzygy answers the question of why I can recognize anima in myself and others and animus at times in women, while thinking in this separable way often feels distancing and awkward.

The Syzygy, Space, and Difference

Andrew Samuels very astutely argues that, from Jung's anima and animus theory, which unfortunately "hamstrings us by its insistence on contrasexuality," we can "extract the theme of *difference*" (1989, p. 97). It is not very fashionable to talk of difference since differences between the sexes has been so compromised by patriarchal bias. The French psychoanalyst Luce Irigaray notes that "sexual difference is one of the important questions of our age, if not in fact the burning issue. . . . But wherever I turn, whether to philosophy, science, or religion, I find that this underlying and increasingly insistent question remains silenced" (1987, p. 118). But it was not silent in Jung.

An important aspect of the syzygy and the phenomenology of difference concerns our deeply ingrained notions of space. While one can attribute different approaches toward space (Erickson 1963, p. 106), and also different images of space, to males and females, the question of difference really requires that we go beyond such separated parts. This new conception of space can be found in the syzygy.

The sociologist Mino Vianello, while not claimed any genetic truth for his arguments, but rather the societal records of millennia, has argued that a female's conception of space is "ovular." By this he means that women give priority not only to intimacy and emotions, but also to what he terms the law of the situation, that is, the attempt to solve problems pragmatically (Vianello 1989). He claims that anything that has to do with an open space to be manipulated is typically male, and he argues that differentiations in spatial conceptions greatly influence thinking.

The importance of space and difference has been underscored by Irigaray, who states that "in order to live and think through this difference, we must reconsider the whole question of *space* and *time*. . . . The transition to a new age in turn necessitates a new perception and a new conception of *time* and *space*, or *occupation of place*" (1987, p. 119).

Carolyn Bynum has shown, in her study of female saints of the Middle Ages, that these women's lives did not follow the pattern of liminality, in Victor Turner's sense, pertaining to male experience (Bynum 1984, p. 108). She is careful not to overgeneralize her results, but they do suggest what I have also noted in clinical practice. Namely, men, having entered the liminal space of the syzygy, will tend to exit in a far sharper way than women, whose lives have more continuity with this sense of space. The women in Bynum's study appeared to show less need for an entrance-exit quality of liminality which men appear to require (ibid., p. 109). Men appear to need more structure than women. This may be rooted, as Bynum contends following Nancy Chodorow's research, in a man's greater need to separate from his mother (ibid., p. 114).

But transcending the effects of spatial distinctions, whatever these may be, will never be achieved through the integration of one or the other attitude toward space. Rather, a new awareness of space, the space of the syzygy, is required.

Jung's major contribution to the central issue of difference lies in his recognition of the syzygy, the hermaphroditic pattern to which people tend to relate differently, yet in which their attitudes toward and perceptions of gender roles can change. It is in this kind of space that integration of Jung's anima and animus occurs. This integration process is not one of heroically splitting one part from another, but rather, recognizing the true mystery of difference.

Once our orientation centers upon the field of the syzygy rather than some allocation of its parts, it appears that gender is not very useful. In a sense, it would be better to do without these gendered terms, *anima* and *animus*, or call them by other names. Perhaps Greek letters would be more appropriate, as in Bion's (1970) alpha and beta functions, notions that are intentionally empty of associative material. Issues such as container-contained or processes such as the alchemical *solve et coagula* (dissolve and coagulate), are even more appropriate. Yet the field of the syzygy, while relativizing the meaning of difference between the sexes, especially as its sense of space is embraced, also retains difference, largely through the mysterious workings of desire.

Desire, as Irigaray says, "requires a sense of attraction: a change in the interval or the relations of nearness or distance between subject and object" (1987, p. 120). This is the mystery of desire; its inchoate nature can be destructive if it obliterates the gap or interval within the union state, yet properly contained, desire creates and fires union. Irigaray speaks eloquently of the dynamics of what seems to me to be the syzygy, noting that if there is a "double desire," man and woman capable of desiring and being desired, then "the positive and negative poles divide themselves among the two sexes (creating) a chiasmus or double loop in which each can move out towards the other and back to itself" (ibid., p. 121).

To recognize difference is one thing, but to allocate different qualities of male and female development or strengths as elements of the so-called contrasexual qualities of the unconscious is another. Women who reach a point in which the "critical experience becomes not intimacy but choice, creating an encounter with self that clarifies the understanding of responsibility and truth" (Gilligan 1982, p. 163) are not necessarily developing their so-called contrasexual qualities. They are developing a capacity for separation. Men who deal with "intimacy as the transformative experience . . . through which adolescent identity turns into the generativity of adult love and work" (ibid., p. 164) are not necessarily dealing with qualities of the other sex. Rather, pairs such as intimacy/separation exist as parts of the pattern of the syzygy. To split them into conscious and unconscious attitudes of women and men is to repeat the patriarchal prejudice toward solar-rational thinking. Seen through the diffuse, linking quality of lunar light, they coexist in both sexes, with a capacity for intimacy certainly more natural for women, as is separation for men. Both are simultaneously there, but not in equal strength. However, unless the cultural canon causes them to be sharply split and one becomes repressed, they will not necessarily occupy positions in the conscious and unconscious aspects of psyche. They may be simultaneously present in the unconscious, or they may align vertically, perhaps split, but side by side rather than conscious-unconscious.

Parts and Unity: Relations Per Se

Thinking in terms of a "man's anima" and a "woman's animus" (or even of each having both anima and animus), while perhaps once useful in Jung's cultural-historical context, is obsolete, rendered so by a paradigm shift in our culture from the analysis of the parts of a process and their relationships to the *relations per se*. This universe of relations is an aspect of what David Bohm called the implicate order (Comfort 1984). Perceiving relations per se forces us to think differently, to enter into an imaginal space, different from Cartesian constructs, a space in which matter and spirit are not separate and opposite but part of a same subtle universe. Who other than Jung himself would have stood more firmly for this shift? Jung's life work represented a paradigm shift away from a mechanistic conception of psyche as comprised of historical elements and their distortion through repression, ambivalence, and splitting. While Jung recognized that conceiving psychic life as comprised of separable parts is necessary "if we are to gain reliable knowledge of the world," he also stresses that

> it has the disadvantage of breaking up, or obscuring, the universal relationship of events so that a recognition of the greater relationship, i.e., of the unity of the world, becomes more and more difficult. Everything that happens, however, happens in the same "one world" and is part of it. For this reason events must possess an a-priori aspect of unity. (1955–1956, par. 662)

Jung related this unity, Bohm's implicate order (which is the same as the *unus mundus* or the pleroma in Jung's writings) to the idea of the subtle body. And at numerous times, he postulated that anima and animus were parts of a syzygy, a union of opposites that can be known in the field of the subtle body (Schwartz-Salant 1986, 1989). This link to an archetypal background was seen by Jung as essential:

nobody can stand the total loss of the archetype. When that happens, it gives rise to that frightful "discontent in our culture," where nobody feels at home because a "father" and "mother" are missing. Everyone knows the provisions that religion has always made in this respect. (Jung 1954, par. 141)

Thus Jung underscores what I find to be his major contribution to psychotherapy: one must deal with the separable parts of the psyche, as in developmental models; yet, these parts must be recognized to contain an "a-priori aspect of unity" and be related to the archetypal structures of the "one world" from which they stem. Otherwise, we lose the meaning that this world alone provides. Jung writes:

Anyone . . . who does not know the universal distribution and significance of the *syzygy* motif in the psychology of primitives, in mythology, in comparative religion, and in the history of literature, can hardly claim to say anything about the concept of the anima. His knowledge of the psychology of the neuroses may give him some idea of it, but it is only a knowledge of its general phenomenology that could open his eyes to the real meaning of what he encounters in individual cases, often in pathologically distorted form. (1954, par. 115)

Our focus upon the "psychology of the neuroses" (for example, in terms of developmental failures) may explain a good deal but, in truth, can also obscure "the real meaning of what [one] encounters in individual cases." I have dealt with this issue elsewhere in reference to clinical experience with abandonment depression (1990), projective identification (1988), and ways that analysts tend to split from a patient's madness (1989). Also, much that appears, for example, as sexual desire and an incestuously toned drive for another person, is actually a desire for the syzygy, either as an event in a shared, subtle space or as an inner union (Schwartz-Salant 1984).

John Layard's study on the incest taboo influenced Jung's thinking in "The Psychology of the Transference" and his understanding of the *Rosarium Philosophorum*, the alchemical text which formed the backbone of that study. Layard stated that every instinctive desire must ultimately be satisfied, and what cannot be satisfied in the flesh must be satisfied in the spirit (1945, p. 282). He published another paper, in 1959, entitled "On Psychic Consciousness," which goes beyond his previous conclusions. In this later paper, Layard discusses the play of energy in the "third areas" that the incest taboo creates and, in particular, the "hermaphroditic consciousness" that can thus be created. He describes how, within these third areas and their creative ambiguousness, "male may at any moment become female, and female become male" (1959, p. 283). It is such third areas that the syzygy signifies and in which incest can be symbolically lived. This is a ritual space, a place or location of transformation.

The Syzygy

The syzygy is an archetypal pattern, depicted in mythology as pairs of gods, or as a mortal and a god when it is closer to a human sphere. It is not an image of the relations between people, but of relations per se. Its locus is the implicate order or pleroma, not the space-time world. To imagine relations per se is a bit like trying to picture four-dimensional space or see music and the intervals between notes. It is like attempting to look at the nature of the love between two people and describe *its* qualities separate from the people that it joins; it is not *their* love that would be described, but the love that joins them, the linking quality that has its own life and own sphere of operations.

The life of the syzygy can be inferred from its effects upon people. We can gain an imaginary glimpse of its presence in the space between people and recognize that it goes through a considerable change of forms. For example, the *Rosarium*, at the outset, portrays two separate people, king and queen, touching left hands. This scene eventually develops into a hermaphrodite which goes through its own transformations. For the alchemists, this development is a great achievement, and it may be seen as a linking of parts of people or parts of an individual, back to a sense of at-oneness, to the "one unity."

The hermaphroditic image in the *Rosarium* is a way of symbolizing relations per se, and each successive image takes on a more developed form, closer to the pleromatic potential of oneness, purified of incestuous and compulsive fusion drives. In Winnicottian terms, the transformed field becomes one of "object usage" rather than one dominated by splitting and projective identification (Eigen 1981, p. 415; Schwartz-Salant 1989), although this process only reaches fruition in the *rubedo* stage, represented in the last ten pictures of the *Rosarium*.

The syzygy is known from numerous images and stories. In the myth of Cupid and Psyche, we find the sacred union existing first in a state of unconsciousness, in the darkness of Cupid's palace. The blissful union is lost when Psyche attempts to become conscious of her beloved Cupid; she seeks the union again through her terrible ordeals, ending with the ascent of the pair to Olympus. The divine syzygy may thus have gained a permanent place in even a patriarchally structured unconscious, but not yet on earth. We know of the syzygy in numerous other places, in the ecstatic embrace of Shiva and Shakhti, in the alchemical *coniunctio*, in the quests of King Arthur's knights, in courtly love, and often in secret form, in the unconscious between two people when the transference and countertransference process has become enlivened. The syzygy, once the center of mysteries of union in the ancient worlds of Isis and Osiris, Tammuz and Ishtar, Kybelle and Attis, and perhaps, although we are never explicitly told, Dionysus and Persephone in Eleusis, went underground with the demise of the religion of the Great Goddess. It kept up a shadowy life in magic and the occult, and in alchemy.

The syzygy can also be known as an internal state, for example, as a union between the ego and images felt as powerfully numinous. These images will usually be portrayed as the opposite sex, but this is also and perhaps primarily a symbolic representation of what is totally "Other" (Samuels 1989, p. 103). In this union experience, individuals of either sex have known a purely inner state of at-oneness and completion. The Other can be the personal mother or father, or other figures, but the union experience cannot be split into personal and archetypal factors. Tendencies to do so stem from a particularly narcissistic development of personality, a development that is relatively devoid of dealing with incest issues.

But the *syzygy* also comprises an experience to be had by two people within an interactive field that their psyches *constellate*. I use this word because it would be incorrect to say that the field is only the sum of the parts, or to even say that it is the result of the interaction of the parts. The latter would be closer to experience, especially if one were to underscore a central feature of the union experience, namely that it releases energy much as in nuclear fusion. In the syzygy, one deals not only with a merger of parts, but with a particular kind of interaction in which a genuine fusion occurs. In alchemy, this is symbolized, for example, by an arrow striking the side of Mercurius. The energy released can be used for good or ill, as in so-called white or black magic. What makes the process of projective identification both difficult to manage and potentially creative is that energy is released in an unconscious way that can lead to compulsion and splitting, but also to a new and transformative awareness including the experience of being contained by another person.

Even this understanding of the syzygy is too limited. Within its precinct, both persons can, through imaginal act and grace, interact in a manner that opens their awareness to a new dimension of space, a liminal experience that links to the "gods" and is different in nature from Cartesian constructs. The experience of this space is such that one feels like both participant in and observer of its processes. Thus, the space is not "out there" or "inside." One is part of this space and separate from it. Understanding the paradoxical nature of the space of the syzygy is essential; it allows a fluidity between "inner" and "outer" that an analysis based on the integration of projections cannot otherwise tolerate.

It is, I believe, a patriarchal bias to insist on the incarnation of the syzygy within an individual, as opposed to it being a shared-field experience. The only way to enforce this bias clinically is to insist upon the integration of projections presumably discovered within the interactive field. One thus experiences the countertransference, which may be related to the patient's transference, but only for the purpose of extracting information about the patient. The field per se is not valued in this approach; its delineation into separable parts is the rule. What is "mine" and what is "yours" becomes the central focus, and what is "mine" becomes a source of information about "you." In this approach, psychic marriage exists at best as a useful state to be dissolved and at worst as a regrettable countertransference. However, the field is also a phenomenon that can transform and engender structure, as if it had a magnetic quality that gathers in split-off, "mad parts" of psyche. This integration process usually eludes approaches that are rooted in the separability and interiority of psyche.

The issue of desire and the consequent unavoidability of a gendered syzygy became stumbling blocks for Jung's theory. Apparently he also found it unsuitable to allow an interactive field that included desire since the dangers of fusion and participation mystique, which blurs an individual self-concept, are considerable. To avoid these inherent dangers, Jung essentially jettisoned the alchemical model initially used in "The Psychology of the Transference" and moved to a model based on taking back projections.

The Anima/Animus Theory and the "Seven Sermons to the Dead"

There is no better place to read of Jung's experiences leading to the anima/animus theory than in his "Seven Sermons to the Dead" (Heisig 1972, p. 215). This "non-canonical" text, written during Jung's dark years (1913–1917) when he explored the unconscious after his break with Freud, is a document of inestimable value for Jungians. His language is the archaic speech of the unconscious; it shows the levels of depth he embraced, and, along with other writings in his "Red Book," it formed the core that his life's work then attempted to fill out. In it, he has recorded his experiences of the pleroma and its essential difference from the distinctiveness of created beings. This was to become a leitmotif in his later work, spelled out most explicitly in *Mysterium Coniunctionis* (Jung 1955–1956, par. 662).

In "The Seven Sermons," Jung speaks of the "Mother"—the spirituality which is to be set "between heaven and earth"—and of the "Phallos"—the sexuality, also set "between heaven and earth" (Jung 1972, p. 387). These may have been precursors of the anima and animus.

The sermons show that Jung was deeply aware of the difficulties of linking pleromatic existence with space-time life. We find him insisting on the necessity of differentiating male and female sexuality and spirit (Jung 1972, p. 387). But the virtues of distinctiveness *and* communion are emphasized: "In communion let every man submit to others," and "In singleness every man may come to himself and avoid slavery" (1972, p. 388). This is a point of view that he did not fully develop as he later veered strongly toward distinctiveness and away from communion. The communion, especially through unconscious fusion fields dominated by desire, can produce a form of psychic "slavery" in which two people can be tied together in a knot of affects that possess them, the negative aspect of the hermaphrodite.

Did Jung to some extent abandon his vision or reduce it fit it into a scientific and expanded Christian framework? I do not think so; it seems to me that he attempted to bring his vision into historical reality and, in the process used what he could of existing concepts and attitudes. He often reworked them, as we find in his treatment of Christianity, and at times, this work and its clinical relevance appear to be his main endeavor, while his visions were of initial significance, at best, and, at worst, a fateful transit through madness. But Jung was a man who knew something deeply, whose soul was imprinted by the passion of his experience.

One could liken Jung's anima/animus theory to scientific practice, in which one attempts to solve an equation whose general solution is far too complicated. Here, instead, certain approximations are made, and the question then is how good these approximations are, what might be the limits of their domain of validity. Nowadays this domain has certainly diminished, necessitating a new "approximation" which brings the syzygy into a more explicit focus.

Clearly, Jung felt the need for parts (anima and animus) to be related to a representation of the "one world" and found the link in the syzygy (1954, par. 115). If Jung's commitment had been only to explore the psyche's phenomenology in terms of apparent masculine imagery in a woman and feminine imagery in a man, there would have been no need to postulate the ordering capacity of the syzygy. One could then study "the anima" or "the animus" and essentially do away with an overriding form that encompasses them both. Jung, however, did not do this, and I believe he followed the path he chose because of his personal and clinical experience.

The Syzygy and Container-Contained

Let us consider experiences of the syzygy within a field of oneness, rather than in its projected parts. This essential archetypal pattern can be experienced, especially if we do not emphasize the analysis of projections. In the interactive field of the syzygy, there is a dynamic weaving of energies that flow back and forth between two people. I think it is likely that Bion's notion of container-contained, while derived from different sources of experience, may be rooted in the syzygy (1970, pp. 72ff). Each person must be able to give and receive, to experience to some degree being a container for the other person and then being contained. It is as if one were alternately the yang force and then the yin. This process becomes distorted under the impact of splitting and projective identification, and the analyst becomes largely the container and the patient the one whose projections are contained. The reverse is also common, leading to the patient acting-out in ways compelled by his or her introjection of the therapist's split-off contents.

The relationship of container-contained is a daily analytical experience. For instance, an analyst may experience intense dislike for a patient and silently contain such affects while wondering about their meaning. After some time of inner reflection, the analyst may find the patient beginning to speak about a fear of intimacy. In this example, hate has been "held" by the analyst, the hate that was meant to distance from need, and when the patient felt contained, his or her true feelings could emerge.

We know how analysts will fight such processes and attempt interpretations in order to feel contained themselves. In its pathology, the container-contained degenerates into parts, container *and* contained. But in its creative form, rooted in the energies of the syzygy, there is a mutual field of containing and being contained. When we feel contained, we may dissolve our rigidities, lower our shield, and when we are the container, we become more coagulated, imaginally holding the other and providing a form. A sense of at-oneness pervades this process in which container and contained can reverse roles. If one partner rejects the need to feel contained, for instance, if the therapist rejects his or her need to be contained by the patient, the creative, interactive field degenerates into "things." The *field of relations* ceases to have a presence, and a group of related things takes over as the object of consciousness.

A special case of container-contained is found in what Jung would call an anima/animus interaction. For example, a woman's confrontation or independent thought may be experienced by a man as attacking his inner feeling life. Her experienced attack lodges within him in his anima and is contained there in an uncreative merger state. He may experience her as being secretly contemptuous of him while denying it, and, in turn, he will tend to become irritable and moody if not enraged and withdrawn. The anima, Jung says, "softens the man's character and makes him touchy, irritable, moody, jealous, vain, and unadjusted. He is then in a state of 'discontent' and spreads discontent all around him" (1954, par. 144). The man will attempt either to flee the field of battle or else fight back in the form of counterarguments, all to the goal of being seen, i.e., of being the contained one. But if the interaction is to be creative, both people would have to ask a difficult question: How are we both creating this situation? This means giving up the power of "being right" and taking the risk of relinquishing control to an organizing "third thing," here to an unconscious couple merged in hatred. If they succeed in such efforts, actually imagining such a "third force," a rhythmical field can develop in which not only does the woman feel taken in, contained, and the man feels seen, the states readily reverse. Out of such a "communion," they may each also see the parts of their own psyches in their initial, negative fusion state. The woman may see her contempt, and the man see his cowardice or passivity, which invites such attacks. Conversely, the man can experience his contempt and the level on which it functions, and the woman can experience her levels of cowardice or passivity that relate to his contempt. Each can experience both the oneness of the interactive field that the syzygy creates and the separated parts.

The syzygy is always a new event, always something one experiences as if for the first time. It is not without its dangers.

> The subject who offers or permits desire transports and so envelops, or incorporates the other. It is moreover dangerous if there is no third term. Not only because it is a necessary limitation. This third term can show up within the container as the latter's relationship with his or her's own limits: a relationship with the divine, death, the social or cosmic order. If such a third term does not

exist within and for the container, the latter may become *all-powerful*. (Iriga-ray 1987, p. 123)

In the initial four woodcuts of the *Rosarium Philosophorum*, one find this "third term" as the descending holy ghost. Later the *coniunctio* forms and becomes the third thing itself, for it has, to a workable degree, internalized the rhythms of separation and nearness. But fusion, the collapse of the gap or interval created by the third thing, is a constant threat. The woodcuts that follow address this issue, transform-ing the syzygy into a container-contained form that holds out the consummation of desire for its greater goal, harmony between the sexes, and between an individual's male and female polarities. Only in the eighteenth woodcut, the green lion devouring the sun, do we reach a stage of a transformed subtle-body of relations. And what is to come of this? The *Rosarium's* imagery in the nineteenth and twentieth illus-trations may have been illuminating in the sixteenth century, but a sexless virgin prefiguring the enunciation, and a risen, albeit androgy-nous, Christ will hardly do now. We need a new ending for this series, an ending that can only be crafted from relations between the sexes.

Dissolve and Coagulate

Today, the very notion of a "woman's masculine side" and a "man's feminine side" is unacceptable to many. While the gendered notion of behavior may have some validity, its widespread use, culmi-nating in numerous persistent and abortive attempts to link personality characteristics and genetics, is definitely a characteristic of patriarchal culture. Qualities commonly ascribed to the animus, such as seeking security and power in logic and truth (Humbert 1988, p. 58) or as a capacity to focus a solar-rational form of consciousness to complement a woman's more diffuse orientation (Castillejo 1973, pp. 77ff), do not have to be designated as masculine or feminine. There are cultures in which these gendered attributes are reversed, just as Lévi-Strauss has shown that allocation of "sacred" and "profane" as fixed attributes are capable of reversal in a given culture. Jung's anima and animus theory is specifically his mythical form of ordering such pairs of qualities. Qualities covered by this theory include:

solar — lunar
mind — body
consciousness — life
analysis of parts — concern for wholes

active — receptive
power — love
focusing — diffuse
rational — irrational
analysis of parts — relations between parts
one — many
open space — closed space
mind *and* body — subtle-body
heaven — earth
culture — nature
sacred — profane
separation — fusion

The allocation of masculine or feminine has been culturally determined. Jung allocated most of the left side of the above list to the masculine and the right side to the feminine. This is not useful as a fixed approach, as Jung would, of course, agree. But how can we allow such "distinctive" qualities without reifying them?

Within the space of the syzygy, the distinction between feminine and masculine is fluid. The alchemists knew this very well; we find it explicitly spoken of in the *Splendor Solis* (1592), wherein we learn that *male* and *female* are terms for two qualities of a process.

> The philosophers say: "Dissolve [the ore] until it is sublimated, then distill and coagulate it; make it rise and fall; dry it inside and out." The manipulations which they name are without number. . . . Among all these, there belongs to this art the two manipulations [dissolve and coagulate]. The philosophers signify them by the two words Woman and Man, or Milk and Cream.
> (McLean 1981, p. 16)

Thus "male" and "female" refer to the operations of dissolve and coagulate, not to qualities allocated to masculine or feminine. Furthermore, each can, in linkage to the other, coagulate or dissolve. There may be a difference between the dissolving that stems from "man," perhaps as solar consciousness, and that which stems from "woman," perhaps as lunar consciousness. One may take apart a structure, while the other may moisten it with a sense of wholeness and unseen linkages to a truth so that it dissolves. "Man" might represent the coagulation that results from the fixative property of clear thought and a conceptual grasp of psyche, while coagulation may come from "woman" in the form of an inward pull toward a sense of contained space, "ovular" in distinction to "open."

The person who acts as container coagulates his or her own energies, while the one who is contained can dissolve the rigid structures of fear that protect against pain. This rhythm can change, so that whoever was "male" at one time takes over the function of what was "female" at another, and vice versa. With this understanding, the syzygy is not at all confined to men and women. For example, a man I worked with for several years came to the point of wanting to leave therapy. He had had this plan for some time and had accomplished the work he came for, in particular, the repair of several previously destructive relationships with men. During the last session, a quality or texture of the space between us began to carry a strong projective-identification dynamic: he could not help but expect that I, like other male figures of his past, would oppose his initiative. There was considerable new material emerging in his psyche at this time as well. I felt the pull to oppose him by questioning the wisdom of his leaving, but instead of acting on this feeling, I "took in" his conscious attitude. I respected his initiative and allowed it to rest within me, without opposing it. In so doing, I struggled with the projected parts of an "opposing father." I believed in him and his integrity, so this act was possible. That night, he dreamed:

> Dream: *I am atop Nathan, and he encourages me to enter him. I am surprised to see that he has a vagina. When I withdraw my penis, it is covered with gold.*

This dream portrays the subtle-body level of the previous encounter (Schwartz-Salant 1986). I was "feminine" and he "masculine." I was the container and he the contained. In the process, his phallic power is regenerated into a golden phallus. Should we see the dream, instead, in other ways, such as his projection onto me of his anima-self contamination? One could, but such an analysis into parts destructively limits the revitalizing capacity of the syzygy.

Anima, Animus and the Alchemical Queen and King

In the *Rosarium*, the queen rests on the moon and the king on the sun. Jung regards the queen as a man's anima and the sun as a woman's animus. However, as parts in the syzygy, the patterns represented by the king or queen can be felt by either partner, but will be experienced differently by males and females. One or the other cannot be allocated to a man's anima or a woman's animus.

Whatever is seen culturally as feminine can also rest upon the sun, symbolic of rational-discursive awareness, and what is seen as masculine can have the moon, symbolic of the diffuse and wholistic nature of lunar consciousness, as its foundation. The third image in the *Splendor Solis* is akin to the *Rosarium's* second woodcut, the left-hand contact, but this transforms in the sixteenth and seventeenth illustrations of the *Splendor Solis* which shows the queen standing on the sun, while the king stands upon the moon! A similar reversal occurs in the last ten pictures of the *Rosarium*, the *rubedo* phase. In the eleventh illustration, the queen lies atop the male, and the *vinculum* or soul, the linking quality between king and queen, that ascends and descends is now feminine, while it was masculine in the *albedo* phase of the first ten woodcuts.

It is possible that these transformations, from male images rooted on solar foundations and female images upon lunar ones, to changes wherein the lunar is the resting place for the king and the solar for the queen, represent a fundamental quality of the experience of *difference*. Such images portray shifts in consciousness that each person may partake with a feeling of sameness nurtured, paradoxically, by a simultaneous feeling of difference. I believe that the alchemists were working with such issues (Can we really say they were unconscious of what they were doing?) and that this effort was only finally crushed in the Reformation, which carried out the "total censorship of the imaginary" (Couliano 1987, p. 193).

Incest and Jung's Ambivalence Toward the Syzygy

In "The Psychology of the Transference," Jung offers an ambivalent analysis of the syzygy. In its form as the hermaphrodite (the tenth woodcut of the *Rosarium*), he rejects it as the height of an immature mind, a regrettable instance of the alchemists's (supposed) lack of knowledge of the psychological process of projection (1946, par. 533). Could Jung not have known of the exquisite awareness of projection in many Renaissance magicians? Giordano Bruno instructs the magician: "Be careful not to change yourself from manipulator into the tool of phantasms" (*Sigillus sigillorum*, II, 2, p. 193, quoted in Couliano 1987, p. 92). "Bruno," Couliano tells us, "warns every [magician] of phantasms—to regulate and control his emotions and his phantasies lest, believing himself to be their master, he nevertheless becomes dominated by them" (ibid.). Numerous such instances could be sighted. Heightened awareness of projection among the alchemists must have been as highly developed as that of the modern scientist for whom processes of projection into matter take a strong lead along the path of scientific discovery.

The Rebis, for Jung, represents the alchemical process being "stuck in sexuality, as always, when the potentialities of consciousness do not come to the assistance of nature" (Jung 1946, par. 533). He believed that the "sexualism of the hermaphrodite" overpowered consciousness and led to Freud's great emphasis upon sexuality, "an attitude of mind which is just as unsavoury as the old hybrid symbolism" (ibid., pars. 533–535). In fact, Jung finds that the hermaphrodite is always regressive — a totally different position than ones he holds at numerous other times in his collected works (Schwartz-Salant 1984) — and represents a fusion of ego with anima or animus (Jung 1946, par. 545). But for the alchemists, the Rebis was a great achievement.

It is especially with the *Rosarium's* woodcuts six through ten that Jung's analysis sharply detours from the alchemical path, a detour prompted by an apparent horror of incest and the unconscious identity with another's psyche. For Jung, the alchemical images depict the goal of "complete individuation" of an individual (Jung 1946, par. 469). The goal is "the union of the conscious mind or ego personality with the unconscious personified as anima" (ibid., par. 474) to produce a union of the two, the self. This road excludes the positive result of conscious "immersion" in an interactive field. Jung's analysis increasingly must then attack the alchemical mind; the *Rosarium's* imagery ceases to mirror his approach to individuation.

It is especially when Jung turns to the body and the *coniunctio* of body and soul that his analysis reaches for the anima and animus and leaves the alchemical path as a degenerate one. He speaks of the alchemists' failure to distinguish between *corpus* and *spiritus* and of their psychological immaturity (Jung 1946, pars. 497ff). Body, for Jung, is taken as that which gives bounds to the ego personality, the ground of the ego (ibid., par. 502). But for the alchemist, the purifications of "the body" refer to the transformations of a hermaphroditic consciousness away from both concretization and spiritualization into a genuine "third thing" which is not devoid of desire. In a sense, this is the goal of the *rubedo* stage of the last ten woodcuts of the *Rosarium*.

In Jung's analysis of the ninth picture, the soul's return to the hermaphroditic body, soul becomes anima; the successful union of soul and body is one in which anima projections have been withdrawn. Then, Jung says, the anima is no longer "interposed between ego and the world," but instead now functions properly "between ego and the unconscious" (1946, par 504). With this development, an uninflated ego, aware of its difference from the unconscious, can join with the anima; One is born of the Two, the self is born. What has become of the animus?

> Here I must point out that very different rules apply in feminine psychology, since in this case we are not dealing with a function of relationship but, on the contrary, with a discriminative function. Alchemy was . . . mainly a masculine preoccupation and in consequence of this its formulations are for the most part masculine in character. (Ibid., par. 505)

Jung then lists a number of male–female collaborations in alchemy, but apparently his main point about the issue of an anima psychology is intended to hold.

It is in the area of body and sexuality, as well as gender issues, that Jung's anima and animus theory is especially problematic. In his analysis of the *Rosarium*, he is forced to the conclusion that the animus is not a function of relation while the anima is, in distinction to his generally expressed ideas that both anima and animus are to become purely functions, divested of their male or female qualities (Jung 1928, par. 370).

If a therapist fears desire, the tendency will be either to withdraw from an interactive field by resorting to a power position of interpretations or else to fuse with the field in a psychological if not physical acting out. The therapist will fail to maintain the sense of a *gap* between these acts, each of which can destroy the creative potential of desire. Desire is the dynamic force in the syzygy. When it is properly contained through reflection upon the purpose of the analytical encounter, which is to create links to the wounded, possessed, and unknown parts of soul, desire moves those within its domain in a relation of nearness or distance.

Jung's anima and animus theory came up against his own great insights on the value of alchemy for modern psychotherapy. The alchemical model, which includes the wisdom of centuries of thought repressed by patriarchal biases, is alert to the mystery of the syzygy and the complexities of difference. I think we can, in our own historical time, regain the alchemical model and its astute insight into the phenomenon of union, separation, and difference, but in a new way unencumbered by the anima and animus concepts.

Notes

1. In her study, *Lyrical-Analysis: The Unconscious Through* Jane Eyre, Angelyn Spignesi (1990) offers an approach to the phenomenology usually discussed under the rubic

animus, but does so in a new and extremely insightful way, unencumbered by such gendered notions, and always mindful of the syzygy.

References

Beebe, John. 1984. The father's anima as a clinical and as a symbolic problem. *Journal of Analytical Psychology* 29/3.
Bion, W. R. 1970. *Attention and Interpretation*. London: Maresfield.
Bradway, K. 1982. Gender identity and gender roles. In *Jungian Analysis*, M. Stein, Open Court, LaSalle, Ill: pp. 275–293.
Bynum, C. W. 1984. Woman's stories, women's symbols: a critique of Victor Turner's theory of liminality. In *Anthropology and the Study of Religion*, edited by R. L. Moore and F. E. Reynolds, eds. pp. 105–125. Chicago: Center for the Scientific Study of Religion.
Comfort, A. 1984. *Reality and Empathy*. Albany, N.Y.: State University of New York Press.
Couliano, I. P. 1987. *Eros and Magic in the Renaissance*. Chicago: University of Chicago Press.
de Castillejo, I. C. 1973. *Knowing Woman*. New York: Putnam.
Eigen, M. 1981. The area of faith in Winnicott, Lacan and Bion. *International Journal of Psycho-Analyis* 62.
Erikson, E. H. 1963. *Childhood and Society*. New York: Norton.
Gilligan, C. 1982. *In a Different Voice*. Cambridge, Mass.: Harvard University Press.
Heisig, J. 1972. The *VII Sermons*: play and theory. *Spring*.
Hillman, J. 1985. *Anima*. Dallas: Spring Publications.
Humbert, E. 1988. *C. G. Jung*. R. Jalbert, trans. Wilmette, Ill.: Chiron.
Irigaray, L. 1987. Sexual difference. In *French Feminist Thought*, Sean Hand, trans. Toril Moi, ed. London: Blackwell.
Jung, C. G. 1928. The relations between the ego and the unconscious. In CW 7:123–304. Princeton, N.J.: Princeton University Press, 1953.
———. 1946. The psychology of the transference. CW 16:163–338. Princeton, N.J.: Princeton University Press, 1966.
———. 1954. Concerning the archetypes, with special reference to the anima concept. *CW* 9i:54–72. Princeton, N.J.: Princeton University Press, 1968.
———. 1955–1956. *Mysterium Coniunctionis. Collected Works*, vol. 14. Princeton, N.J.: Princeton University Press, 1963.
———. 1972. *Memories, Dreams, Reflections*. New York: Random House.
Layard, J. 1945. The virgin archetype and the incest taboo. In *The Virgin Archetype*. New York: Spring, 1972.
———. 1959. On psychic consciousness. In *The Virgin Archetype*. New York: Spring, 1972.
McLean, A. 1981. *The Splendor Solis*. Edinburgh: Magnum Opus Hermetic Sourceworks Number 8.
Samuels, A. 1989. *The Plural Psyche*. London: Routledge.
Schwartz-Salant, N. 1984. Archetypal foundations of acting-out in the transference-countertransference process. In *Transference and Countertransference*, N. Schwartz-Salant and M. Stein, eds. Wilmette, Ill.: Chiron, pp. 1–30.
———. 1986. On the subtle body concept in analytical practice. In *The Body in Analysis*, Nathan Schwartz-Salant and Murray Stein, eds. Wilmette, Ill.: Chiron Publications.
———. 1988. Archetypal foundations of projection identification. *Journal of Analytical Psychology* 33:39–64.
———. 1989. *The Borderline Personality: Vision and Healing*. Wilmette, Ill.: Chiron Publications.

_____. 1990. The abandonment depression: personal and archetypal factors. *Journal of Analytical Psychology*, forthcoming.

Spignesi, A. 1990. *Lyrical-Analysis: The Unconscious Through* Jane Eyre. Wilmette, Ill.: Chiron Publications.

Ulanov, A. 1982. Transference and countertransference. In *Jungian Analysis*, M. Stein, LaSalle, Ill: Open Court, pp. 75–85.

Vianello, M. 1989. *The Sceptre and the Bowl*. Unpublished manuscript.

Disguises of the Anima

Ann Belford Ulanov

The Bridge

Through experiences forced on me by my clinical work, I have come to the idea that the anima or animus maps routes to certain experiences of the Self which bring us more into life, which make us face reality. Anima or animus forms a bridge, across which the contents of the Self come to address the ego, to put questions to our very existence. These questions seem to issue from an other—personified as an anima or animus figure—who says, in effect: You must deal with me, confront me, respond to me, even if it is to reject me, but here I am and you cannot escape.[1]

These Self experiences make us feel that life is worth living. They color our perceptions with excitement and awe at the very fact of being.[2] It makes no difference what our age or sexuality, whether we are single or married, celibate or divorced. We all must face and answer the other who confronts us from a sexual departure point opposite to our conscious gender identity. We all share the task of putting these parts

Ann Belford Ulanov is a Jungian analyst, member of the faculty and supervising analyst for the C. G. Jung Institute of New York City, and Christiane Brooks Johnson Professor of Psychiatry and Religion at Union Theological Seminary. Her many books include *The Witch and the Clown: Two Archetypes of Human Sexuality*, and *Religion and the Unconscious* (with Barry Ulanov) and *The Feminine in Jungian Psychology and in Christian Theology* and *The Wisdom of the Psyche*.

of ourselves together to make an identity for ourselves, with its possibilities and tribulations.

In focusing on the anima/animus bridge, I am expanding on Jung's notion of these archetypal figures as "unwelcome intruders" who compel our attention through their irresistible and indefinable attractions as dream and fantasy personages or, in projected form, their lure to other people. By making the personifications of these complexes conscious, "we convert them into bridges to the unconscious. It is because we are not using them purposefully as functions that they remain personified complexes" (Jung 1928, par. 399). To the degree that we actively try to understand them, "the personified figure of anima or animus will disappear. It becomes a function of relationship between conscious and unconscious" (ibid., par. 370).

Where then does the bridge take us? Right to the Self, bringing us, as conscious and unconscious move each other, to a closer meeting with life and the reality made available to us when our psyche is opened up. We are more pliable and open to ourselves. Reality beckons in our own particular colors.

The image of bridge helps us to focus on its function of linking the ego world, and its ways of operation following the laws of directed thinking, with the Self world, characterized by nondirected thinking. Each, ego and Self, has its own aims and values; they link through the contrasexual factor.

Anima and animus do not provide a set content, but rather a dynamic function or process. When we slap the animus label onto people, as if it always meant the same thing, we are articulating a dysfunction of the bridge. It has, in fact, broken down. The animus, for any given woman, can never be made to fit reductive generalizations; it is always highly individual. For example, a professional woman with postdoctoral training found that her animus figures — whether in dream or reality — consistently appeared as big, silent men, utterly nonverbal, who stood calmly next to her or gently lay over her, to "earth" her, to connect her to her "deeper self." Another woman, who felt herself dumbly inarticulate, married her husband because of his ability to talk brilliantly. Years later, she sought analysis because she thought that if he did not shut up and listen to her, she was going to kill him.

We share among us the same function of anima and animus as bridge between ego and Self. Where we differ is in the contents that walk across that bridge, even though we can describe them in general as issuing from another departure point, opposite to our conscious gender identity. The anima and animus are not just types of consciousness, as some revisionists suggest, insisting that we all possess both (Bachelard 1969, chapter two; Whitmont 1980; Hillman 1972; Kast 1986, chapter eight). That makes the content a set one, always the same no matter where or in whom it turns up. But the anima/animus contents that cross that bridge insist on their individual particularities. They do not permit reduction to the terms of culture-bound prejudices, and they are not merely the products, as some feminists assert, of Jung's own sexism (Reuther 1983, pp. 190–273, n. 9; Miller 1976, pp. 78–79; Goldenberg 1976).[3] Both of these views miss the epochal nature of Jung's insight, however "clumsy" it seems to be, even to him.[4]

As we know, one foot of the anima or animus complex stands in the personal world, shaped by introjected objects and images — the significant persons of the opposite sex in our early life, images of the masculine and feminine in our culture, our inherited physical makeup. The other foot stands in the objective psyche, functioning according to its laws of contiguity, similarity, association, simultaneity, and the range of physical to spiritual poles of the archetype (Jung 1952). Here the contrasexual figure confronts us with particular archetypal images that constellate the objective psyche in relation to our personal, physical, and cultural life. That is why, for example, when an animus content replaces that of the adapted ego in discussion, we feel invaded by something wildly irrational, with tinges even of madness. We've got hold of a fish out of water, the animus that swims in the unconscious. When we recognize it as such, its tendency to throw opposites together takes on a revelatory light, rather than a crackpot dimness or frightening disruptive glare.

The contrasexual bridge functions to connect the worlds on either side, not to merge them. The contrasexual are border figures, taking us from one to another sexual departure point, from the personal to the collective, the conscious to the archetypal, the ego to the Self. So what seems spiritual, in effect, whether we live with meaning or futility, shows itself as all mixed up with the sexual, in effect, how we put ourselves into shared existence with others. What seems private turns out to be social, for our struggles to connect with an other at our own center also has roots that extend from a center far outside us. In this struggle, we feel not as if on some isolated journey but intimately bound up with other people, a woman with other women and with womanliness, and even though a woman, like a man identified with men's points of view, almost in the skin. At the same time, we know that the other sex, however we experience it, also feels bound up with us.

The spiritual expands the sexual view to a wide and flexible contemplative gaze onto all kinds of coupling, while the sexual draws the spiritual into the most specific here-and-now interaction with another concrete human being. Sexuality both forces us toward incarnation and pulls us across the borders of our ego identities toward otherness, toward the center. The Russian philosopher Solovyev said that only sexuality is strong enough to counter our egotism (Solovyev 1945, pp. 25, 35, 77).

Sexual responses, then, have a spiritual function as well as a bodily one. They act to pull us through into another center, bigger and more encompassing than the ego, what we Jungians call the Self. But this anima/animus region where sex and spirit tangle and conjoin can also be the place where heart and soul get broken, become addicted, compelled to do things against their best interests. We fear this place. There we can be hurt. There betrayal can strike us down. In defense, we make steely vows of revenge against betrayers and against ourselves for opening so far. There is the instructive example of Scheherazade. Without her help, the sultan in the famous *Arabian Nights* situation would have fulfilled his vow to execute every woman with whom he lay. She stopped him by appealing to his imagination with her thousand tales on a thousand nights. She slowly opened in him a space of interior contemplation.[5] As long as we resist finding the helper in each of us, we will go on reading headlines in newspapers across our world that tell of a woman who hires a thug to kill her husband, of a man who beats his girlfriend to death, of elders sexually abusing children, of rape, of contempt between the sexes. Anima and animus affect our society as well as our spirit and our sexuality.

People come to us as Jungian analysts because of their difficulties in these areas. They feel unalive, deeply frightened by a seeming inability to make intimate contact with another, or in an urgent state where they feel split almost in two. If something does not change quickly, they think of killing themselves. The psyche brings these dilemmas and all sorts of fitting images to express them and body clues to their resolution. We ask the psyche where its energies are heading, what it is trying to bring about.

It is possible to map the territory of these experiences that speak of Self, whether achieved or approached or missed, through anima and animus. I find this map of great practical usefulness in my work. It cuts through dense fields, to move toward the point of it all. I find myself, in relation to this theory, trying to do what Vladimir Horowitz said about his performances: "I play music behind the notes. I search for it and play from this other side."[6]

I am interested in the way anima and animus usher in the Self, and in the space of emptiness behind the notes of the theory, where our God-images stop and the presence of the Holy is evoked by the Self. I see, in the two case examples I am about to give, that I have always been interested in this space, for they span more than twenty years. Work with the first man began in 1968 and was finished, finally, with his death, in 1975. Work with the second man, the son of the first, began just recently and, although interrupted, will continue. The anima/animus theory made it possible to map these men's experiences so that one could die without going mad and the other could live because he confronted and chose his life.

Disguise

What makes these cases of father and son of special interest is that both men, allowing for individual variation, suffer the same disguise phenomenon of the split-anima. This disguise presents itself to a man's ego at first as an almost intolerable conflict of choice between two females, the wife and the other woman.[7] To be caught between two women and unwilling to choose is a choice in fact—for death. Life hangs in the air, unlived. The man is caught in suspended animation. The anima in retreat represents death; her disguise, a shroud. Yet, in both these cases, we can see the anima engineering through the split a way of coming to the Self, of making a bridge to that other country, so foreign and so enticing to the ego.[8] Each of these men moved from suspended animation to real election, choosing to receive the feminine in himself. In this way, analysis informed by the idea of anima and animus shows itself as much more than interesting material. It is life-supporting; it speaks for life, not for death.

Both men, in their transference, used me as the anima bridge.[9] This allowed them to come into relation with the unconscious contents that had sought their attention. The contents were of such importance that they not only disrupted their lives but threatened to end them if left neglected, unintegrated. As the men met the task their psyches set them, they could begin to dispense with me. Their anima was functioning as an inner bridge across which ego and Self were meeting.[10] Something large is demanded of the ego in such situations, or more accurately, everything is demanded. The ego must venture on that bridge and cross over to Self country, but it cannot do so securely until the anima becomes a sturdy connecting link.

The father sought treatment at the age of forty-three, after twenty years of marriage and three sons. The son, youngest of the three, sought treatment at age thirty-one after ten years of marriage and no children, although in the course of treatment he had a son who died the day he was born and who was named for the father. The father came to me through referral from a colleague treating his wife; the son sought me out because his father had spoken of his work with me and told him to see me if need arose. Need did arise for the son, fourteen years after his father's death. The father came for two hours of individual work a week for three years, then group therapy, with irregular individual sessions, for another three years. The son came one hour a week for eight months. Both traveled from several states away to undertake analysis.

Both men were deeply unhappy, although they expressed their unhappiness differently. The father said if it were not for his children, he might consider suicide. He and his wife got along as friends, but were hopelessly locked in sexual struggle, he wanting it, she feeling the demand excessive. He quickly saw his need for affection as exorbitant and put the hard question to himself, "Am I a taker, not a giver?" This was painful since he had committed himself to a helping profession, knowing it as his vocation. Bouts of guilt laid him low. He was uneasy in not having discovered his vocation until after his marriage, in work his wife hated, which robbed her of her hope of working together in the wilderness, as they had planned. He felt guilty about his sexual desires and the anger his wife aroused, not only by denying him sexually and saying she found him unattractive, but also her general deprecating attitude toward him, "telling the truth when it does not need to be told." His wife wanted him to be celibate; he felt he could not and would not be, and then he felt guilty because of the resultant affairs. The aggression with which he was not in touch turned against him, in dreams of pouring gasoline on himself to destroy himself or of going into a house where he might be castrated. In these dream plots lurked the motif of son-lover sacrificing his manhood to mother-goddess.

The son expressed his unhappiness directly, saying he had the fantasy of living a life where he would be "true to himself." In a dream at the beginning of analysis, he was in a plane that would not take off for lack of fuel. His mother was on it, too. When it flipped over and he fell out, a man who was there did not help him. He struggled out of the plane to find himself "on thin ice." He felt dissatisfaction with his marriage. He and his wife were good friends, but lacked sexual passion and all the excitement about living together that came with it. He felt anger at his wife's moody withdrawal and negativity about herself,

which made her "not nice to my friends." He did not feel guilty about
his affair. But he did feel torn apart, desperate that he was unable to
decide what to do, which woman to choose. At one point, suicidal
feelings threatened him, as they had his father. He presented his problem as conflict between two women, which his father had known, too,
but the son saw clearly that he was "being dragged somewhere" and
that "the answer was within," even though he could not yet find his
"own truth."

The principal disguise of the anima in both men was an insoluble
conflict between two women.[11] The father felt bound to his wife for the
sake of his boys and his profession, a public one where he was passionately committed as well as very successful. He did find sexual happiness
with another woman, and more—laughter, sensuality, intimacy, emotional expression, intensity, and, above all, acceptance of all of him. He
felt life was not worth living without the sexual connection.

The son felt bound to his wife by the security of their home and
the land which he had worked hard to purchase and through fear of
breaking his wife's heart. She was "sad and depressed," and he had
worked hard to help her, leading her to face her feelings of abandonment by her father and to go abroad with him to see her father after
many years of separation. Before their marriage, while they were at
different colleges, he had tried to break off his relationship with her,
but had found no better alternative and could not bear to hurt her. Yet
he still had "no desire to kiss her," had "no woman feeling about her."
He wanted to sleep with someone else before leaving the city where he
worked and relocating. And then he fell passionately in love with this
other woman. He knew it mattered to him to be important to her ("not
just a dick"), indeed, to try to change her life, too. With her, he felt
pressed to know where he was and what he felt, not to "fall asleep" in
his life. "I feel like a man with her," he said. A level of primordial
sexual fire ignited between them. He said she could not "control" her
sexual response to him; it would overcome her. "She smells me and
responds." This he found deeply exciting and reassuring.

The split-anima for both men set security, life investment, loyalty,
consideration, and responsibility to children against igniting sexual fire
and spiritual aliveness but along with them a feeling of being unhoused
and ungrounded. The father's conflict accented the strain between his
persona—his beloved profession—and his secret sexual life. The son's
conflict was lodged more in his ego and what was his true path.
Although for both men the affair lasted some time—for the father off
and on for five years, for the son intensely for two years—neither could

choose that sexual option. The father, for example, had another brief fling and then a more sustained relationship before he ended his marriage and went to live as a single man. The son struggled slowly toward realization of the anima fire within himself, toward a real life in himself rather than in either woman, and chose to test his marriage by recommitting himself to it. He did not want to start all over again with another woman for he felt he had never really chosen his wife in the first place. He had "to give 100%" to the marriage before he could discard it. Thus the anima disguise, when it dissolved and functioned within each of the men as his own bridge to the unconscious, lead to a greater sense of life in himself rather than carried by a woman. One man chose to live alone, contrary to anything he had ever expected of himself, and, in his sudden confrontation with death, he found himself wholeheartedly choosing the Self. The other chose for the first time to be really married, although he had been married in name all along.

The split-anima disguise can best be summed up by citing two dreams, both of which were dreamt after much analytic work. The father saw himself, in his dream, in a room in a house between two other rooms in which stood his wife and the other woman, opposite poles of his anima fascination. Each woman had a revolver and wanted to shoot either him or the other woman. Each is stayed in her action by the fact that the other could see her and take aim and perhaps shoot first. The father felt trapped, as well as pulled apart. But he also felt a change in himself in this dream. He saw he had shifted away from asking, "What can I do to end all this?" He no longer felt a suicidal temptation. He now asked, "What is the meaning of this suffering?" He was living consciously with the tension of the split. He even felt that his suffering helped him to help others through his work (see Ulanov 1982, p. 82). In the son's dream, the "other" woman came to his home, where his wife was. "They were forced to converse, or at least be in very close proximity." The two opposing sides, security and instinct, began to draw together.

The Wounded Feminine

Behind this split in the anima lay a wound to the feminine. The father experienced it with his wife, the son with his mother. The mother, in her turn, suffered the wound to her feminine self through her own father. In cases like this, we can see the suffering of generations, passing on wounds that have not been healed. We also see the difference consciousness makes. The son's analytic work began at a better place than the father's, thanks to the work his father had done in his own analysis. He bequeathed his son a psychological legacy.[12]

Growing up, the father felt himself to be his mother's confidant. She loved him, he said, in a positive way, but with something sexual missing. His father, he remembered, was demonstrative and affectionate but ruthless in business and spoiled and worshiped by his mother. In analysis, he began to see how he had lived in thrall to the Mother in her archetypal manifestations. He depended on his mother's approval, remembering no fights with her or any need to gain his independence. He found it intolerable when the woman in his extramarital relationship was mad at him. He felt "doomed" when his wife told him that she felt "blah" about him. On the other hand, he felt cheered and rejuvenated when he was accepted and loved by a woman. He saw, after a while, that he was at the beck and call of the woman's responses. Even his suicidal feelings or self-castration dreams came to seem to him proof of his bondage to the Mother. Gradually, he was able to distinguish between his feelings and his needs. He stopped whimpering and became strong enough to face his wife's anger and her own affairs and the other woman's anger and hurt that he was not going to marry her.

Looking back, he felt wonder at having been drawn to his wife, whom both his parents had urged him to marry. She was so opposite to his mother, not at all the approving, accepting, maternal type, but rather a girl-woman, a sort of Artemis figure, confident in nature and of her own athletic prowess. We could speculate that the marriage had promoted his differentiation from his boy-to-mother stance and permitted him to incubate the opposite sex in himself. Suffering his wife's sexual rejection, he could begin his journey to free himself from endless orbiting around the feminine-as-mother. He would no longer renounce his ownership of his own sexual impulses. Thus he smashed the son-mother containers, both in his wife and with the other woman.

A second woman with whom the father had a long and important relationship was a young prostitute, some decades his junior. Sexually, he said, she reminded him of his first extramarital partner. But the terms were clear and up front from the beginning, although the relationship soon became personal. He brought her to his house and into his community after he divorced his wife. He wanted her to see his world and to meet his sons. When she did, she said there was no way she could compete with that. The match could not become a merger, so eventually they parted on good terms. What struck me was his effort to bring the opposites together and let each side know the other, to own both of them. The effort helped heal the wounded feminine in him, which had led to such enslavement to the mother that his own anima had barely emerged, leaving him for so long in his split-anima condition.

The father's wife had originally attracted her husband, I think, because she had approached him from a departure point radically different from his mother's. She came as an equal. She was bold and adventurous as she moved through the world and into nature's wilderness. She prized honesty over acceptance or approval. She got mad and froze him out in disapproval of what she saw as his hypocrisy—his excellent reputation in his community while conducting a secret sexual life. She owned her own affairs and felt she was not representing herself publicly as a paragon. She felt that his heavy-handed sexual needs robbed her of her own lightness of being. She linked her husband in her mind to her father, who had scornfully criticized her as a woman and as a wife, finding her woefully inadequate on both counts. Her father ignored his own marital difficulties which had ended in estrangement from his own wife except for a persona face they turned to the world together, as the proper couple. Everywhere there was secrecy, betrayal, withholding of warmth, sexual unhappiness. Hurt piled on hurt.

The wife was wounded in receiving and then again in trying to present all of her feminine self. The wound first came through her father's scorn of any female person and her mother's impotence in asserting an alternative. To receive an other, a woman has to be someone in herself, must be able to meet and inquire about herself. The wife felt this self-possession in the woods, but not with her husband, her sons, or her lovers. She was always looking for it and wanted to find it. Her wounded femininity resulted from her inability to possess and present the full feminine self she longed for. Her animus did not function as a bridge between her ego and the Self, and so, in her ego, she felt insecure as a woman, while the raw animus pronouncements filled in all the deficits. Her insecure feminine presence was no help to her husband's unemerged anima and left her son only the more depleted.

All these wounds to the feminine descended upon the son's life. As the youngest in the family, with his brothers away at school, he bore the brunt of his parents' unhappiness as they struggled toward divorce. Even prior to that time, he had felt himself "a self-sufficient child," independent of his mother, neither giving nor receiving affectionate hugs and kisses. He saw his mother always struggling under the burden of living up to her father's respect. He did not feel she protected him. Even living with her after the divorce, he felt it was he who took care of her: "I knew my responsibilities." It was what his father wanted him to do: "It was right to do it and I was happy to do it." He felt she had a special relation to him, but not he to her. At the age of seventeen, after his father died, he was already independent of his mother, although pulled in to advise her as she contemplated a second marriage. He described himself as being matter-of-fact in his role of advisor, not overly compassionate. He had "removed" himself, feeling that his life was "together" and hers chaotic by comparison. He did not want her advice when he fell into his own torments. Dependence was not possible: "She never pays for dinner when we go out."

He felt angry with his mother, at her lack of self-confidence and later at her trying so hard not to be a burden to him and his wife when he married in his early twenties. He found himself impatient with her low self-esteem which resulted in "attracting all the energy and attention to herself." He admired her capabilities, which were apparent whenever she was in the woods or at her job and which altogether vanished in personal contacts. When his own son died, after one day of life, he had to tell his mother to stay with them at the hospital. "We needed a parental figure there at a moment of parental despair. But I had to tell her how to do it."

He felt his father never had to be told how to be a father. His father had given him a real conviction of what life was about, and, in the way he had dealt with his dying, had freed him from the fear of death. His father made him feel special and loved for the person he was. He knew his father's pride in him for enjoying and participating in life. His father had, in fact, told me, many years before, that this son was a "lovable, genuine boy" and very much "his own person." He felt that he was important to the son and worried, when he was dying, that the boy had to "carry such a load."

Father and son shared a football metaphor for the "game of life." The father, when a senior in college, played on the junior varsity football squad, because he loved the game. The son, when he failed to make the starting lineup on his high school team, knew he had not disappointed his father—for his father, life was a game to be entered into, no more, no less. In contrast, his mother's father played only to win. He knew about his father's sexual troubles, although not in great detail, and thought his father was stupid and lazy in the way he dealt with them. He "ought to have resisted." During analysis, he dreamed about being chased by a grizzly bear in a mink coat and this recalled a boyhood experience when his father's young prostitute friend kissed him goodbye at the end of a visit, wearing a mink coat. He remembered the touch of her soft lips on his mouth and knew in a flash what drew his father: "I wanted to sink into the coat." When later he fell passionately in love, he felt he really understood his father.

When his father died, he saw that his father had forgiven himself "for being who he was; he celebrated himself as human, faults and all." For the son, death's destructive blows had come earlier in life, when his beloved dogs were killed by cars. His father had always felt he would die young and had often spoken of it to his sons, saying he felt prepared. The father had suffered an early heart attack, discovered, he said, because "my heart hurt," but the father and I also approached his premonition of death in terms of the archetype of the son-lover yielding up life to the embrace of the Great Mother. After his father died and his ashes were spread, the son felt his father constantly with him: "I have a foot on the other side; part of me is on the other side. And yet part of him is here. I feel comfortable where I'm going, so I'm not afraid of death; it comes back in how I live life." His father gave him, in death, an anima bridge to life. The son took it and grew a womanly receiving presence in himself.

The son's capacity to embrace life stood out in the midst of his grief over his own baby's premature birth and death. He named this son after his father, accepting it as the darkest time, one of great sadness. Yet he was able to gather his family and friends around himself and his wife and to know "confirmation of all that light you felt from everyone coming back to you." He felt "held by all those people" and said, with great feeling, "Confidence is allowing yourself to be indebted to others." He felt his little son's gift to him was the determination to talk openly with his wife about their relationship. He would not risk another pregnancy until things felt right between them.

The son's ability to depend on his family and draw from their love increased, I believe, as a result of his analytic work. We had discovered that he had hopped over the trauma of his parents' divorce mainly because of the wound, the split in his own image of the feminine. The mother image for him broke into the familiar division of what Jungians have called the elemental and transformative feminine, what Winnicott calls the environment and instinct mothers (Jung 1952, chapters 5–7; Neumann 1985, chapter 3; Winnicott 1965a, pp. 75–80). As a child, he held himself to "self-sufficiency." What dependence he allowed himself he transferred onto the house. After the divorce, when he moved away with his mother, he missed the house deeply. This dependency, in turn, transferred to his wife, the land, and the house he felt an urgency to own and worked so hard to buy, complete with family dog. The holding function of the feminine, its grounding aspect, which can be depended upon to support one in being, he transferred into his relationship with his wife and their home. After the rupture of his parents' divorce, he turned to his wife-to-be and became a member of her family. It provided a holding environment.

He dealt with the unmothered part of himself first by mothering his mother and then his wife. Part of the intense urgency he felt in trying to hold himself together over his split between two women was, on the one hand, to feel he would "be orphaned" if he gave up his wife and home and, on the other, that he would lose some essential piece of his soul if he gave up his affair.

Some of the reliability of the feminine on which he could depend transferred to me. When the other woman got angry and said she hated him because he would not see her, he panicked. Later, he told me that he knew he could call me, "but knowing I could meant I did not have to; I felt attuned to inner feelings and confidence in myself." I think he was able eventually to let things fall apart with both women because his dependency need was reliably met in the analysis.

He discovered the instinct side of the feminine only with his partner in the affair. He had not known it before either in himself or with a woman. But it was like a soul; it could not be lost.[13] In contrast, he and his wife lived like Hansel and Gretel. With this other woman, he reached across an inner split between security and aliveness to embrace the spontaneous impulses that felt truly personal instead of staying in his usual identification with the defenses that controlled them.[14] I think the other woman reflected back to him the validity and value of those impulses, allowing him to claim them joyfully. He risked aggressive feelings with the other woman, letting himself really want experiences that colored outside the lines of his defined security. That he could only find access to these impulses outside his marriage, in the breaking of convention, symbolizes the outlaw status of these impulses within him. More controlled than lived, these impulses fell into his shadow and could only be contacted again through shadow behavior. He allowed himself to experience desire, recklessness, aggressive pursuit, and intensity of sexual expression and satisfaction. This heightened his sense of the split between his craving for the security of a known framework and his seemingly uncontrollable thirst to follow where his passion led.

He reached a pivotal point in the analysis when he could no longer hold the split together. Consciously, he relinquished control and let things "fall apart." In the midst of the pain he felt in making his wife suffer and hurting the other woman, too, what surfaced was grief over his parents' divorce and his lost home. He took the risk of feeling all his mourning, for his mother and his father, for his childhood house, for his wife, for his woman friend, for his dead son, for himself and what he had missed as a boy. He concluded, "This is the biggest change. I can let things fall apart. I don't have to control everything." He faced all of his reality.

Around this time, two dreams signaled deeper change. In one, the son was trying to reach a place farther down the coast where there stood a Greek temple, "like Sounion, in Greece." He had been there on a trip with his mother at a time when he did not have to take care of her but was free to have his own experiences. The temple's location recalled the poignant moment in the ancient myth when Theseus forgot to hoist the sails on his ship whose color would signal to his father that he was returning safely after killing the Minotaur. Aegeus, his father, not seeing the right signal, thought his son was dead and dove to his death in the sea. My patient said the myth was about "a country divided against itself and that is me. Two women battling for me, but it's really my battle manifesting itself in two women. Why didn't the father know, or see the colors? It's such a tragedy. It makes me think of the hair colors of my two ladies, for they are opposites like the black and white sails of Theseus." I thought, here is a man facing the split-anima in himself, finding a way in his masculinity to hold the feminine in himself. I wondered then if the allusion to the king's death signaled the death of the son's attachment to his father, so that he could now find his own solution to the split-anima problem.

The second dream, a week later, seemed to confirm this guess. In it, two porpoises approached him as he was swimming in the water. "I was flanked on each side. I reached out and held onto the dorsal fin of each one. I was being carried over the water by the two powerful porpoises. I could feel the water rushing all about me as my arms were opened as far apart as could be. The water was made turbulent by the speed and the power." Immediately, he thought the two fish were the two women and saw his split between them in a new way. If he let go of either fish, he would sink. He had needed to hold both to "keep from going under." But they were fish and not women, and so the image led him to see the two as aspects of the one. We asked what the psyche intended in changing the women into dolphins. He felt that it was to get the projection off the women. For me, the dream dolphins seemed to correspond to the usual symbolic meaning of a psychopomp, destined to carry the soul to the realm of the dead, to ultimate reality, and thus to be associated with the redeemer.

The son's wound to the feminine consisted in the split between the holding and instinctually enlivening feminine. What died was the projection of those two aspects onto the two women. What was redeemed were the psychic realities he was now able to find within himself. He had changed his life in many remarkable ways, showing the transformations that can happen when the ego faces the conflicts brought by the anima. Changes occur to the ego (which includes others), the shadow, the anima, and the Self (which includes other people, too, in a collective way).

Transformation: The Father

In all psychological work, no perfect answers develop. But subtle and decisive changes happen if the work goes well enough, and so it was here, with both father and son. For each man, the anima came to function as bridge between ego and Self, and this affected them both in urgent, life-and-death instances. For the father, it made possible what might be called a blessed death. Not only was he at peace with himself, given over to the source of life, but (to follow the traditional notion of a blessed death) other people who came in contact with him then felt they had been blessed with something peculiarly their own. For the son, it meant taking hold of his life in a new way, consciously carrying his own wounds and seeking his own path. These two lives show us, I believe, both the ragged imperfect state of human solutions to problems and the somewhat larger-than-human effects of an integrated anima functioning as a bridge.

Both men's egos changed, enlarged. They found their missing pieces hiding in the shadow. Thus, the shadow changed, too. The ego integrated bits of it. The anima aided the task by pushing shadow parts under the ego's nose all the time and thus differentiating itself as articulator of the unconscious, as in the *albedo* stage in alchemy (see Jung 1984, pp. 53, 55, 258; 1944, par. 333–335). The father's dream of the two women with guns showed him that he had to deal with two anima carriers full of murderous hostility, each to the other. In life, he had to deal with his wife's confrontations of his "hypocrisy" in protecting his public persona by hiding his sexual activities and with the other woman's refusal to carry his sexual life for him, her threats to expose him, and her pressure on him to face up to his waffling and need to please. I stood on the anima bridge, so to speak, pointing out the way each woman carried the burden and the effects of his secret split, instead of him doing this himself. In his work in group therapy, others took the same tack, always pushing to make him see his evasions of what the split meant, his use of the women, his hiding behind an image of affability.

What he found when he looked at the split was bits and pieces of missing aggression that belonged to his ego. Dreams tossed up images of guns. He was shooting and killing, or he had the enemy in his sights and was supposed to kill him and found he couldn't, but then the enemy shot his best friend, which made him sob with remorse. Or he was once again in military service, going back "to the man's army," living in communal barracks and urinating in a huge urinal that took up one whole wall with cascading water. Or he had to deal with a raucous group that drove a giant diesel locomotive through his place of work. He suffered seeing how much energy he devoted to weaving and dodging his ego tasks in order always to please, to make no one mad at him, to be the good boy pleasing to the other whom unconsciously he cast in the role of all-accepting mother. He had to face that he was negating life with his suspended animation. He dreamt of another of his sons (who he feared was too "good" and who, interestingly enough, joined the Marines), telling him to stir up the fire on which they would cook their steaks. And then, "rats came out from everywhere."

He tried hard to deal with all the rats, which toughened his ego, making it more realistic, and benefitted others in his life. He stopped blaming his wife for his sexual problems and took responsibility for his own actions, realizing it was not just her rejection of him that set him off into an affair, but his own dissatisfaction with their relationship. He faced the other woman's wrath and pain, decided not to marry her, and told her so. He managed to see it through enough with both women that, although he made them angry, they also saw and respected his firmness in deciding he could not go on with two lives, and, surprisingly, they won through together to a level of genuine cordiality. He bought a motorcycle and enjoyed it hugely. For once, his enjoyment did not depend on his community's approval, although in fact they did approve. He made public his decision to separate from his wife and their subsequent joint decision to divorce and carried the consequences for that to his reputation and work. Altogether, he felt more independent, not "swept all over the place."

The reduction in his fear of aggression freed up more energy which went into his work. That, in turn, deepened and flourished. Being more realistic about his own disabilities made him both tougher and more compassionate of the weaknesses of others. It is not too much to say that, at this time, he had a formidable and often decisive impact on people's lives.

Instead of trying to get a woman to fill deficiencies in himself, to stuff her into the holes in his being, the father received and held his deficiencies like an empty space inside him that he could increasingly accept and allow to be empty. He began a new relationship with a woman who, it seemed to him, combined in herself the opposite qualities of his wife and the other woman. He decided for the time being not to marry nor even to promise that he would in the future, but simply to allow himself to be, a single man, a man in his own right, holding his empty space himself. The anima projected itself much less and came to function much more as an internal bridge to the Self. He had reached a place of emptiness where his god-images could leave off and the presence of something other could make itself known, which showed dramatically in the way he met his death.

We see a change not only in the ego and shadow when the anima begins to function as a bridge, but also in the anima itself. The ego toughens; the shadow becomes more integrated; the anima projects less onto others and becomes more of an articulator of the unconscious, and that is what puts something different into the world. The anima functioning as a bridge strongly and distinctly affects the ego, making it more masculine, with its own special spiritual qualities—connecting the ego to the Self and social elements as well, changing others' lives, helping them across their bridges to reality.

When shadow aggression is not integrated adequately, as was the case with the father, external reality is not external enough. As a result, a man tends to use others, principally women, as characters in his own inner drama of needs and shoring up. In bouts of sexuality, a man is apt to approach his partners essentially as selfobjects, props for his fantasies. This is a nonlife, a shrouded life, a disguised one. He is not apt to take in much of what comes his way or take advantage of what reality brings him. He then wastes life and its great opportunities. Caught in a consuming attitude to counteract the inner emptiness he fears, he uses and disposes rather than really living and feeling gratitude for life. Gratitude, after all, is a positive force and an essential one in our lives, gathering all of us into our shared existence. This father was, I believe, a good person and so his benefits from analysis were not only shared with others, which happens automatically in such a changed personality, but also brought to others because he so much wanted them to benefit from what had happened to him. This accounts, in part, for his "blessed death." He ended up alone, but with a remarkable long day's dying that gave much to many people.

In the lengthy dying, he completed the task on which he had worked so hard but had not finished in his living. He was suddenly struck down by a rapid, rare brain disease. It opened up all of the troubles that had initially brought him to analysis. The prognosis of the disease was that it would ravage him, causing psychosis before death. My patient feared that his long-contained, secret life would spill out into the public when he became psychotic, as the disease threatened.

Suicide once more presented a solution. There he was again, back at the beginning, fearing for his reputation, keeping secrets, afraid of disapproval, tempted to defend by destroying. We worked sporadically at this point, because of his need for constant physical treatment and his increasing disability. But we worked enough to see how all the great differences had been put into place. The old problems jumped up again, ready to assault him; he was back in the same old place. But the man himself was different because of all the work; this new man reacted to the old threats in a new way.

He used his aggression. A teaching hospital heard of his affliction with this rare disease and wanted to examine him. He did not like the way they treated him, as simply a thing to be tested, not a person facing the end of his life. He contacted his sons and made them take him away, back to his home, where he wanted to die. With me, he was able to locate and articulate his fears and link them up to the old ones we knew so well, despite increasing loss of function, first his balance and sight, then his muscular coordination, and finally his voice and hearing. He drew openly on his past work, and he drew on me to reach further into his present reality. This brought a relief of pressure, but suicide still beckoned. He had some dreams that helped. In one his watch stopped, which we took as referring to his impending death. In another, there was "a bad guy in the trunk of my car. Should I turn him in or keep driving? He's tried to get me. Now I've got him." He dreamt of being in "the worst battles of North Africa (in the Second World War, in which he had served), wounded, hot, face down in the sand with no water."

His transference had been to me as trusted guide and colleague, not mother or hoped-for sexual partner. Those parts were fully cast. Now the urgency of his illness pushed me into spiritual issues of the most intense kind. He drew on me and on our analytical connection to lead to real life, not to enactments of fantasies that would shut him up against life. We asked basic questions: What could the meaning of this illness be? Toward what end might this disease's threat of psychosis be moving? What could be the purpose of the threat of exposing his long-held secret, which he had learned to live with but had not fully accepted?[15]

A way opened. He voluntarily and completely gave up the escape route of suicide, offering it back to the source of life from which he had come, from which he had received all he had known of life. He felt this as an intensely personal offering of what he had to give, all he had feared and wished for, back into the hands of God. That empty space in him yielded a fullness of feeling that made him want to offer even his sanity and his terrible fear of losing his sanity, his fear of exposure, everything, to the power that had created him. In dying, he achieved a depth of acceptance he had not found in life to that point. He reached beneath the split of both public and secret life to deliver himself over utterly, as he was, fears, splits, and all.

I saw him the day before he died. Although he could no longer speak, I knew he knew me as I spoke to him and read him a favorite psalm. He made whalelike noises, as if hailing me from a great distance, from the midst of the "blue fog" he lived in now, which he had spoken of on previous occasions. What amazed us those last days was that he did not become psychotic. His was the only one of the recorded cases to have missed that fate. Thus he was spared what he most deeply feared, because, I believe, he faced his fears and willingly submitted to them and offered them up.

The anima that functions as bridge to the Self engenders, in Jungian language, faith in the Self, that it can be reached and trusted and relied upon. It will hold the ego. When it is reached, the Self is always shared. We do not know the Self in isolation. As Jung put it, where the Self is genuinely constellated, it creates a group, a true gathering of persons.[16] And many people did gather around this man's bedside. Some members of our therapy group came to see him, and his death was written up in the national press. From all these sources, I saw how his reaching the Self gave others access to their experiences of the Self, too, in the most individual, idiosyncratic, and deeply felt forms. For myself, I knew a permanent shift in my commitment to the analytic methods, theories, and practice that seek to enlarge consciousness. My conviction about the value of these activities deepened while at the same time an empty space widened where questions could appear both to challenge the whole analytic endeavor and to confirm it.

Faith in the Self showed in the son's analysis, too, although not in any form of dying but in an increase in the living of his life. The largest change in the son's ego was that it grew big enough to hold as its own the split-anima, formerly projected onto two women. He now wanted all of his life to be available to be lived in an unmistakable reality. He saw the split as between security and sexual needs, between a long line of continuity built up with land, house, home, and wife, and the spiritual explosion of seeing and being seen as an assertive sexual man. In his outer dilemma of having both a wife and another woman, he was searching for an inner way to heal the split between his dependency need for a reliable other and his need to live from his personal impulses instead of controlling them.

Claiming the split as within his own psyche changed his treatment of the two women. He saw that he had taken his wife for granted, bundled onto her a whole fabric of projections centered on his own mother needs. He saw, too, that helping her with her bad moods was just more of the same. He discovered now that he had always been a bit afraid of his wife's moods, that he felt bound to "her leash," even though he had helped tie it. He was angry, "tired of pulling feelings out of her," and wanted to "cut the leash" and "bring the woman out in her." He understood now that he had not "chosen her" when they married. I understood this to mean he had simply assumed her presence in his life, much as a boy counts on a mother's presence behind him as he goes out into the world. This assumption accounted, I think, for his lack of feeling guilty about his affair. When he told his wife that he had not "chosen" to marry her, she took off her wedding rings, not wanting to put them on again until they both chose to be married. She also, he said, dropped her moodiness. It just fell away, she told him, because when you lose a child and maybe a marriage, moods "just don't compare."

Early in his analysis, the son had wanted his wife to see an analyst, making it a condition for continuing the marriage. Then, as he took up his own problems, he let go of all his conditions, leaving his wife to decide about her own psyche. He shifted to a larger ego; he ceased being his wife's mother and started to carry his own wounds.

His wife's reaction to his affair, he said, was upset, grief, and, it is not too strong to say, a kind of unconditional loving. She gave him, he said, "a gift of forgiveness." She wanted to hold onto her relationship with him and made that clear from the start of his disclosures. She was hurt by his betrayal but managed to carry it, leaving him free to find his way back to her or away. This deeply moved him and allowed him to go further with the removal of his projections onto her. He found he was holding nothing back from her now in the sense of saying, "This is who I am." It did not include reporting details of his activities with the other woman, but only the emotionally significant fact that he loved her. The energy that used to go into taking care of his wife now returned to him, and he told his wife that he wanted her to say what she wanted and thought and felt sexually for him, and he wanted to be and do the same with her. Nothing less would do for them both. The death of their baby gave him, he felt, a deep resolve to relate truly to his wife before they risked another pregnancy. It was a "rebirth based on honesty." I saw him addressing his wife, as if saying, "receive yourself and come out to me with who you are. Find out if you want me and me you."

He chose to give his wife "one hundred percent," as he put it. If that did not work, he would leave, but he could not leave without having ever arrived. He was closing the wound to the feminine, passed to him through his mother, who did not receive all of herself and could not present it to him, because of her father's scorn. Feeling connected to his own sexual passion, no longer projected onto and lodged only with the other woman, he wanted to see what might ignite with his wife. His way was unsafe, quite unguaranteed. He did not know it would turn into a renewed relationship. But this was what he had to do. He even seriously entertained moving out of the house and off the land, terrible decisions for him. He was afraid he was "just settling in" because it was too hard to let go of his wife and home. So he allowed himself to think and talk about moving out and that broke the unconscious tie. "That was sufficient."

With the other woman, he went through much guilt and pain. In the jargon of the trade, his wife was the environment mother and the other woman the instinct mother (Winnicott 1965b, pp. 182–183). He used the latter to risk a ruthless experience of his instincts toward which he had not reached before. This was her gift to him. He remembered that at the beginning of the affair he had wanted to have such an effect on her that she would live differently after knowing him. He wanted to change her, "impact" her, "know that she had a vision because of me." He felt he knew "what was important and what was not because of Dad and the way he died; it changed me forever."

He loved this other woman and went on loving her and felt deeply distressed by her pain and his own at their parting: "it tore me apart." He felt they had both learned, had both given a lot to each other, but he had to face both himself and her with the fact that he did love her but not enough to change his whole life. He talked with her whenever she needed to reach him, but chose not to see her. He felt depressed and very sad, feeling they had met at the wrong time in their lives. He went on loving her but no longer lived the love with her.

One of the reasons for his choice was that his ego now owned his sexual passion instead of having to project it on the woman. He knew it now as real in himself, as an integral part of himself, and as something that could leap up in response to other women as well. It was no longer attached only to this one woman. From this he knew he had to contend with it directly. Changing his life around to start another marriage and build another home was not going to change the task that confronted him. He could imagine a good and compatible life with this other woman, but it would not differ much from what he presently lived with his wife. He took up the management of his sexual and spiritual passion, rather than making the woman its keeper.

He had made direct contact finally with his sexuality and with his guilt over using the other woman to do so and then not staying with her, and he faced as well now his depression over losing her. Other shadow bits pressed to be integrated into his ego. Aggression and anger came up on the job with his boss. He did not mind being called down for something he did wrong, if he was spoken to calmly and rationally, he said, but he hated being yelled at. I saw that the split between the sense of the feminine he depended on to hold him in being and the feminine that instinctually aroused him left him identified with controlling, rather than experiencing, his spontaneous impulses. Faced with yelling, he would first get hurt, then explode with rage. This linked up with the bear in the mink coat that had threatened him in his dream. Although the bear recalled the impulse to surrender to the soft lips touching his mouth, it also evoked terror at the bear's power: it could devour him! This led him to speak of how he differed from his father, thus reaching out for some of the bear's power. In addition to the bear symbolizing a positive mother or, like Artemis, fostering the growth of the young, all its masculine associations came to my mind. The bear can represent a warrior's strength or military energy, a kingly beast. The bear can stand for a mediating figure between heaven and earth, as well as symbolize the obscure *nigredo* of *prima materia* in alchemy. In the dream, the bear chased him and he had to defend himself and fight back. He contrasted himself again with his father. He wanted to integrate the passion; his father could not. He saw his father as reaching passion but never integrating it. His father seemed compelled to respond if someone said they needed him, whereas he, the son, wanted to understand things in his own terms and choose accordingly. It was important to him, for example, that the other woman know he loved her even though he was choosing not to build his life with her. He was all the personages in the dream and wanted to own them all— the hunter, the hunted, the female in the coat, the man who could fight.

Claiming the anima within him affected not only his ego and shadow but also his living toward the Self and his transference to me. His transference was not unlike his father's, to one neither mother nor lover, but rather a sort of guide standing on the anima bridge. I offered a perspective leading to reality, to life. I represented a counselor whom increasingly he came to see as within himself, a firm binding to reality, to life. Sometimes he wanted me to assume an answer-giving function and was annoyed and frustrated with me for not literally fulfilling this assignment. When he chose to suspend his analysis for the time being, for the sake of significant choices he had made in his work, I agreed that was right. I saw his analysis leading into a large reality available to him as his psyche opened up to him. But I expressed disquiet over the dream he brought to the last session and raised the possibility of his continuing analysis because of it. He chose, however, to follow his plan, guided by something within himself that had replaced me. We parted warmly, open to resuming work at a future time.

Living toward the Self was made possible as his ego enlarged and pressed on him a long hard look at his work life. Unlike the "problem with women," where he "needed help," he said, he felt he could "handle" his job problem. In short, he said, his job "is not my vocation." He had undertaken a business career to make money, had succeeded, had acquired the much-desired house and land. "I gave up a lot for security; even though it seemed too easy at twenty-two to make all that money. Now I want to pursue what matters to me." This meant changing careers now.

He stood fast with this decision even though his friends in business thought him demented and it meant a great loss of income. He was turning in a new direction, which required new training. Although unclear as to its outcome in a specific job, he felt certain in choosing this direction. He saw what he called "a void in myself" which the other woman filled up. "Now I must do something about it and that means my work." In reaching toward the Self, he felt a great sea change in priorities and the need to give something of value into the world. It was on this basis that he decided to suspend his analysis. He had had to come a great distance to our sessions, and his new school schedule and rearranged work schedule left him with no time for such long trips.

His last dream moved me very much. He found himself in an airport, "a no man's land with the potential to go everywhere." There he was to meet a male, a friend, whom he identified as "sort of promiscuous, that is, sex for sex's sake." Then the dream climaxed: "As soon as I saw him, I shot him. No sooner had I done it than I was aware that while he was hit, I had felt the bullet go into my brain and lodge there. There it would stay like a splinter of wood. There is no retrieving it except by time dislodging it. Neither pain nor despair. A natural end. I go on and live." When he mailed his check for that last month, he wrote a note saying he would be in touch later: "Until then I remain the man with a bullet in his brain."

He had read a piece I had written on transference that included a passage about his father's death and his father's dream about the two women taking aim, each either to shoot the other or his father, and being prevented from doing so (Ulanov 1982).[26] He said, in association to his own dream, "Here was Dad's dream trying to avoid shooting and here I am shooting." He also recalled one of his beloved dogs who had lived for years with a .22 bullet in its head. The bullet was the other woman, he thought, and his disengagement from her sexually. He felt good about the dream: "This part of me causes me pain and I carry it and I accept the wound." I was moved by the image but also disquieted: being shot in the head is terrifying, and his father had died of brain disease. Yet this son had found what seemed to be at first just a sexual adventure and had turned into a life-changing love. His suffering, his acquiescence, his carrying it and choosing his own path touched me.

Can it be said, in conclusion, that the anima as it came to function as a bridge between ego and Self for each of these men ushered in vital changes in which each man's ego became more masculine, shadow bits became more integrated, and the anima more an articulator for the unconscious? Each of them, one in dying and the other in living, felt himself faced with the awesomeness of life and answered it with a desire to give, to give over to its center in the father's case, to give into the world in the son's. The father finds he is able to offer up his wound in the crisis of his death. The son consciously carries his wound into his life. Could it be that the anima, disguised as a split between two women, as a split between two kinds of mothering, as a wound to the feminine, is really the disguise of the Self putting itself forward to the ego in an irresistible way? This leads to mystic precincts.

Although Jung was not a mystic and explicitly disavowed "faith," eschewing both compliance and will power as substitutes for immediate experience, does he not bring us finally to a faith, or to multiple faiths in the Self (Jung 1938, par. 8–11; Jaffé 1989, chapter 1)? Is this not the work of all analysts, finally, a leading to the Self? The anima and animus archetypes engender experiences of the Self coming into being, calling the ego to leave its country and journey into strange territories to take up new life, real life. As Jung put it, "One must be able to suffer God. . . . God needs limitation in time and space. Let us therefore be for him limitation in time and space, an earthly tabernacle" (Jung 1975, vol. 1, pp. 65–66).

Notes

1. Examples illustrate this confrontation: a man dreamt of a sick woman trying to run after him in the sand. He was repelled by her. She called after him in protest, saying that the only way she could get any attention from him was to whine and complain to him.

A woman dreamt she was on an important journey. As she drove along in her car, the roads became more primitive, finally going off into a wilderness on a dirt track. There at the end of it stood a stark man, "looking like John the Baptist," as if waiting for her arrival. He had immense authority and spiritual presence and "there was no way I could avoid meeting him."

A woman dreamt of a man she respected who was fishing up out of the watery depths a cure for incurable disease. After speaking about it to everyone, he came over to the dreamer and kissed her, saying he would love her forever (Ulanov 1971, pp. 256–257).

2. Lecturing on this subject once in North Carolina, a member of the audience asked what distinguished these Self contents from, for example, shadow materials. I found myself spontaneously answering that Self contents have to do with life and death. I have no quarrel with the bridge analogy being used in relation to the shadow, or for other major psychic complexes, like the persona, but there is a different feel to the contents addressing us. Self contents coming across the anima/animus bridge do not face us with the bad in ourselves (or, for some of us, the good, if we think of ourselves as bad). Self contents put questions to our very existence.

3. This is not to say, however, that Jung's theory is problem-free or without the mark of his time in history (see, for example, Ulanov 1971, pp. 335–341; Ellenberger 1970, pp. 293–294, 708–710).

4. Jung himself says, "Take for instance *animus* and *anima*. No philosopher in his senses would invent such irrational and clumsy ideas. When things fit together, it is not always a matter of a philosophical system; sometimes it is the facts that fit together" (Jung 1975, vol. 2, p. 192).

Animus and anima appear at the threshold to the Self. They usher in Self experiences. They occupy the lowest place on the ladder into the Self. Clumsy as this theory is, it occupies a place on a par with Freud's discovery of the oedipal complex, Klein's of the depressive position, Winnicott's of the false and true selves, Kohut's of the self that precedes experience of the instinctual drives. Here Jung makes accessible to us, through image, symbol, and theoretical construct, our experience of our own sexuality, as it is, not as it should be. Jung shows us that we cannot ask, What kind of woman (or man) am I, let alone answer it, if we are not also asking what way an other lives in us from a sexual departure point opposite to our own gender identity. The person reaching toward wholeness is the contrasexual person; we are not either-or, nor neither-nor, but both-and, self and other, same and opposite. We cannot possess the object of the opposite sex except as an image. So there opens between us a space of spirit where imaginatively we experience but do not possess the world of the other. Symbols get born. In the midst of sexuality and body presence, then, Jung gives us a way to talk about the spiritual component of sexuality, not as something tacked on, but as its central motif, opening to us, indeed, addressing us, and asking for our response in all the body push-pulls of impulse and need, desire and appetite. Jung penetrates "this difficult field of extremely subtle experience" with these figures of anima and animus which are the "cause of that deep human need to speak of souls or daemons at all" (Jung 1931, pars. 92, 82). Thus he offers a counter argument and a counterpart to Freud's oedipal complex.

Freud had an experience of anima that seemed to him frightening, dangerous, threatening to put him into the passive position, overcome by music, religious illusion, or the "mudtide" of the occult. The anima looked enviously on his chief member, perhaps even plotting to rob him of it. Thus Freud puts her in her place, definitely second in importance. He constructs his Oedipus theory from the male point of view, never inquiring what happens from Jocasta's perspective, let alone the little girl's.

The oedipal battle between fathers and sons is made too simple because it omits dealing with the incomplete mother, which is less an anthropological issue of generations fighting for her favor as it is a mother who does not present herself and cannot do so *because* of the sins of the fathers. This feminine deficiency passes through male succession, just as the deficiency of animus is passed on through the mothers.

Jung approaches the mystery of the human person with all of our deficiencies and sufficiencies, which engineer as well as express themselves in sexual tangles, including the oedipal, with as much conscious security as possible, without dissipating the mystery. It is not the job of a theory to substitute scientific certainty for mystery. With the symbolic concepts of anima and animus, we have a way to talk about a depth dimension. For the anima and animus do not only pull our egos across their borders toward the otherness of others and through that into the otherness of the Self, but also pull us from consciousness into the unconscious (both personal and objective). They speak not only of the sexual opposites, but also of the opposites of conscious and unconscious. (Jung 1944, par. 192; Jung 1955–1956, par. 104; Jung 1952, pars. 264, 335, 451).

5. For a discussion of this rescuing anima, see Ulanov and Ulanov (1987, pp. 250–254).

6. Cited by Karl Hass, Radio Station WMNR CT, December 1989.

7. I have not used the term *mistress* because there was no question of financial support nor of providing shelter, clothes, etc. These were deeply emotional relationships.

The split of the anima can present itself in other opposites, too, such as a man feeling that his inner life leads him one way and his outer life another, or his spiritual needs oppose those of the flesh, etc.

8. Jung sees the anima and animus living in a world different from our own, "where the pulse of time beats ever so slowly . . . their aspect is . . . so strange that their intrusion into consciousness often blasts into fragments the all-too-feeble brainpans of unfortunate mortals. Anima and animus contain the greater part of the material which appears in insanity, more especially in schizophrenia." They are "elusive wraiths," "fragmentary personalities," "always strangers to the conscious world"; they "permeate the atmosphere with a feeling of uncanny foreboding, or even a fear of mental derangement" (Jung 1939, pp. 23–25).

9. This kind of transference is one of the main types surrounding the anima, in contrast to another main type where the analyst herself receives the sexual projection. For discussion, see Ulanov (1982).

10. The animus also functions as a bridge, hence the function of anima and animus is the same, but subtle and decisive differences exist, too.

When one is in touch with a well-functioning animus, one is in touch with the truth by which one lives; when one is in touch with a well-functioning anima, one is in touch with an animating connection to being (see Jung 1955–1956, pars. 232, 646).

11. Marie-Louise von Franz comments, "the anima behaves very paradoxically, or else she splits into two opposing figures, between which consciousness is torn this way and that, until the ego begins to concern itself with the task of individuation. It is only when a man begins to have an apprehension of the Self behind the anima that he finds the foundation on which he can escape her pulling and tugging in contrary directions" (E. Jung and von Franz 1970, p. 262).

12. For discussion of the effects of a father's anima on a son's development, see Beebe (1985); see also, Ulanov (1977).

13. By soul I mean both of Jung's meanings—the "partial personality" of the anima and also the Christian meaning of an inner doorway to God, about which Jung says, "it has the dignity of an entity endowed with, and conscious of, a relationship to Deity" (Jung 1944, p. 10, see also, pp. 8, 9, 11).

14. For discussion of controlling instinctual life with the result of loss of vitality, see Winnicott (1988, pp. 85–86).

15. These are examples of what Jung calls the synthetic questions, in contrast to the analytic ones, from the prospective point of view, in contrast to the reductive one (Jung 1943, par. 121–140).

We can also see this split of private secret and public life as an example of Jung's exploration of the relationship between the anima and the persona (Jung 1984, pp. 52, 75, 79ff).

16. "The Self, the very centre of an individual, is of a conglomerate nature. It is, as it were, a group. It is a collectivity in itself and therefore always, when it works most positively, creates a group" (Jung 1975, vol. 1, p. 508).

26. In my opening remarks for the discussion of this paper at the Ghost Ranch Conference, June 2, 1990, I added these comments about the transference-countertransference dimensions of these two cases.

In the work with the father, I found myself arranged and rearranged in different ways. Here he was, a man successful in his profession, a veteran of combat with the rank of sergeant, standing with courage for unpopular causes in his work, yet before women as if a boy. Sympathetic to his suffering and worried about his suicidal impulses, I resisted being his mother-approver, feeling myself in an opposite place—still, not jumping on cue, not always hospitable to the boy-mother need. Yet he had a sense of humor, and we erupted into laughing more than once. He got his split-anima to a liveable place, where the two women in his dream no longer were going to shoot. But the split was not fully resolved when he stopped treatment. That happened, I believe, in his dying and the short, intense work we had time to do in relation to that.

His sexual transference to women did not shift to me. It was all taken up with the various women in his life. Also during his treatment I was marrying, and then later pregnant, and still later nursing. I was all taken up. There was a deep abiding connection between us, so he called when he heard he was dying, and we were able to take up and accomplish that last piece of work.

With the son, I was associated nearer to the world of his parents than to his own and the sexual projections were all taken up with women in his life, so they did not (yet) fall on me. This is a different experience than I have had in other cases where the work focuses on anima issues. There the erotic tone of the transference is intense and seems to be the necessary heat to match and dislodge the intensity of where the man feels stuck as, for example, in one case, in what the man called his lifetime of perversions.

With the son, too, a deep sense of the being of the other and respect for it helped weather periods of negativity because I did not answer everything or speed things up or fix them. I managed to weather periods of worry about his suicidal impulses.

In general, I think with Masud Khan, that countertransference works best when it works silently and is used and folded into the patient's life. The patient's life and relation to reality, both societal and psychical, both religious and pragmatic, is what matters. The particular danger of overemphasis on countertransference-transference dynamics, and especially, I would suggest, in anima/animus situations, is that the analysis and the analytical interaction or field can substitute for the patient's life and then for the analyst's. In analytical jargon, it means the analytical couple can substitute for the ego-Self couple: the process of analysis can substitute for the process of living toward the Self and thus for the deepest aspects of life.

The issue for me is not in the theory of anima/animus, but in the living of the anima/animus situations which bring us into the center where we feel and know we are in the center of life. We know that this is it. What is here in this moment is what really matters. This is the immediate experience that Jung stressed so much. This theory—for all its clumsy confused nature and awkward language—is the only one I know that approaches this kind of experience on its own level.

References

Bachelard, G. 1969. *The Poetics of Reverie*. Daniel Russell, trans. New York: Orion.

Beebe, J. 1985. The father's anima. In *The Father: Contemporary Jungian Perspectives*, A Samuels, ed. London: Free Association Books.

Ellenberger, H. F. 1970. *The Discovery of the Unconscious*. New York: Basic Books.

Goldenberg, N. R. 1976. A feminist critique of Jung. *Signs: Journal of Women in Culture and Society* 2/2.

Hillman, J. 1972. On psychological femininity. In *The Myth of Analysis*. San Francisco: Harpers.

Jaffe, A. 1989. *Was C. G. Jung a Mystic?* Diana Dackerland and Fiona Cairns, trans. Einsiedeln: Daimon Verlag.

Jung, C. G. 1928. The relations between the ego and the unconscious. *CW* 7:123–304. Princeton, N.J.: Princeton University Press, 1953.

———. 1931. Mind and earth. *CW* 10:29–49. Princeton, N.J.: Princeton University Press, 1964.

———. 1938. Psychology and religion. *CW* 11:3–105. Princeton, N.J.: Princeton University Press, 1958.

———. 1939. *The Integration of the Personality*. Stanley Dell, trans. New York: Farrar and Rinehart.

———. 1943. On the psychology of the unconscious. *CW* 7:3–121. Princeton, N.J.: Princeton University Press, 1953.

———. 1944. *Psychology and Alchemy. CW*, vol. 12. Princeton, N.J.: Princeton University Press, 1953.

———. 1952. *Symbols of Transformation. CW*, vol. 5. Princeton, N.J.: Princeton University Press, 1956.

———. 1955–1956. *Mysterium Coniunctionis. CW*, vol. 14. Princeton, N.J.: Princeton University Press, 1963.

———. 1975. *Letters*, 2 vols. G. Adler and A. Jaffe, eds. R. F. C. Hull, trans. Princeton, N.J.: Princeton University Press.

———. 1984. *Dream Analysis*. William McGuire, ed. Princeton, N.J.: Princeton University Press.

Jung, E. and von Franz, M.-L. 1970. *The Grail Legend*. Andrea dykes, trans. New York: Putman's.

Kast, V. 1986. *The Nature of Loving: Patterns of Human Relationship*. Boris Matthews, trans. Wilmette, Ill.: Chiron Publications.

Miller, J. B. 1976. *Toward a New Psychology of Women*. Boston: Beacon.

Neumann, E. 1985. *The Great Mother: An Analysis of an Archetype*. Ralph Manheim, trans. Princeton, N.J.: Princeton University Press.

Reuther, R. R. 1983. *Sexism and God-Talk: Toward a Feminist Theology*. Boston: Beacon.

Solovyev, V. 1945. *The Meaning of Love*. Jane Marshall, trans. London: Geoffrey Bles.

Ulanov, A. B. 1982. Transference/countertransference: a Jungian perspective. In *Jungian Analysis*, Murray Stein, ed. LaSalle, Ill.: Open Court.

———. 1971. *The Feminine in Jungian Psychology and in Christian Theology*. Evanston, Ill.: Northwestern University Press.

———. 1977. The search for paternal roots: Jungian perspectives on fathering. In *Fathering: Fact or Fable?* Edward V. Stein, ed. Nashville, Tenn.: Abingdon.

Ulanov, A., and Ulanov, B. 1987. *The Witch and the Clown: Two Archetypes of Human Sexuality*. Wilmette, Ill.: Chiron Publications.

Whitmont, E. C. 1980. Reassessing femininity and masculinity. *Quadrant* 13/2.

Winnicott, D. W. 1965a. The development of the capacity for concern. In *The Maturational Processes and the Facilitating Environment*. New York: International Universities Press.

———. 1965b. Communicating and not communicating leading to a study of certain opposites. In *The Maturational Processes and the Facilitating Environment*. New York: International Universities Press.

———. 1988. *Human Nature*. London: Free Association.

The Role of the Anima in Analysis

Peter Schellenbaum

Introduction

In recent years, some Jungian analysts, among them James Hill-man and Verena Kast, have made the image/concept of the anima the object of critical scrutiny. During C. G. Jung's lifetime, characteristics of the anima, regarded as determining the nature of the feminine in the man, were accepted without question. Today, influenced by women's growing efforts toward autonomy, these characteristics seem much more to be the product of historical imprint. Moreover, there is a demand to stop defining the nature of the masculine and feminine, because misuse of definitions seems unavoidable and has served to cement outmoded power relationships.

Of course, this does not decrease the importance of an on-going confrontation with what Jung had termed the anima and the animus. On the contrary, these images of the feminine and masculine psyche are emerging only now in their full dynamic, because their understanding is no longer bound up in an unconscious patriarchal entitlement to power. This should become clear as I develop my theme — the role of the anima in analysis.

Peter Schellenbaum is a Doctor of Theology and graduate of the Jung Institute, Zurich, where he currently serves as analyst, training analyst, supervisor, and lecturer. His English publications include *How to Say No to the One You Love* and *The Wound of the Unloved*.

Definition of Terms

With this premise, any discussion about the anima must begin with a definition of terms. Contentwise, the suprapersonal anima, insofar as it refers to the feminine pole in the human, is difficult to distinguish clearly from the personal anima—that deposit of one's experience with the feminine accumulated over the course of a lifetime. All considerations on this matter are merely a waste of energy. It is more fruitful in any given situation to get a feel for the play of energy between the masculine and the feminine poles in the psyche and conceptualize on the basis of this.

For this reason I also agree with Hillman and Kast that the archetypal images of anima and animus are effective within both sexes. Even in a mature individual where the feminine and the masculine interact with a certain amount of consciousness, it becomes clear that in every individual there is a certain degree of consciousness and unconsciousness adhering to the masculine as well as to the feminine pole. In every individual, both poles evince an archetypal character; they are not only the result of chance imprinting, but belong like masculine and feminine genes to the humanity of both.

Decisive as this may be, in both men and women, the same reciprocal dynamic toward increased consciousness and integration is inherent in the anima and the animus. This is evident today in analysis with men who have renounced the old masculine attitude of dominance and have become receptive to the feminine outwardly in women and inwardly in their own souls. It is in every sense wrong to identify one's own sex with consciousness and the opposite sex with unconsciousness. I repeat: both men and women have a degree of unconsciousness with respect to both the personal as well as the collective unconscious. So it becomes superfluous to assign the concepts anima or animus to the opposite pole and the shadow to the same-sex pole. The term *shadow* refers to a psychic content which is nearly conscious although repressed, but which can be raised to consciousness. When we speak of anima and animus, we refer to all those life processes that are rooted in the archetypal, those processes which are autonomous, unavailable, and, at least in part, not integrable.

By anima then, in relationship to the psyche of the man, I understand the generally less conscious and less developed feminine pole, and, in relationship to the psyche of the woman, the generally more conscious and more developed feminine pole.

Jung often characterized the *anima* in the man as compensating a one-sidedly masculine *persona*. For this reason, in the East there is neither anima nor persona: "In the Eastern view the concept of the anima, as we have stated it here, is lacking, and so, logically, is the concept of a persona. This is certainly no accident, for, as I have already indicated, a compensatory relationship exists between persona and anima" (Jung 1928, par. 304).

This remark of Jung's about the compensatory relationship between anima and persona is thus related to the concrete historical informing of the Western patriarchal man. Does this mean that, with the reduction of the persona, the anima also diminishes? In the above quote from "The Relations Between the Ego and the Unconscious," it appears this way. In any case, in his later writings, Jung did not discuss this any further. Influenced by his interest in alchemy, in the end he saw in the anima the archetypal feminine opposite in the inner *coniunctio* within the masculine and feminine. All images of *coniunctio* are symbols of the energy-charged experience of an optimal psychic tension. For this reason also, it can never be precisely stated what is "really" masculine and what is "really" feminine. What woman and man can experience with one another is a shared building up of tension: the polarity between them. Contentwise, this is related to opposition. Still, because these opposites have always appeared in historical patterns, it seems sensible to proceed at any given moment from the polarities lived in reality and to strive toward the now optimal connecting of the two poles, within partnership as well as in one's own psyche.

For these reasons, I prefer to see animus and anima as masculine and feminine *poles*, and not as masculine and feminine *principles*. A principle should be clearly definable as such. This is not precisely possible in the description of a masculine and feminine principle. We always remain at a loss to explain why that which is not definitely masculine and not definitely feminine should be easily ascribable to masculine and feminine principles. When we use the categories masculine and feminine to mean a masculine and a feminine principle, we get into endless entanglements. We make statements about masculine and feminine nature and then immediately relativize these with references to historical influences, only to have to state that we can't be certain where these influences begin and end. I prefer to proceed from the one undisputed fact relating to human existence: the primordial attraction, even fear, that men experience with respect to women and women experience with respect to men. I want to proceed from the psychic energy gradient inherent in the polarity between male and female and its correspondences in the individual psyche.

In Chinese philosophy, yin and yang also appear exclusively as the interplay of polar energies. Here, too, it is not concerned in the final analysis with definition of what should be masculine and what should be feminine, but rather with the dynamic set up by the opposing poles. It is in this sense that I would like to have the following discussion understood.

The Psychic Energy of the Anima in Analysis

The original concept of the anima did not yet contain definite images of the feminine: the holy, the whore, the muse, the femme fatale, the demon of death, the guide into the unconscious, and so forth. It contained rather the formless and goalless *animating energy*. In analytical work, only when we discover intuitive and instinctive access to this vivacity as such, beyond all later decisions, classifications, and moral judgments in the form of praise and blame, can we experience the reality and autonomy of the unconscious. Sometimes I have the impression that we Jungians know well, all too well, in what forms the anima appears. We know it so well that we also simultaneously know just what form the next developmental step should take: Aha! You have dreamt about a loving, giving mother. Now you must finally realize that an adult does not have life given to him any more, but has to work hard on his development. We interpret and join the interpretation to a moral postulate. Admittedly, this is the psychology of consciousness and a therapy oriented toward the development of conscious awareness, even though we proceed from constructions of the unconscious. But in employing such therapeutic coercion we inhibit the healing forces arising from the unconscious.

For Jung, the anima is above all the *natural archetype of living being*. He calls her a *factor*, thus, an agent not dependent on consciousness. She is *a priori to all animated utterances*, above all, those of which we are ashamed because they don't correspond to the picture we would like to have of ourselves. She is a priori to all our moods, reactions, and impulses, the determining factor of our possibility for self-expression. She is *that which lives of itself and causes us to live* (Jung 1954, par. 56).

There, in the situation where life wells up most intensively, where it excites, seethes, exerts pressure, impels forward, confuses, loses the old orientation, discomfits, floods one with fear, awakens hope, confronts one with radical leave-taking; there, the anima is at work. Where this happens, a psychic *gradient* develops, flowing away from an outmoded life pattern toward something as yet unknown, away from a highly esteemed value toward something undervalued until now. For this reason, Jung described the anima as the personification of the inferior function and as the representation of the inferior feminine gene in the male body (Jung 1954, par. 58). According to this amplified image of the anima, I understand her as the representative of that human psychic life process toward which, at any specific time, the most libido or life energy flows. To a certain extent, the anima is always situated on the moving point of an individual's drive toward development, on the point of the strongest pressure toward individuation.

The original appearance of the anima is thus one of Dionysian oneness. She is life, life that moves apparently without plan from one point of concentration to another. Only when we entrust ourselves to her do we begin to sense her in-dwelling coherence. The Greek god Dionysus reveals himself to us in the same way in the ordering rhythms of music and in the inner coherent logic of cathartic tragedy — but then only when we cease to struggle against him, lest we be torn to pieces or driven to insanity.

In the end, the art in analysis for any individual is the *optimal dissolving of resistance* to the anima, in the sense of her original meaning as life-bringing energy. It has to do with *admitting the anima in her meaninglessness* (Jung 1954, par. 66): she doesn't offer any interpretations, but rather confuses and involves one in goalless being. Without *breakdown*, the *breakthrough* which belongs to any initiation cannot happen. In the moment of breakdown, one sinks to a final depth (ibid.).

As long as there is in us the slightest secret motive regarding definite, achievable progress, we are evading the anima. Such thoughts play an important part in Jung's ideas. Why do we find them far less often in works by Jungians, where the spotlight is certainly on detailed and definite anima images, but the imageless, meaningless, as yet formless and chaotic anima as a priori to life is hardly mentioned.

I believe the answer lies in the creeping helplessness that Jungian therapists experience in the face of the fundamental task to permit the *"life without the need to know why"* to be lived (Eckehart's "Worumwille"). With respect to a dream, for example, it is much easier for us to interpret the symbolic pictures than simply to surrender ourselves, together with the analysand, to the flow of life.

The main question that confronts us is: How can we in our depth-psychology therapy bring the anima into play in the original sense of the word as the anima-tor?

In answer to this question, Jung suggests the path of *dialogue*. Dialogue with the unconscious corresponds to the *middle way of Tao*.

The middle way of dialogue runs along the border between inner and outer, between being at the mercy of the outer world, and adapting to this, the reality principle, which arises from the necessity to hold one's own in a partly strange, even hostile environment, on the one hand, and, on the other hand, being completely at the mercy of the inner world that impells ultimately toward dissociation.

Jung speaks in this connection of a conversation with one's own serpent. This is the disturbing factor in the middle of the supposed paradise of our everyday harmlessness and downplaying of facts. If we as analysts seek above all a "comfortable rapport," the snake with its unreliability and its unpredictable movements is uncomfortable to us. We then misuse our analysand's positive transference to maintain a hollow psychic truce that avoids the conflicts that need to be addressed. Some "eternal analyses" come about through the eternal avoidance of the serpent-anima as an incalculable vital energy.

In contrast to this, alertly entering into the dynamic of the dream symbol in discussion and active imagination as the middle way between day and dream, as well as giving form to the inner pictures by means of drawing, painting, and modeling, can induce a fruitful dialogue with the anima. The unconscious appears in this way. The subjectivity of consciousness is relativized by the "objective psychic" opposing us as dialogue partner. An aggressive affect, for example, will neither be devalued nor denied. Instead, judgment-free questions will be put: What do you want to say to me? What neglected aspect of my self seeks expression in you? Is there some necessary delimitation that you want to force from me? Are you signaling some life task that needs tackling? Or, what in my life would you like to destroy? A particular attitude or relationship, or a particular behavior of mine?

Such a dialogue with the anima should, according to Jung, last as long as required for a subjective feeling of peace and satisfaction to set in. It is an inestimable instrument of analytical work.

Yet, precisely because Jung specifies dialogue, colloquy, two opposing positions, and the distinction of subject and object, it seems to me that he doesn't quite do justice to the original conception of the anima as unitary, undivided, undifferentiated vital energy. She requires an empirical path that is also unitary and undivided. Only then is the healing path of the dialogue open.

For several years in group work I have sought to connect psychodrama in dialogue form to the energy-laden way in which a definite emotion seeks a suitable mode of expression. On several occasions, I noticed that the dramatic path of inner confrontation taking place in the psychodrama was blocked at a decisive point: always at the point where emotional traumata of early, preverbal childhood were stirred up. When I, as leader of the psychodrama, let the play go on despite the emotional barrier, the play would become inauthentic and could no longer lead to the desired cathartic release. Quite the contrary, it would increase feelings of alienation in the protagonist.

For this reason, I interrupt the psychodrama at such a point, sit down near the protagonist, and often touch him. Or, I hold him in the moment and let the inhibited emotion resonate in me. This can take the form of pain or sorrow, bottomless abandonment, or powerless fury. The entire life force of the person to whom I am so close in this moment now concentrates in the unredeemed emotion. By means of an appropriate invitation and/or a physical touch, I make it easier for him to identify completely with this emotion, *to be* this vital force, *to be* the anima. This is not at all a compulsive anima possession — I will address this shortly. A process of free self-experience and free self-expression is thus set in motion. The presence of the therapist gives the protagonist the necessary trust to stay on the unknown and uncertain track of his most powerful emotions.

This empathy on the part of the therapist is necessary in the fullest sense of this word. He or she is the resonating body responding to the client's still-unconscious, still-unlived emotions. For example, this means that, in participating in the life of the client, the analyst already consciously experiences a feeling of abandonment while the client is still suffering a muffled, unexplainable emotion whose nature remains unconscious. The client transfers the unconscious wave of emotion to the therapist, who consciously receives it, lets it run its course in him and in this way, without a word, lets it flow back to the client. Thanks to this reinforcement, the patient begins to accept the emotion heretofore inhibited and permits it to live.

Often the experiencing of one emotion leads to the experience of another; for example, an impotent fury is finally permitted to live, and this in turn can lead to the experience of a deep desperation. In the end, this emotion work leads to an intense feeling of happiness that is able to incorporate one's entire unhappiness. If this feeling of peace is achieved, the interrupted psychodrama can proceed, and with a completely new feeling tone. The now reopened path of dialogue often leads to an unexpected solution. Only now can it lead to catharsis and a restructuring of life.

I call the direct connection of the analytic dialogue, as Jung meant it, to the experience of an emotional process *psychoenergetic*. It is also enormously fruitful in the analysis of individuals. I am convinced that it does justice to the dual aspect of the anima as primordial unitary life force on the one hand, and as projection-shaping factor on the other. Without this connection, we are barred from access to those disturbances that are rooted in a phase of life that is determined by the unitary experience of symbiosis.

For the analyst, this connection is often very uncomfortable. He cannot install himself in the center of his work any more. The anima snake sees to it that he doesn't turn an analysis into an orderly stroll. Thanks to the joining together of dialogue and emotional work, it will most certainly never be boring and will make of him literally a more lively and original person. Jung's oft-repeated remark regarding a dream, or perhaps an affect, "I haven't a clue what this dream (affect) means," is no joke. Whoever opens himself completely to the dynamic of a dream, affect, or emotion experiences the breakdown of all his comfortable certainties and convictions. For a time, there will be no safe watchtower from which he can observe and order events. In the final analysis, the tiny light of his continuing consciousness is his *complete attentiveness* to what is happening, or better, his attentiveness *within* what is happening. Indeed, this is indispensable.

The analyst's alert, undivided attention is transferred to the analysand, who now no longer feels himself quite so much at the mercy of unfolding events. Perhaps he has been prone until now to experience his anima in a state of defenseless receptivity, passively exposed and flooded. In this case, images of the devouring mother are constellated. But now, aided by the analyst's contagious attentiveness to the inner flood of images and emotions, *passive* receptivity can be transformed into *active receptivity*. His anima no longer expresses itself in the images of the destructive *devouring mother*, but appears perhaps in images of *psychic pregnancy* or pictures of inner fertility.

It is important to experience and understand the anima not only in terms of archetypal images, but in terms of archetypal attitudes and primitive patterns of human behavior. When the emotion that accompanies such a basic psychic attitude or primitive behavior is made conscious, it often expresses something deeper and more central to the hidden archetype than even an archetypal image can do. The emotion is more primitive than the image. When we are working with an individual and this flood of emotion is released, the structuring and meaningful flood of images is also activated. The basic attitude of the mature anima, active receptivity, stimulates the pouring forth of images which further individuation in this way.

In this basic attitude of active, alert receptivity attributed to the anima, two longings will be simultaneously fulfilled: the paradisiacal longing for a happiness that will be given to us, and the longing for freedom and self-actualization. The last is experienced in association with the first.

Anima Collusion Between Analyst and Analysand

Psychiatrist Jürg Willi defined *collusion* as the predominantly unconscious interplay of specific roles between partners. The partners engage in this as a means of defending and surmounting feelings of fear and guilt which they have in common. They cannot renounce these behavior roles because they feel bound together by fate (Willi 1980, p. 39). By *anima collusion* between analyst and analysand I understand the enacting of roles in which the main problem is that both of them are partially or completely unconscious with respect to the anima.

I will first discuss four collusions arising between a male analyst and a male analysand, after which I will discuss collusions between a male analyst and a female analysand. I leave it to the women among my colleagues to pursue further the collusions that can develop in the practice of a female analyst.

Anima Collusion Between a Male Analyst and a Male Analysand

Each Encounters the Other in Terms of an Unconscious Aversion to the Feminine

This occurs within his own psyche as well as in the outer world. Between them reigns a sort of unspoken agreement to avoid the entrance to the dark cave that could lead to initiation and rebirth. On the surface, both have fallen prey to the one-sidedly masculine ideals of separation and autonomy, linear thinking, rights-and-rules oriented order, hierarchical structure, instrumentality and the "objective" viewpoint. Deep down, both are mother-dependent and cannot dispense with the protection of motherly persons. They are deficient in thinking and in a sense of self-reliance and courage. On the one hand, each mutually confirms and strengthens the other in his attitude of "manly" distance to inner and outer worlds. On the other hand, they are blood brothers in the bonds of longing for the maternal paradise.

Such an analyst wards off everything coming from his analysand which signals the sort of uncontrolled, spontaneous vitality which should and must be supported by resonance. He mobilizes the feeling of manly solidarity against the unconscious need of his analysand finally to engage in a life-affirming affect, emotion, or mood. He does not permit the analysand to pursue the trace of his own feelings, to finally experience vitality in itself and push through to the source of a natural self-reliance. Through his demeanor alone, this analyst without saying a word admonishes to discipline and restraint. He himself feels incapable of dealing with the living flood of emotions which could erupt from his analysand. He has an unconscious fear of losing the feeling of masculine solidarity and of being left alone if the analysand no longer entrusts himself to him, but to the anima as inner guide.

Such an analyst doesn't experience this with all analysands, but perhaps with one. With one, for example, whose anima is particularly strongly inhibited and who for this reason constellates a corresponding inhibition in the analyst or, with a great investment of libido, unconsciously seeks to constellate this inhibition in the analyst. Or, the analyst experiences this with another analysand whose emotional vitality could break out with such fury that the analyst unconsciously feels himself to be overburdened.

Like all the collusions which follow, this situation doesn't deserve to be termed *analysis*. In it, the impulse toward a vital oneness and to an acceptance of the anima as guide to the unconscious is suppressed or repressed. No wonder that in such an "analysis" either very few dreams will be remembered, or, if they are remembered, they will not be discussed in their disquieting and disturbing aspects.

Analyst and Analysand Encounter in Unconscious Anima-Possession

Addiction to the dissolution of emotional boundaries characterizes both. Both fall under the spell of Circe or the anesthetizing song of Lorelei or the Sirens and seek their vitality in the passive, expectant attitude of the child — risking the death of the psyche for this reason. In a symbiotic way, they are at the mercy of their emotions. The bond between analyst and analysand nourishes for both the illusion that two blind men together can see, that two men possessed by their emotions can together find reason and order. Mutually, they goad each other into more and more emotion-laden events, obliterate the borders of sentimentality, confuse touchiness with sensibility, and resentments with healthy aggression.

An anima-possessed analyst goads the suitable analysand into paroxysms of emotion, in order to feel alive himself through passive participation. If the analyst is in general a rather inhibited man, he feels dependent on this analysand to break through the barrier of his emotional inhibition. If the anima-possession is rooted in the basic structure of his personality, he feels himself to be validated by his analysand. In both cases, he acts out consciously or unconsciously a homoerotic inclination, so that his analysand cannot integrate his own homoerotic tendencies.

Such an "analysis" is lacking in both structure and meaning. There is a risk of psychotic inundation and dissociation with especially endangered patients. But in every case, passive longings that cannot be satisfied will be awakened and nourished in the analysand. Sooner or later it happens that the analysand expresses his growing disappointment and frustration in anger and aggression. An anima-possessed analyst is not in a position to provide the necessary alert and selfless resonance to these aggressions which are directed at him. For this reason, such an "analysis" is often broken off in belligerence: both feel wounded, offended, and frustrated because the other cannot serve as the good mother. In favorable cases, the analysand seeks a new analyst. In unfavorable cases, he sinks into discouragement and depression.

This example of a collusion between analyst and analysand represents an intentionally one-sided exaggeration in order to promote awareness of related, but somewhat weaker collusion tendencies.

In the collusion of a mutual anima-possession, dream and fantasy play an important role. These are used merely to heat up the feeling climate. Interpretations that contribute to a structuring of the situation are treated as superfluous. There is no genuine dialogue with either the unconscious or the partner.

There Is a Conflict Between the Analyst's Anima and the Analysand's Need to Define Boundaries

The analysand feels himself to be driven into a corner, run down, and oppressed. The analyst acts out his own fear of contact, his own lack of spontaneity and directness, and unintentionally directs fervor and emotional warmth at an unsuitable object, an analysand, an analysand who can be guided into the emotional track only with great respect and reticence. His anima is like a shy deer seeking haven with a hunter disguised as analyst. With this analysand, the analyst believes he can completely be the anima, completely be the feeling bond, completely be the animating energy. And, indeed, he can be, because he knows that the analysand is backing away from him. The unconscious, unrelated anima of the analyst colludes with the similarly unconscious and unrelated animus of the analysand. The analyst is emotional and feeling-toned and the analysand is cut off from his feelings and lamed. Both attitudes mutually confirm and strengthen each other.

In the beginning, the analysand came to precisely this analyst full of hope, because he sensed in him a readiness to approach him emotionally. Nevertheless, bitterness soon took the place of hope because of the unrelatedness of the analyst. The breaking off of this analysis is also difficult, because hope and disappointment have been in conflict for a long time.

Eventually every interpretation on the part of the analyst provokes fear and defensiveness in the analysand, and it would be important for the analyst to admit his own lack of emotional relatedness with respect to this analysand.

The Analyst Defends Against the Anima Identity of His Analysand

Here we find the fourth anima collusion between a male analyst and a male analysand. In this case the personality of the analyst probably has compulsive aspects: he is unspontaneous, controlled, and cautious in his emotional expression. His anima expresses itself more or less in the image of a young, reticent girl or a holy virgin. The anima of the analysand on the other hand appears perhaps in the image of a whore, who propositions the other with no respect for the niceties. Because the two anima figures are related to each other as opposites, antipathy and defensiveness develop easily between the two opposing players in the analytical discussion. The analysand will become even less respectful of distance and the analyst reacts with even more aloofness than with other analysands.

In the beginning, the analysand senses a hope of achieving, in dialogue with exactly this analyst, more distance to the outer and inner worlds, more perspective with respect to psychic interactions, more order and structure in shaping his own life. Nevertheless, the analyst is not capable of promoting by means of participative attention the transition from a chaotic to a fruitful and creative emotionality in the analysand. This "analysis" also leads to a polarization incapable of healing.

As in all forms of anima collusion, it would be necessary for the analyst to gain consciousness and openly discuss with the analysand the polarizing collusion of the transference and countertransference which is driving them. The holy anima of the analyst is split off from the whore anima—he projects the latter onto the analysand, who provides a suitable hook. From the side of the analysand, this projection runs in the opposite direction. A discussion of such a psychodynamic connection instills in the analysand a feeling of solidarity and a sense of being understood. In being together with this analysand, the analyst gains a chance to access with no "ifs, ands, or buts" the unconditional a priori of his own vital energies and, in the experience of their numinous power, also to learn to accept the analysand in all his fascination. Now both can start down the path of coexistent emotion and dialogue which constitutes a fruitful analysis.

Anima Collusion Between a Male Analyst and a Female Analysand

All that was discussed above is relevant to a great deal of what is to be said here. For this reason, I am limiting myself to specific instances. I want to remind the reader that I use the term *anima* not only for the masculine, but also for the feminine psyche. In the woman, the anima also has a numinous character and is only partially accessible to consciousness. Of course, the degree of consciousness with respect to the anima, understood as the feminine pole in the human being, is higher in the woman than in the man, as there is more correspondence to the development of the woman's identity. The anima of the woman is also the guide to the unconscious, if often in a more sisterly, familiar way than is the case in men. On the other hand, it can be that the animus of the female analysand might connect to the more dominant, better developed, nearly conscious animus in the male analyst in order to strengthen the more mysterious masculine pole, the animus, in herself. In the steeper gradient of this polar psychic dynamic, she might experience the life force more intensively. This means that, in working together with the analyst, she would like to gain support for all those characteristics in herself which in men tend to be stronger and more frequently found. It is unimportant to what extent these derive from nature or are socially conditioned. It is the dynamic interplay of the polar opposites in her own psyche, their relationship to the environment, and beyond this the integration of undervalued and neglected aspects of her personality that is important.

Analyst and Analysand Encounter Each Other in Shared Unconscious Aversion to the Feminine

This occurs in their own psyches and in the outer world. In a woman, this aversion is all the more tragic because it contains an aversion to her own sexual identity. It leads to alienation from the self and makes her dependent on the patriarchal world of the man. Concretely this means that such a woman in analysis finds herself once again in a degrading dependency on a man. Given the cramped condition of the masculine aspect of her personality, she can never be the equal of a man. She will always feel inferior to him because she denies the dominant feminine pole in herself. She will reject as not appropriate for herself everything that pertains to devotion and surrender, bonding, empathy, nurturing, and preserving. Please understand me clearly: I am not making any statement about the feminine, I underlined that at the beginning. Rather, I am proceeding from the characteristics that such a woman experiences as feminine and for this reason stifles.

If the analyst now joins the analysand in mutual aversion to the feminine, in that he one-sidedly and regularly glorifies "manly" values like competition, achievement, separation and autonomy, and cool detachment in thinking and feeling; if he emotionally does not perceive his analysand as a woman, and thereby neutralizes the enlivening vibration between male and female; if he rejects this particular woman in her femininity, then he creates an insurmountable power gradient between the superior and the inferior "man," between himself, the real man, and his analysand, the castrated "man."

In every patriarchal analyst, this hostility to the feminine finds at least a note of resonance. Here neither technique nor the analysis of transference and countertransference comes to the rescue. Here the one thing that can help is if the analyst himself can set his feet on a physical and emotional path of experience on which he can encounter the anima as a fundamental, undifferentiated life force having neither purpose nor goal.

Analyst and Analysand Encounter Each Other in Unconscious Anima Possession

This collusion is also a power relationship, this time to the disadvantage of the analyst. Because his identity is masculine, he experiences his own inferiority in the male-excluding triumphal procession of the feminine. He gets pulled into the vortex of his analysand, permits her to manipulate him, and falls under the spell of her feminine fascination. The archetype of the devouring mother constellates ever more strongly in the analysand. If she had originally sought out this analyst in order to find her way to more consciousness and structure together with a male partner, she now experiences with him (once again!) the weakness of the masculine and the destructive dynamic of her female personality. Discussions with the analyst become more and more chaotic. Helplessly she acts out her chaotic emotionality and makes more and more unreasonable demands on him. She may telephone day and night, come too late or too early or at the completely wrong time, fail to pay, etc. — presumably in the unconscious hope that a man, this man, her analyst, will finally stand up to her, bring his manly strength to bear and delineate himself from her with a liberating clarity, enabling her to free her animus from the embrace of the anima, thereby leading her to conscious and constructive behavior. Because all this doesn't happen with her analyst, who is at the mercy of this motherly vortex, the unconscious unholy alliance between anima and animus gains even more strength in her, and she tries even harder to injure the analyst and destroy him. If she finally succeeds in this, she is left behind alone once again.

If, on the other hand, the analyst comprehends the nature of the challenge mounted by such an analysand, he can learn to help her in that he helps himself. This means he keeps her assault within bounds by establishing the limits with matching strength and, in taking his stand, remains in a feeling relationship.

There Is a Conflict Between the Relationship-Seeking Anima of the Analyst and the Delimitation-Seeking Animus of the Analysand

This collusion often occurs between an analyst who is undifferentiated and even obtrusive in his feeling statements and a shy, retiring, sensitive, and discreet analysand. She needs time and trust to venture her feelings. A tactless analyst who has no respect for distance only increases her need for shelter and delimitation. The emotions of the analysand are the more blocked the more the two roles polarize in this collusion. Now the analyst must practice granting the necessary freedom in a differentiated feeling relationship. This analysand requires his anima in its most mature form; namely, as Sophia, wisdom, who joins love to gracious distance, in order that she can find distance to her habitual flight reflex and eventually be able to open up her feelings to a man.

There Is a Conflict Between the Analyst's Need for Delimitation and the Relationship Needs of the Analysand

In this last anima collusion, the analysand is unconsciously seeking, in the sense of a neurotic compulsion, to repeat the painful confirmation that for her there is no love in the world. She appeals to the feelings of the analyst to turn to her in such a way that, in case he hasn't perceived and understood the connection, he reacts only with defensiveness and rejection. If this stirs up the early childhood complex of the unloved child in the analyst himself, and if he is not conscious of this, growing aggression will inhibit his relationship to the analysand. This analysand will seem to threaten his well-being and autonomy. He doesn't realize that the relationship and love-seeking needs of his analysand are founded on a deep fear of her own lack of vitality and the pain of an early wounding in her own life.

The analyst must open himself to the related pain in his own psyche in order to be accessible for the wounded anima of his analysand. Then she can eventually lose her fear-induced, feverish intensity and arrive at the relationship function which achieves her goal.

Because the dominant emotion of such a woman is fear, she doesn't find her way to the Thou despite repeated exaggerated efforts at nearness. She is equally unsuccessful at finding the connection to her own unconscious. Her anima is a restless female ghost who drifts unredeemed from place to place in search of relationship, but always runs into walls. Such an analysand means a challenge to the analyst not to let himself be infected by the hopelessness of this searcher for love. In her presence, he must feel a love of life clearly and strongly — so clearly and strongly that the infection occurs in the opposite direction, and the analysand can let go of her old pain and the attitude of negative expectation that goes with it.

Conclusion

In our time of increasing effort toward relationship, understanding, and communication, the maturing and integration of the anima, as Jungian psychology understands it, plays a central role. The concept of the anima should nevertheless find its way back to its original meaning as natural archetype of the vital force itself, as imageless and meaningless life. Otherwise, we become entangled in anachronistic discussions about the nature of the feminine, instead of seeking ways in which we can awaken the anima as numinosum in ourselves and in the individuals with whom we work. Precisely because in our time there is a growing fascination with the anima, the analysis which seeks only to dissect and achieve distance has seen its day. Experiential therapies, in which the body-and-soul human beings can express themselves in their manifold emotions, approach more closely the need for an immediate experience of the vitalizing energy of life. Nevertheless, internalizing this vital energy requires, in addition, a dialogue with the images that take form during the process. The interplay of the paths of emotion and dialogue enable the anima to awaken in analytical work.

Additional Comments

Why am I of the opinion that we must speak of *anima* and *animus* as archetypal images in *both sexes*? In answer to this question, I want to note three points which were brought up and discussed at the Ghost Ranch Conference where I presented this paper.

First, it was often mentioned (Louis Zinken, for example) as a counterargument that the term *anima* is related to an image of the woman that was derived from a male point of view. This *masculine anima image does not correspond to the feminine self-perception*. My reply: this is true to a certain extent. Still, the *reason* for this lies for the most part in a *lack of dialogue* between men and women. The psychically isolated man in the patriarchate castes the anima image in pictures of fear and longing for this reason. These images are thus unrealistic because of the isolation of the man.

In a comparison of the *dreams* of men whose understanding of themselves is rooted in the patriarchal tradition with those of men who coexist in an open, flexible, and lively dialogue with women, I have observed that the former, in fact, display anima images that are completely split off from feminine self-experience, whereas the latter have images of the feminine in the unconscious that are very similar to images of the feminine in women.

The second group of men corresponds to the *Zeitgeist* of our time. In the future, this tendency will undoubtedly become even stronger. Jung himself belonged to the old partriarchal school. His intense fascination for women did not correspond to an equally intense, seriously taken dialogue with them. His inner dialogue with the anima had a character that was partly compensatory to his deficient perception of the real woman.

Archetypal images do not arise directly out of the human psyche. They are also made of the stuff of the world, and thus of the stuff of a definite period of time. The hidden archetype is merely a psychic readiness system which connects with the concrete world to form archetypal images.

I presume that Jung's idea of gender-specific archetypes derived in one sense from the inner separation of his anima from the real woman, in other words, in a lack of dialogue.

A second counterargument maintained that the man has a "lack" with respect to femininity, just as the woman has a "lack" with respect to masculinity. But every *lack signifies relationship* (Louis Zinkin). A psychic void is a *space*, a *field*, an *interval*, that calls forth emotions like *longing* (desire — Nathan Schwartz-Salant), *love*, and *fear*. This *creative void* exists with respect to the *opposite sex*. This is as it should be; nevertheless, it also exists, although usually to a lesser extent, with respect to *one's own sex*. This, too, is never completely conscious to us, never completely available; we are never completely identical with it. There exists an archetypal *difference* here, too, which signifies relationship. I refer to this "lack" when I refer to the animus in the man, and the anima in the woman.

In this connection, I agree with Polly Young-Eisendrath that men and women are not members of one of two clubs.

The relationship function between man and man I call the animus in the man, and the relationship function between woman and woman I call the anima in the woman.

Third, my *most important argument* in favor of the renunciation of gender-specific archetypes is the following. As I have described in detail, the most fundamental meaning of the *anima* is *archetype of life*, just as the fundamental meaning of the *animus* is *archetype of the spirit*. This is exemplified in many places in Jung's work. Life and spirit are inseparable, and most certainly in the same way in a man and in a woman. At this depth in the human psyche, gender-specific attributions make no sense whatever. In the self-experience of the child, too, that is, in the earliest self-experience of the individual, gender-specific differences play a subordinate role, and they play no role whatever in any central sense. This is demonstrated most clearly in body-related therapy in which the emotional working through of early feelings of abandonment and an early insufficiency of love takes place in the same way in both sexes.

However, if we ascribe the anima as archetype of life and the animus as archetype of the spirit to both sexes, then we must do the same also with respect to all the other images associated with the anima and the animus.

References

Jung, C. G. 1928. The relations between the ego and the unconscious. In *CW* 7:123–304. Princeton, N.J.: Princeton University Press, 1953.
————. 1954. Archetypes of the collective unconscious. In *CW* 9i:3–41. Princeton, N.J.: Princeton University Press, 1959.
Willi, J. 1980. Die Zweierbeziehung. Hamburg: Rowohlt.

The Anima of the Analyst — Its Development

David I. Tresan

I

Most Jungian analysts, when asked, generally say that the anima has personal importance for them, but no one is quite certain of how to encompass the concept. This is true of highly seasoned and well-trained clinicians, but it is certainly more true of the person in the street or for therapists of other traditions for whom the concept is either totally unknown or, at best, baffling. For all its charm, the anima seems either badly neglected or misunderstood by most, which is both curious and unfortunate because the concept (or is she a fact?) is unique in psychology and its elaboration by Jung is brilliant. Clinically, for instance, nothing in psychology explains nearly so well the dynamics of the male in the second half of life; the concept of the ego-ideal, which comes closest to it, is still totally off the mark. Why, then, one may ask, is the concept of anima not better known, better understood, and better received? So, too, there is the question of why the concept has not been more generative among those who do know of it. Pitifully little research, writing, and elaboration of theory has been done, and hardly

David I. Tresan is a faculty member of the C. G. Jung Institute of Northern California and conducts a private practice in San Francisco and Mill Valley, California.

any at all if the work of James Hillman is exempted. This neglect applies to Jung as well; he did not significantly expand the concept further during the last thirty-three years of his life. This paper is a study of the anima as an elegant, subtle, and heuristic psychological apperception. I seek the sources and development of the notion (as Hillman (1985) labels her) both in Jung's personal psychology and his theory — they reflect one another — but I begin with my own meetings with her.

I was introduced to the concept of the anima in the first year of my analysis when I was informed that my dissatisfaction with my wife was actually an anima problem. At once, I seized on the explanation with great vigor and great relief. It meant that there was something important I did not know about men and women, that I could preserve my marriage and stay with my wife because it and she were not truly deficient, and that my problems all stemmed from an unfair comparison of my wife with another woman who was not even real. I was delighted, came right home, and shared the good news. My wife wondered what it was I had discovered, as well she might. After all these years, I am still trying to explain it, and so I am writing for her as well as for myself. At that time, though, my enthusiasm could not be dampened by lack of understanding. The entire idea of anima conjured up in me adumbrations of past, often secretive lusts and longings that I had put aside to become responsible to family, profession, and adulthood. Could these facts and my fictions all live together in some harmony? Even the notion was wonderful.

Thus, I first came to understand anima as a woman within my psyche to whom I was related and who could be critical of actual real women, like wives. Moreover, she could produce bad moods when unhappy and could also project herself into real women, whom one was cautioned to resist because the attraction belonged to the anima and not the woman. This phenomenological formulation, although theoretically correct, did not serve me very well, either personally or professionally; the idea had no real life, and the only therapeutic tool derived from this understanding was an appeal to the will to suppress those errant fantasies, moods, and urges. Even when successful, this did not cure anyone of anything.

Unsatisfied, I turned to Jung's *Collected Works* to find out more about anima. Jung's three most complete formal statements about the anima are found in "The Relations Between the Ego and the Unconscious" (1928), "Concerning the Archetypes, with Special Reference to the Anima Concept" (1954), and "The Syzygy: Anima and Animus" in *Aion* (1951). In these, the concept of anima falls basically into two parts. The first is simple and easy to understand: the anima is a man's feminine counterpart. It means that, in his personal unconscious, a man has qualities generally considered feminine—such as relatedness, softness, and receptivity—which he needs to integrate into his ego-consciousness in order to be whole. The second aspect of anima is archetypal and more complex; however, if this aspect is not understood, then the deepest meaning of anima is truly not understood. To begin, the anima in her archetypal aspect is both a symbol of the entire collective unconscious and also the personifying factor that bestows anthropomorphic form and affect on all archetypes and manifestations thereof, including herself. It is as if by reflecting on herself, she gives rise to consciousness, affect, and form. The concept of *anima mundi* and material from cabalistic thought are useful for examining this aspect. Jung knew both of these traditions.

Jung says that the anima as a psychological idea first appears in the sixteenth century (1951, par. 26, n. 3). It is plain, though, that its earliest ancestor, even psychologically, was the concept of the *anima numdi*, the world soul, as elaborated in detail by Plato in "The Timaeus." To elaborate on Plato's concept, imagine the world soul as coextensive and synonymous with the entire universe, and imagine one person's ego-consciousness as one single human on the earth. Imagine, then, that the entire universe is a hologram such that any small piece of it is an exact replica of the whole. Now, imagine each person having such a piece, in effect, having the actual entire universe in his or her piece of the hologram. Individual difference lies in the distinct coloring that each person imparts to each replica of the universe. Imagine also that although each person's universe is infinitely larger than him or her, the ego can envision it as a woman who can be any size, even smaller than the ego itself and that each ego-consciousness, that is, each person, can have a dialogue with this universe qua woman. Moreover, remember that although reduced in size and personified as a woman, the piece or scintilla of *anima mundi*, now simply known as anima, contains within it all of the things in the universe, both those experienced as tangible and those experienced as imagined or internal. Imagine all of these things, and you approach the idea of anima in her archetypal dimensions.

Jung also drew from the Cabala and from its central work, the Zohar, which dates from at least the thirteenth century and perhaps as early as the second century A.D. He refers to the Zohar at length in *Mysterium Coniunctionis*; however, in his treatment of this work, Jung ignores the fact that the concept of the Shechinah can be a very personal and psychological notion, akin in many ways to his notion of anima and in other ways actually more sophisticated and beautiful. Shechinah translates as "indwelling" and is the immanence of God on earth and, to my understanding, also the immanence of God within man. She is known as God's radiance which shines in all things and is the only manifestation of God that man can know except for the written Torah. Monotheism is not offended by her (so say the Cabalists) because she is a symbolic aspect of God and not a reified mythological figure. In other words, as the ineffable enters the realm of human perception, the Shechinah is the first manifestation, the first emanation, of God's energy, his will, and as such, she is the symbol of the reality and essence of all things, their "ontos." She is said to descend as the Sabbath Bride on Friday nights, she accompanies righteous men when they travel away from their wives, and she is present when ten or more men gather for ritual prayer. Like the anima, she can be experienced as an actor in a play for which she is also setting and plot. She is both figure and ground at the same time (personal communication, Rabbi Gedaliah Fleer).

There is psychology in the notion of an upper and a lower Shechinah. For the purpose of explanation, allow me to simplify greatly the cabalistic Tree of Life. Imagine an average tree, perhaps an oak, and think in terms of its three natural divisions: foliage, trunk, and roots. Let the foliage represent the sefirot (or archetype) called Daat or knowledge. This sefirot is also known as Leah, the first wife of the biblical Jacob, and is said to be the upper Shechinah. The roots are the lower Shechinah, also known as Rachel, Jacob's second wife and Leah's younger sister. Rachel is also known as Malchuth, meaning kingdom, the sefirot that symbolizes God's immanence on earth. Man, who is the tree trunk, is Jacob. He turns first to the upper Shechinah as Jacob in the Bible first marries Leah, and in this upward pursuit to Leah, he is called by his higher name, Israel. Israel comes to Leah through prayer, and she gives him inspiration in return. As in the Bible, Israel has many children with Leah, many inspirations, but few with Rachel. In her compassion for her younger sister, Leah helps Jacob know how and when to approach Rachel to impregnate her. When Jacob and Rachel do come together conjugally, it signifies the coming together of the written Torah (Jacob) and the oral Torah (Rachel). Since the oral Torah — the Talmud and the Mishna — explains how the written word of God should be interpreted, the union of Jacob and Rachel symbolizes the word of God brought into the conduct of daily life. In more secular words, this theosophical drama means that earnest and reverential seeking leads to inspired and meaningful behavior which, in turn, infuses daily life with ineffable wisdom and joy. In other words, like the anima, the Shechinah relates us to the world within and the world without, the world above and world below, and links them all.

Jung, in his genius, recognized the immediate relevance of this kind of material. He rediscovered and reformulated religion and philosophy as psychology, heuristically available to every man. Like a religious imperative, the anima concept implies a lifelong commitment to a way of life; namely, a continuing dialectic between ego-consciousness and the unconscious qua anima. The anima, Jung says, is not a figure such as " 'the guardian of the threshold' and all such hobgoblins" (these belong to occult practices) but the "middle path of psychic autonomy, a conception that has not entered the philosophical mind of our time. To make people understand this 'middle way' has been my particular effort" (1984, p. 222). Over time, this middle way has been addressed as the *mundus imaginalis* (Corbin 1972), liminal space (Stein 1983), subtle body (Schwartz-Salant 1982), and "esse in anima" (Jung 1921, par. 66). In "Thresholds of Initiation" (1967), Henderson speaks of a constant psychic state of immanence that obtains after many alternations of incubation and release. Immanence is a continuing state inbetween incubation and release, a state characteristic of individuation, the "middle way."

When the anima becomes active or causes symptoms, Jung says she is signaling ego-consciousness to be attentive to a rift in the psyche. He uses the metaphor of a gap on one side of which stands the anima and on the other ego-consciousness. A bridge is possible, according to Jung, that brings the two sides together, and this potential for bridging he calls the transcendent function (1988, pp. 1231–1232).

When present, my own anima's lightness and good cheer recalls my youth, for she carries memories of the love that we, she and I, felt for the warm summers in Tennessee where I grew up, the balmy nights and the lush, hot, coruscant days. I recall the yellow green thickets of vegetation, the friendliness of everything and everyone. I would lie in bed at night, my head by a window screen that was being gently rubbed by the tender leaves of bushes moving in the soft breeze, all the while listening to the radio in the dark to 1940s dance music from an unknown orchestra atop the roof of some far away hotel and hearing in the distance the faint whistles of unseen trains. The world was wonderful in those moments, and the future had promise of sweet things to come. This is still alive in me, the joy of it all, although its ambience is much too simple and young to fuel a certainly more complex adult life.

I was young, unformed, and unconscious in those days, for I was a child and my anima was mother. A maternalized anima always seems to accompany an immature ego-consciousness. For me, this youthful bower of mine held my young Eros snuggled up to his mother Aphrodite's loving bosom. What has remained unchanged are the religious overtones of those times, for my anima still senses design and designer in all this beauty, and she is always mildly seeking the source of it, sensing it to be accessible to me first through feeling.

The anima is more present as a psychological and psychic fact than is the Self. It seems to be the role of anima to function as the immanence of the Self like the Shechinah is the immanence of God. In a paper on the father's anima, John Beebe underscores the ubiquity and psychological importance of anima. He finds it:

> helpful to think of the anima as the emotional attitude a man takes towards anything he reflects upon. (1984, p. 277ff)

In a comment on his paper, Rosemary Gordon rebukes Beebe's idea of anima on several counts, but most importantly, feels that his definition is so "vague and all-inclusive that it can be of little practical use — except to confuse" (Gordon 1984). Rather keeping with Beebe, Jung himself, in the 1925 seminars, said he had:

> thought for a time that the anima figure was the deity . . . the dominating spirit of the psyche. I practically threw the whole metaphysical problem into the anima." (1989, p. 46)

Again with Beebe, Hillman postulates that the base of consciousness may well lie in the anima experience and that the ego may best function as a "trusty janitor" (1985, p. 92). So, too, does Donald Meltzer (a neo-Kleinian) invoke his mentor Bion to suggest that the unit of psychological life is, indeed, the emotional experience:

> The Ego becomes the horse, shying at every unknown object in its path, always wanting to follow in the way it has gone before; while the unconscious internal objects become the rider directing it relentlessly towards new developmental experiences. (1988, p. 8)

Consider this: Where in psychology have we seen the mighty ego compared to the animal? The dumb beast is always reserved for the unconscious. This will unsaddle Freud, of course.

Gordon further criticizes Beebe for not differentiating between mother and anima and for not recognizing the anima as the figure that takes a man away from his mother, "lures him away from his parental home, out into the dangerous world." I think that Gordon is right in that the anima does and must lure the man from the mother, mother as both personal mother and as unconsciousness. However, Beebe is correct also. The difference is that Gordon speaks to an immature ego-anima configuration, while Beebe speaks to a more mature and stable liaison.

Development of anima from young to mature is always a problem and, when it occurs, is always hard won. It is some of my own struggling in this service of maturation that I want to take up in the next section.

II

Early in my training, while conducting an adolescent group therapy session, I was asked by my coleader if I thought a girl in a young male patient's dream was the young man's anima. The answer tumbled unbidden out of my mouth: I said that he was too young to have an anima. Although I was fifteen years older than the patient, I was speaking of myself, for I know now and evidently knew then in a subliminal way that something in me had not seemed born, differentiated, and discerned such that it warranted the discrete name of anima. It got born in time, or at least, I discovered it.

The formative experiences I shall tell you about happened over a span of about six years during the early part of my analysis and psychiatric training. They are experiences with patients, and what I shall talk about is over and beyond and antecedent to transference and countertransference issues. It is with a certain level of his own development that the analyst or therapist enters the work with a given patient, and that level of development presents a limit to the work that can be done. In this regard, it is the extent to which the psyche of the analyst has awakened that is the extent to which he enhances or retards the awakening of the patient's psyche, irrespective of the former's technical knowledge. This awakening is symbolized by the waking of the anima. My story unfolds through my interaction with three women.

The first experience was with a patient who was not formally my patient. I was a psychiatric resident in a hospital on a therapeutic community ward where patients and staff intermingled freely when not in various small, large, or dyadic group meetings. Each patient was assigned to one psychiatric resident who was both individual therapist and treatment manager. In short, a very attractive and nubile twenty-five-year-old woman patient assigned to another resident took a liking to me, although I had had virtually no contact with her other than an occasional passing greeting, and over a period of four years her liking became an avowed loving and took on frankly delusional and psychotic dimensions.

If you have never been actively pursued against your will without knowing why and without knowing how to stop it, then you do not know a certain kind of terror, for terror it is, even if you are pursued with love rather than malice, both of which feel strangely close together in such situations. I felt strange and uneasy when told that this woman had returned to the hospital from time to time to inquire about me in the corridors. Once she came back to the ward and just looked at me for a while. In time, she became pregnant, and I received a note assuring me that she would not reveal that I was the father. Other notes began to address me as Christ, husband, lover. She accosted me on the street to my house, fell on her knees, and grabbed my legs, pressing me to her. The hospital administration would not help (she had not been a patient there for a long time at this point) nor would the staff psychiatrist in charge of the daycare program where she was then a patient. She tried to enter my house when my wife and I were not home, telling the babysitter on one occasion that she simply wanted to see the dining room table, and she began to stand on the corner late at corner late at night trying to look into the windows from across the street. I became exhausted and outraged, feeling besieged all the time, never knowing when and where she would appear, and fantasying madly about the harm of which she was capable, for she had truly become evil for me. One night about midnight, the door bell rang. I rose from bed, went to the door, pulled back the curtain a little, and saw it was her. Cracking the door, I hissed, "Go away! Leave me alone! Leave my family alone!" Suddenly there was an explosion, and shrapnel flew through the door into the vestibule. I dived for the floor, yelled to my wife to turn off all lights, and crawled to the fireplace to get the poker. She had fired a gun at me, and I was going to protect myself and my family (our youngest, an infant, was asleep in a room that opened onto the front porch where the woman stood). As quietly as possible, poker in hand, I lay on the floor, called police emergency, and reported a break-in in progress with an armed assailant. Two squad cars converged on the house with sirens ascream and lights ablaze. Officers with drawn guns confronted this woman—her hands held high—on my front stairs and arrested her on my complaint. She didn't have a gun. She had thrown a pot of geraniums at the door.

I will tell you later what became of this woman, but at this point, I want to tell you, instead, what it was about myself that predisposed to what happened, what I resisted learning, and what I finally did learn.

My stint on the therapeutic community ward was my first assignment as a civilian doctor. I had gone directly from medical school to a military internship and tour of duty, and from there to residency. Having chosen a residency that was reputed to be one of the best in the country, I invested it with great authority and, although I brought a certain amount of warmth and kindness to it, I was largely ruled by a dedication to taking responsibility and handling situations. I had had virtually no training in dynamic psychologies, and for me Freud's genetic reconstruction as an in-depth way to understand all behavior just did not work. I thought I welcomed direct and authentic engagement, but I was much more frightened of open contact than I knew at the time. Meanwhile I was concerned about the economic and emotional well-being of my young family. The discontent that I felt with my wife was not simply anima based but based instead on the need for more mothering, for more nurturing. And my wife needed the same, for we were both overburdened.

The backdrop for this setting was San Francisco in the middle 1960s. In fact, the therapeutic community ward later became the first youth drug ward in the country, and for me the sociological clash of values reflected my own inner cash. I was basically achievement-oriented with traditional structures, values, and goals in a profession that was demanding great openness and in a city that, in part, was being taken captive by Dionysus. A fellow resident whose life had been very ordered became personally involved with the hippies on the ward and then with the counterculture and finally ended his exploration by killing himself. Many of us were in trouble. Only the wisest with the most related and supple of animas could cope with all this. And mine was a poor, dumb, undeveloped thing, a natural thing, a burdened and frightened little creature whose consort was an overworked and callow ego. The nurturing mother anima of my youth had fled the field.

In a dream, during this time, I was a doctor in a long white doctor's coat like I had worn in the military. However, I knew I was actually in my psychiatric residency, and I was treating patients by a special method which consisted of shining a white light on them and then a black light, one held in each hand. The alternate application of these lights was the treatment. In retrospect, I think I had the right idea and the right treatment symbolically, but it was mechanical, and I was girded by persona. What was most lacking was eros of any sort. In another dream, I entered a bar, and Lyndon Johnson, the president, was the bartender. The bar surfaces made a square, and he was inside the square, and the only thing on the counter was a prominent cash register. I was caught in power considerations and the only sign of eros was the bar setting, a rather degraded symbol for it. I have no recall of any prominent female dream figures around this time. I do recall having written a sad little poem some time before when I was in a terrible funk. It was about a poor little girl and it started, "Poor wrinkled waif of bloodless earth. . . ." I am afraid that this was the state of my anima.

It is only in retrospect that I realize how frightened I was of change, how stuck in collective ways, how concerned with a security based on power and persona, how truly constricted in feelings, how in need of nurturing I was, of a mother, of the warmth and succor of the warm summer nights of childhood. My fear of this essentially harmless patient (and she was harmless) was a fear of losing important controls. I could not extend myself to her or explore her connection to me, lest I be overcome by I-knew-not-what. Jung speaks of a projection of the anima, but the actual dynamic was like this: my little anima had fled at the onslaught of a determined, dedicated, committed flesh-and-blood woman who had chosen me to be her savior and who in turn was determined to replace the feminine in my life, both the inner and the outer. My anima abdicated completely because she was weak and shy, unformed, without convictions and tested values, without guidelines for holding her own ground in conflicts, and she was clearly aware that she and I had unwittingly triggered an avalanche of eros which we could not handle or diffuse. The pressure of the patient to supplant my anima, although the concreteness of her attempt felt truly mad, fascinated and, at the same time, terrified me. To defend myself, I stood on my legal rights and my innocent righteousness. In court, the day after her arrest on my doorstep, a kindly brother of hers unexpectedly appeared and asked the judge to have compassion on his chronically ill sister. The judge asked who had brought the complaint. After I rose and told my story, he said to the brother that this man (me) had his rights, too. Tears of gratitude and relief came to my eyes. I thought that the law properly applied was a wonderful therapy and that I had cured my problem forever. The patient was incarcerated for evaluation in a state hospital for a short time and has never again sought me out. I saw her once more a year later on a street near my office and could barely recognize her. she was as obese as she was once thin, and her face and eyelids were heavily swollen, almost closed. She was certainly heavily medicated, for her motions were slowed and she seemed retarded. As I passed, she gave me a very sweet smile and silently mouthed hello. I am pleased to recall that she still had a twinkle in her eye.

I continued to function well enough as a therapist, it seemed to me, but I was more aware of the dangers of women patients. I especially kept a careful and respectful distance from those I found attractive, but I was finding many women attractive and was aware of frequent lustful feelings. I comforted myself by postulating that I was recapitulating the psyche of Asia Minor during the first and second millenia B.C., when the great goddess called for orgiastic ceremonies to celebrate her. At the time this untuited insight did not help me. With male patients I felt safe, but were they safely cared for by me? I remember once taking a man into the yard behind my office to show him the meaning and order of the universe in the shape of a tree, and as I explained it all, I trembled with the unassailable truth of the analogy. So much for analyzing with too much anima. What I really did not and could not talk about with any ease or depth was eros as it related directly and personally to me. I was in touch with the numinosity of the archetypal anima, but my personal relationship to her hardly existed. I had no sense of the dimensions of my problem, but I was soon informed.

Soon after my experience with the first patient, I found myself irresistibly attracted to a new female patient in my office practice. She was strikingly beautiful to me: her face, her body, and her mind. I was mesmerized by her, stunned, and unable to think well or to speak at times. Although I had no formed sexual fantasies about her and no plans to do anything but conduct therapy, the atmosphere in the room was almost always incredibly thick with emotion. After several months, this patient began to act often like a four- or five-year-old, and she began to treat me mercilessly for reasons I could not fathom. She would refuse to come in from the waiting room on occasion, and when exhorted by me to do so, might scream, which would completely unhinge me. Once in the room, she would sometimes crouch in a corner and refuse to move to a chair. She told me that I did not know how to treat a little girl. This was true. I was confused, frustrated, angry, and felt humiliated and helpless. Then she would turn mean and play tricks like leaving her keys in the office (not true) and making me come back from home (miles away) to open the door at the end of the day. To add to my confusion, I continued to feel in her a sexual and alluring quality and felt I discerned in her an adult sexual interest in me. In this emotional climate, she would ask to sit on my lap. Was this the little girl or the woman? I felt like stone and could not reply. I anticipated each hour with an increasing degree of terror until finally, about a year into the work, I sat down opposite her at the beginning of an hour, looked up, and saw two small, soft, skin-covered hillocks protruding from her forehead. I actually saw them, and I had never before knowingly hallucinated. I was incredulous, but they wouldn't go away, and I could hardly speak during the entire hour. I knew I was in the presence of Pan, and was panicked. I stopped our therapy shortly after that, telling her that I felt I could not handle the closeness. In truth, I could not even tell her that, for fear she would talk me out of it, and, instead, I explained myself somehow in terms of Jung's Rosarium pictures of the transference, which left me personally out of the problem. By this time in my life, I was exhausted and emotionally spent. It took me months to recover from the emotional fatigue this experience caused, during which time my patient load dropped to almost half of normal for which I was grateful.

In this second case, I irrationally adored this woman. She was bright, full of life, lovely, playful, psychological, and adoring of me, but more than that, from the very first meeting there was a mysterious and instantly cataclysmic take that persisted. She seemed to fit criteria I had had without knowing I had had them, and I and my anima were delighted to have her move in. We were delighted except that we were also appalled, for the entire situation completely offended all of the personal and professional values by which I lived. She was appalled and frightened also, I think, and regressed. I see now that we recapitulated an incest problem with the father (psychological incest, I think, for I know of no actual physical component) and that I was incapable of carrying the transference, as perhaps the father was incapable of providing safe and nonexploitative parenting. She had not come to therapy to be devoured or otherwise exploited, and I had not undertaken to treat her to gratify myself. Actually, her eros functioning was young but healthier than that of my anima, and I could not tolerate so much encounter without fear of being swamped by affects, that is, by my very unconscious. Eros had become a problem that permeated my entire life. The solution of it was not a gratuitous task any longer, and professional persona counted for naught.

A third patient that I was seeing during this same period shared my reserve and fear of eros. Her mothering had been cold but she had shared spiritual interests with her intellectual father. She and I were polite and restrained with one another but could talk meaningfully and excitedly about deep and relevant psychological matters without being overcome by emotions. She had a gift for expressing archetypal material in beautiful ways, and I was genuinely touched by her productions and her depth. Regarding our personal connection, an early dream of hers had an ice man tramping the world with little masses of cold fog under his arm; he was adversely affecting all the relationships in the world. I had a dream in which I gave her a pristine little kiss on the lips. The fog dissipated some, and we worked together. In time, her feminine fury came forth in full power with a hatred of the patriarchal bias in the culture, of me, and of other men and boys who she felt had hurt her. She and I weathered this reasonably well, and we continued to develop. She was very moved by her deep archetypal experiences, especially around the feminine, and, over time, she changed appreciably and so did her life. After some years, our work ended well.

In this third case, the patient's character and personality allowed me to work within the limits of my young anima's development. In this way, the patient and I were well matched and truly both developed together. I present this third case, in part, to shore up my self-esteem since I still feel a certain shame about the first two cases, but it seems that the unconscious often teaches through turmoil and failure. After the shock of these cases, I came slowly and over years to learn about eros. Jung cautions that it is important to have subdued the shadow before proceeding to confrontation with the anima, but for me and for him, too, and perhaps for everyone, this is possible only theoretically. It is only through such difficult encounters that I ran fully into the intrinsic contradictions between a shadowy, narcissistic loving that would possess the loved object and a more mature kind of loving. The separating out of shadow from anima is part of the work itself, and it is the grip of the anima that holds one to the task of confronting shadow.

Led to it by Hillman, I am taken with the similarity between the myth of Amor and Psyche and anima development. Anima is not synonymous with the Psyche of the myth, but in their early, immature stages, they seem identical. Both need to wake up and grow up, and I can see all of the travails of Psyche in the minutiae of the experiences I had with my three patients. Consider, for instance, the first task of sorting the seeds. For me, the cells of the body are the seeds, and the activity takes place at the level of the vegetative or autonomic nervous system. This system works like the ants in the dark; it is not under conscious control and not consciously discerned. The natural Pan is still in charge. What the human participant does experience is the suffering of the burning Eros. In truth, this first task is an excruciating initial ordeal in the conscious pursuit of eros, for it is the body and body-Self at its deepest level that, through the torment of love, is being seasoned and tempered in aphrodisian fire. Those who try to slake the pain through gratification delude themselves, for the object is not satisfaction but a sustained experience leading to initiation and growth through a psychophysical trial. Without this initiation the flesh remains forever vulnerable to inundation by affect, and those who never complete this stage are caught in the numinosity of unconscious images and urges.

Recall that in the myth the driving force of the drama is Aphrodite's jealous rage at Psyche's beauty; in effect, the myth is a cosmic and cosmogonic beauty contest between Aphrodite and Psyche, between the old and the new. My involvement with my first two patients was graceless at best, unconscionable at least, and truly ugly from the point of view of considered and thoughtfully humane behavior. Like Actaeon after seeing Diana nude, I ran from the dogs of my affect lest I be torn to shreds, but Aphrodite would have understood my panic and condoned the events as inexorable. For her, neither I nor my behavior were necessarily ugly. In the first case I cite, I ran from a patient who experienced the ecstatic rush of raw nature through her animal being. In the second case, it was I who experienced the rush. These raw emotions in pursuit of a perceptible loved object are the stuff of antiquity; this is Aphrodite's kind of love. It is rather Psyche, the new order, that would find me ugly and wanting, for her beauty and love is to be found instead in the recognition, succoring, and cherishing of that spark intrinsic and unique to the individual human, the spark that is the potentially self-conscious core and agent of growth in each of us, the spark that bespeaks an incarnate Self, in sum, the psyche. It was the psyche, the wholeness, of the patients and of myself that I abandoned. The love of Aphrodite had come naturally from my youth, but in itself was not suited to therapy, and I had not yet learned how to know Psyche as well as Aphrodite and how to love her as well.

The next section deals with Jung's developing anima. I shall start with the young Jung and show you how, after an insensitive and then probably painful start, he struggles with her for the greater part of his life.

III

From 1895 to 1912, from age twenty to thirty-seven, Jung was involved with three women who were his patients and with whom he seemed to cut his early teeth around eros issues. The first was Helene Preiswerk, his cousin and the subject of his doctoral dissertation on occult phenomena. Like my first "patient," she was not formally his "patient" but like me, he also referred to her as such. Jung's total unawareness of her obvious love for him (see Goodheart 1984) gives a clear picture of the insensitive state of his anima and feeling at that time. It seemed nonexistent.

> I asked one knowledgeable Zurich acquaintance of Jung about his seemingly callous and perhaps even destructive attitude toward Helly. This authority thinks that Jung had been naive rather than callous in his attitude toward his young cousin, and said, "He did not understand yet that women are not scientifically but personally interested in things." (Zumstein-Preiswerk, quoted in Goodheart 1984, p. 33)

The seances occurred probably from 1895 until 1899 and Jung's dissertation was published in 1902 when he was twenty-seven years old. He married the next year, 1903, apparently with deference to good collective values and not ostensibly to his anima. The next year, 1904, he began to treat Sabina Spielrein and became very emotionally embroiled with her. Totally aside from any considerations of sexual involvement with her, it is patently obvious from Carotenuto's careful work that Jung's eros was engaged in all of the excruciating ways we well know and still hear about even forty years later in "The Psychology of the Transference." Jung's meetings with Spielrein ended in 1909, but he wrote to her until at least 1913, and she to him until probably 1918 (Carotenuto 1980, p. 128ff). In 1910, now thirty-five years old, Jung began to see Toni Wolff as a patient, and, in 1912, he began his personal relationship with her. It is unclear whether their formal relationship had ended before 1912 (Kirsch 1983, p. 91). What it does to the development of an analyst and to his anima to live out his eros longings is not well known even today; we better understand the dangers to the analysand.

In these three women — Preiswerk, Spielrein, and Wolff — there is a progression from what appears to be gross unconsciousness of eros to a seemingly mature relationship of a married man to his mistress. Jung is twenty years old at the beginning of this progression, thirty-seven at its end. He has just bridged his midlife mark, which he puts at age thirty-five (Jung 1954, par. 146). He has not yet arrived at the concept of anima and his first book, "Psychology of the Unconscious," does not have the word *anima* in it. In this first writing of what later became "Symbols of Transformation," the hero is reborn through a *hierosgamos* with the mother (Jung 1920, p. 264) but with a spiritualized mother, the hero having sacrificed his animal aspect. Jung does not correct this conception and introduce anima into this first book until 1952 when he revises it extensively.

Jung's development around the feminine had really just begun at age thirty-seven and had not reached its apogee by his having taken two women into his life namely, Emma and Toni Wolff. Four years later, about 1916, when he is forty-one years old, he hears the feminine voice (Jung 1963, p. 185ff) that tries to seduce him into believing that he is doing art rather than science. The psychopathic patient to whom he imputes the voice is a continuing challenge to him from the feminine quarter. I agree with Carotenuto (1982) that this psychopathic and artistic patient was Sabina Spielrein, who was still writing to Jung in 1916 while she was also very much in touch with Freud. No one had a deeper potential to touch Jung emotionally, for in her was the convergence of Jung's probably most incendiary encounter with eros through a woman and his equally enormous encounter with it in his difficulties with Freud.

The point is that the feminine continues to pique and challenge Jung in a way that he experiences as negative. In "Septem Sermones ad Mortuos," written in 1916, the same year that he reports hearing that first feminine inner voice, in Sermo VI, Jung writes: "The daemon of sexuality approacheth our soul as a serpent . . ." and "The serpent hath a nature like unto woman" and "The serpent is a whore. She wantoneth with the devil and with evil spirits; a mischievous tyrant and tormentor, ever seducing to evilest company. . . ." (Jung 1963, p. 388) It is still only the mother of "Psychology of the Unconscious," the spiritual mother, the "Mater Coelestis" (Sermo V) who is the good feminine, the nurturer. It may be argued that this is archetypal and not personal material and that the use of it to characterize the personal Jung is unwarranted. Notwithstanding, the personal ramification of this material may be even more poignant, for what Jung has woven in "Seven Sermons to the Dead" is his myth, or one of the myths of his life, which, in part, addresses, as all such gnostic-like creation myths must, the problem of how pure essence or will emanates down into and becomes the dross of the material world. How this intrinsically paradoxical problem is solved in any particular myth says something about the world view of the author and is a kind of credo. For Jung—in keeping with the biblical account of the fall—woman and evil are joined together in a moral penumbra.

In a signal talk that he gives to the Eidgenössische Technische Hochschule in 1916, still the year of the anima voice, Jung lays out the psychology of the collective unconscious with a clarity greater than ever before (or after, in my opinion). It is in this talk that Jung is said to have first used the word *anima*, but this is not so. In the 1917 English translation, he word *anima* is absent and only in the 1928 revision of this talk (which became the essay "The Relations Between the Ego and the Unconscious") is the term added. In lieu of anima in this talk, the split between the ego and the autonomous psyche is said to be bridged and healed instead by "phantasy" regarded "hermeneutically, as an actual symbol" instead of "semiotically, as Freud does" (Long 1917, p. 468).

The word *anima* first appears in print in "Psychological Types" (Jung 1921), where it is found twice in the text and twice in the definitions section. In the text, the term is introduced under the heading entitled "The Worship of Woman and the Worship of the Soul." Here Jung says that the lady for whom Dante adventures in the lower and upper worlds is:

> exalted into the heavenly, mystical figure of the Mother of God — a figure that has detached itself from the object and become the personification of a purely psychological factor, or rather, of those unconscious contents whose personification I have termed the "anima." (Jung 1921, par. 377)

And the second occurrence:

> These attributes [Jung has just listed sixteen superlatives] reveal the functional significance of the Virgin mother image: they show how the soul-image (anima) affects the conscious attitude. She appears as a vessel of devotion, a source of wisdom and renewal. (Jung 1921, par. 380)

Here is the anima at last but synonymous still with the mother. The dangerous and autonomous anima associated with Spielrein has not yet come together with the good anima associated with the mother. Jung is still trying to understand how to regard the feminine for man both as a salutary psychic factor and as a functional link to actual women. He is having a hard time reconciling the two, for he simply does not feel comfortable yet with the nonmaternal feminine. Regard what he says to Esther Harding during a supervisory session in 1922:

> analysis requires a new adaptation from a man, for to sit still and patiently try to understand a woman's mind is far from a masculine attitude. The only time he does it is as lover to his mistress: he will not do so for his wife, for she is only his wife.[!] In love, his anima shows him how. He then takes on a feminine tenderness and uses the baby talk he learned from his mother; he calls on the eternal image of the feminine in himself. But [in analysis] that won't do. [The male analyst] has got to learn the feminineness of a man, which is not the anima.[!] He must not let his masculinity be overwhelmed, or his weakness calls out the animus in the woman patient. (McGuire and Hull 1932, p. 26)

At this time Jung thinks that it is the mother who teaches the anima how to be soft and feminine but that by no means must a man use his anima in analysis. Too dangerous. He invokes, instead, a "feminineness of a man, which is not the anima" to circumvent the danger. Jung may be referring to the feeling function as distinct from anima but that's the last we hear of this idea. Twenty years later, in "Psychology of the Transference," the anima seems unavoidably present in analysis. Call out the animus, indeed; more likely Jung's anima in 1922 would call out Eros and Pan. Mother, shadow, anima: they are still mixed together in 1922. By citing the 2nd century A.D. experience of the shepherd Hermas as an example of someone who converts worldly love to love of the mother church, Jung suggests that the only way out of this dilemma is through a complete spiritualizing of love (1921, par. 381).

In 1922, Jung is forty-seven years old; he continues to have these kinds of difficulties with the anima until he is at least sixty-nine years old in 1944. His formal statements of anima theory in the Collected Works do not essentially change after 1928 ("The Relation Between the Ego and the Unconscious") but what obfuscates the study of Jung's actual anima development during these years is the fact that in the 1950s he revises many of his earlier works. For this reason, the actual state of Jung's relationship to anima and his attitude toward women is better found in documents that were not open to his revisions. I speak of the almost continuous series of English seminars that he gave from 1925 through 1939 and which have been recorded in detail by the participants; also the biographical works by Barbara Hannah and Aniela Jaffe, Jung's collected letters, personal testimonies about him by many individuals, and various recorded interviews (see Jung 1980, 1984, 1988, 1989; Hannah 1976; Jaffe 1984; Adler 1973; McGuire and Hull 1932).

In the 1925 seminars, Jung acknowledges that he now knows that Helene Preiswerk had fallen deeply in love with him and that her affection had influenced her behavior and even her "cheating" (i.e., faking voices), but he seems to remain merciless in his lack of remorse or any other kind of feeling about the whole affair. He concludes his reflections by the insight that:

> Her life is an illustration of the principle of enantiodromia because starting with the thing that was most evil in her, namely her willingness to cheat and her general weakness and silliness, she passed by steady progression to the opposite pole where she was expressing the best that was in her. (Jung 1989, p. 6)

And what was that best? A few years of successful dressmaking before an early wasting-away death. This seems to me a rather dispassionate and uninvolved summing up by Jung. It's cold and demonstrates little emotional empathy for this young woman.

In the 1925 seminars, Jung also fully acknowledges Miss Miller of the Miller fantasies as an anima for him. He speaks of how shocked he would have been at the time of his writing "Psychology of the Unconscious" to have even entertained the idea that he himself had a fantasy life. After amply owning that her material should be seen as pure projection from him (although it probably fits her case also) he says,

> and so I assimilated the Miller side of myself, which did me much good. To speak figuratively, I found a lump of clay, turned it to gold and put it in my pocket. (1989, pp. 27–31)

A bit better on the owning-up side. Not great on compassion for Miss Miller.

In these seminars of 1925, Jung is ever wary and critical of the anima. Whenever he speaks of her, it is negative, uncomplimentary, or, at least, ambivalent. He underscores at length the negative qualities of Salome: her snakelikeness, her ruthlessness, her cruelty, her evil, and her capacity to induce madness as she almost did to him in a dream (1989, pp. 92–99). He claims the anima induces "vulgar or banal" thoughts, and "collective notion(s)." And look at this:

> The animus is not necessarily a power figure. The anima, on the other hand, is usually a power figure. She appears in that way from the very beginning. (Jung 1989, p. 146)

In the Dream Seminars (1928–1930), Jung's discussions of anima seem more balanced. He is still working out his thoughts on many aspects of the concept:

> Now, if I have a skin of adaptation for the conscious world, I must have one for the unconscious world too. The anima is the completion of the man's whole adaptation to unknown or partly known things. It was only very lately that I arrived at the conclusion that the anima is the counterpart of the persona, and always appears as a woman of a certain quality because she is in connection with the man's specific shadow. (Jung 1984, p. 52)

In the Dream Seminars, when Jung speaks of shadow affecting anima, he speaks only of the danger of occult practices and inflation (ibid., p. 55); with regard to malice, he imputes it to the intrinsic nature of anima and not to the possibility that her attitude toward him may simply reflect his own toward her. After lauding her as a femme inspiratrice, Jung says, when the anima is behind a man there is also some trap, as if the incentive were somehow wrong, or as if it were done with only half his brains, as if it were not the whole man, his complete personality. (Ibid., p. 57)

Suspicious though he be, Jung does grant the anima an essential freedom:

If a man cannot project his anima, then he is cut off from women. It is true he may make a thoroughly respectable marriage, but the spark of fire is not there, he does not get complete reality into his life. (1989, p. 140)

In the Vision Seminars (1930–1934), Jung's intellect seems to have taken a firmer grip of the anima (and animus) concept. He has become markedly more severe and seems to have come to some kind of an answer for himself regarding how she should be (man)handled:

When a man is able to distinguish between the objective situation and his mood, when he no longer allows his mood to blindfold his mind, but can acknowledge that it is peculiar and set it apart, that is the beginning of the imprisonment of the anima. After a while he will be able to say to his mood: You have not the right to exist,[!] I will put you in a test tube to be analyzed.[!] Of course that means a great sacrifice . . . to bottle up the anima requires a superhuman effort . . . the anima is imprisoned for the purpose of transformation. (Jung 1980, p. 239)

So the suppression of the animus or anima is an act of extreme violence and cruelty. (Ibid., p. 241)

And

In the Middle Ages, when a man discovered an anima, he got the thing arrested, and the judge had her burned as a witch. (Ibid., p. 194)

And

This is not a devaluation of the mind of a woman; a man's mind is very much the same if it is unoccupied. Moreover men have an anima, who has her own special devices. But the unconscious mind of any woman is forever weaving plots and they are usually of a very immoral kind from the standpoint of respectability. (Ibid., p. 509)

This is all rather harsh and points up the ongoing struggle between Jung's ego-consciousness and his unconscious qua anima, and in this struggle Jung has decided to dominate. Moreover, he seems to take the liberty of identifying anima with actual women. It is as if he has finally, long after the fact, figured out how to deal with Spielrein in him. I do not think she would have liked it.

In the Zarathustra Seminars (1934–1939), his calumny of the anima continues and worsens. She is deceptive, clever (Jung 1988, p. 1167), uniformly disagreeable (ibid., p. 1232), and responsible for queer feelings in a man when he is alone (ibid., p. 729). Salome comes under attack once more in many of the seminars (e.g., ibid., p. 944). Of the anima in general, Jung says,

> on the one side she is an inferior woman with all the bad qualities of a merely biological woman, an intriguing and plotting devil who always tries to entangle a man and make a perfect fool of him; yet she winds up with that snake's tail, with that peculiar insight and awareness. She is a psychopompos, and leads you into the understanding of the collective unconscious just by the way of the fool. (Ibid., p. 751)

In fact, over the five years of the Zarathustra Seminars, every statement about anima appears to contain some rejoinder, warning, or disapprobation. The least ambivalent I can find is when Jung says of her:

> That is an excellent example of what the anima can do in a critical moment of life. (Ibid., p. 1247)

What she has done at this extremely important juncture is to advise Zarathustra so cryptically that her message is not understood.

I have asked myself why Jung is so particularly ill disposed toward the anima in the Zarathustra seminars. I surmise that, on the one hand, it has to do with Nazi Germany, for Jung uses Zarathustra throughout the work to point up how all people "east of the Rhine" (which includes Nietzsche/Zarathustra) have a pathological relationship to the feminine, are unconscious of it, and are subverted if not perverted by it (Jung 1988, p. 597). Jung's ambivalence about the anima is reflected in how dangerous he thinks she was for Nietzsche and for the Nazis. These seminars are also a criticism of Jung's own youthful regard for Nietzsche's Zarathustra. (Jung couches "Seven Sermons for the Dead" in similarly unconscious language (McGuire 1989, p. 7).)

Barbara Hannah tells that:

> once when Jung was angry with the anima-possessed behavior of one of his men assistants, I tried to ask if he was not being overly severe. He replied that was quite true, but did I admit that he had managed to come to terms with his own anima. (Hannah 1976, p. 125)

The lesson is that it is possible to come forcefully to terms with anima since Jung had. I cite the passage to point up the continuing manhandling attitude.

In 1941, in an interview with Suzanne Percheron, Jung speaks:

> Inside himself a man depends on his reputation, one must not damage him there. . . . To recognize a great error can be fatal for him, because by this he risks losing his authority.

I, for instance, if in certain matters my wife would notice my errors, or if she showed me that she notices them, I would be afraid of my wife. Because then she shows me that I have not been conscious.

(But you would at least like to know this.)

Yes, provided that it is not too strong and perhaps also that it comes from myself. That is why women need to be extremely diplomatic. (Jensen 1982, p. 52)

Women are a magical force. They surround themselves with an emotional tension stronger than the rationality of men. . . . Woman is a very, very strong being, magical. That is why, I am afraid of women. (Ibid., pp. 52–53)

There is a paradox here. From 1912 until 1944, from ages thirty-seven to sixty-nine, thirty-two adult years, Jung's personal psychology and the psychology he expounded centered about a process of confrontation between ego-consciousness and the unconscious. This process began at midlife with a waking to the importance of the unconscious. All renewal, rebirth, transformation, self-realization, and individuation derived from this process of confrontation with the expressed goal of approximating and reconciling the ego with the contents of the unconscious. The paradox is this: the anima, the very symbol for Jung of the entire collective unconscious, is treated consistently by him, that is by his ego-consciousness, like a most dangerous and decidedly untrustworthy figure hardly available for an enduring reconciliation. So, too, to an avowed degree women in general, whom he identifies repeatedly with the anima.

Why this continuous warring? Why this mistrust? Prior to 1944, Jung had accepted in effect that the ego and the unconscious were forever opposed, more or less, and that any real merger was theoretical. His continuing standoff, "mutatis mutandis," with the anima was only what was expected, for it reflected for him the *de facto* situation between ego and the unconscious presumably through old age and unto death. In truth, though, what happened to Jung in 1944 at the age of sixty-nine was another transformation of a different dimension. Instead of perennially grinding away at the opposites forever, assimilating ever more contents of the unconscious, Jung experienced the "coniunctio" as an immediate felt experience, a metanoia, a quantum change of heart and mind, a kind of consummation of the process that he had not anticipated. He did not see it coming. He did not plan it.

What does Jung say and know about the coniunctio as a goal before 1944? In the early thirties, in the Vision Seminars, Jung states that if you imprison your anima (or animus), it will solidify and become a stone and then a diamond when "your self-control, or non-indulgence, has become a habit . . . a fait accomplit." At this point someone asks him if he has ever seen such a diamond, if any patient ever reached the diamond. His reply:

> You must never ask such questions—whether we have seen a savior or a holy virgin. It is absolutely certain that we have not . . . (but) perhaps one day somebody will possess a diamond. When one talks of such things, one does not possess them; and when one possesses them, why talk? (Jung 1980, p. 240)

This is how he defines the goal in 1940:

> I have therefore called the union of opposites the "transcendent function." This rounding out of the personality into a whole may well be the goal of any psychotherapy that claims to be more than a mere cure of symptoms. (Jung 1939, par. 524)

In contrast to the way many people think of change within a Jungian analysis and in contrast to Jung's 1944 experience, this quotation is a very mild affirmation of the work. It smacks of the kind of ego learning that makes a person better and better or more and more whole by incremental assimilations of unconscious material rather than the kind of transformative process that heals through a wholesale metamorphosis of psyche.

Jung does not use the word *coniunctio* in any of his seminars until November 1938, and then only in an erstwhile reference to alchemy (Jung 1988, p. 1407). It is not yet psychological for him. The first time that Jung uses the word *coniunctio* in a personal letter is on March 10, 1941, when he replies to Karl Kerenyi, who had written to him about Goethe's Aegean Festival. Jung writes:

> you have touched on a central problem of the unconscious [the "conjunctio"] which seems to me exceedingly difficult to handle. . . . This complex of motifs [e.g., the "coniunctio," the "hierosgamos," and the "homunculus"] is a labyrinth in itself, an indescribable tangle of problems, and I fear that my thoughts about it, although they have been going on for years, have still not got to the point where I could trust myself to say anything responsible. (Adler 1973, p. 295)

Jung is sixty-six years old at this time. Sometime between 1941 and 1944, he is working on the first part of *Mysterium Coniunctionis*, which is published in 1946 as "The Psychology of the Transference." In this he speaks at length of the coniunctio but the concept is still very intellectual and theoretical. In the introduction, this is what he has to say of the goal of union:

> The goal is important only as an idea; the essential thing is the *opus* which leads to the goal: *that* is the goal of a lifetime. In its attainment "left and right" are united, and conscious and unconscious work in harmony. (Jung 1946, par. 400)

Something happens to Jung by the end of Chapter 7, the point at which the pictures of the Rosarium start to become quite arcane. He has obviously had the experience of 1944 and has not yet digested it. (The latter part of "The Psychology of the Transference" was probably written after 1944.) Regard the following statement from this latter portion:

> The psychological interpretation of this process leads into regions of inner experience which defy our powers of scientific description, however unprejudiced or even ruthless we may be. At this point, unpalatable as it is to the scientific temperament, the idea of mystery forces itself upon the mind of the inquirer, not as a cloak for ignorance but as an admission of his inability to translate what he knows into the everyday speech of the intellect. I must therefore content myself with the bare mention of the archetype which is inwardly experienced at this stage, namely the birth of the "divine child" or — in the language of the mystics — the inner man. (Ibid., par. 482)

This silence is not typical of Dr. Jung prior to this time. Scientific description of archetypal material is his forte par excellence, and he is ruthless in the couching of it. Here he has yielded to an immediately felt experience of sufficient enough magnitude to silence him, although it be unpalatable to his temperament.

At this point, I want to flesh out what I have been talking about as the experience of the opposites in contrast to the goal of uniting the opposites. Then I want to talk about the implications of this for Jung, the man, during the years from midlife to 1944, from age thirty-five at which time he marries to sixty-nine at which time he has his coniunctio experience.

One way that I envision psychic and lived life for every man and woman is that for many years, often for an entire lifetime, I postulate a constant movement by everyone between pairs of opposites: security — insecurity, childhood — adulthood, work — play, single — married, this job — that job, diet — feast, etc., including the whole litany of syzygies in the Eriksonian developmental stages. Each partner of each of these pairs I envision spatially as existing 180 degrees apart on the periphery of a circle that itself can be thought of as symbolizing a single life, a single psyche. The circle may also be seen as Fordham's original self that must deintegrate for growth to occur. Over the years, I envision a person's ego-consciousness crisscrossing this circle, going back and forth between multiple opposite choices on the circumference (e.g., trust, mistrust, etc.), and by so doing, passing through the center of the circle with each transaction. When, over years, that center has become extremely well trod and relatively stable and constant as a felt and recognized psychic fact and when the locus of one's self-awareness passes from the flitting between opposites to the residing near that center, then the experience of an integral Self replaces a feeling of relative divisiveness, fragmentation, disintegration, or deintegration. With regard to Jung specifically, his continuing involvement with the opposites as reflected in his ongoing struggle of his ego with anima does not bespeak a pathological condition but rather a measure of relative personal development toward a stated goal, the reconciliation of opposites, and a subtle measurement of it at that. In no way do I regard Jung's continuing struggles with anima as pathological. I see them as a specific feature of his own unique and very full life, a feature which has certain implications for him and for us. What he did not realize before the experience, and what few before him outside of a purely religious context had ever realized in articulated consciousness, was that the experience of the center can come in a pure and felt way and as a quantum advance rather than as a rational and linear incremental increase of well-being based on having satisfied some quota of running back and forth between opposites.

While I was tracking the development of Jung's anima, my curiosity kept returning to the fact that, in his material, Jung kept deriving the anima from the mother, especially so in the early years around 1912 and 1921 when he made mother and anima synonymous but also continuing over the years. This is so with just one exception: in 1927, in "Mind and Earth," Jung allows that:

> The most striking feature about the anima-type is that the maternal element is entirely lacking. (1931, par. 75)

This was, he said, because the anima is not interested in procreation but in a personal relationship; as such, she stands totally apart from the mother-imago. This very interesting but lesser known paper must have been revised in the 1950s and if not, stands as an isolated island in the development of Jung's thoughts, for as late as 1937, Jung says unequivocally that:

> in other words, the anima develops out of the mother as the animus develops out of the father. (1988, p. 1157)

Not until Jung writes *Aion* does he deliver his final judgment on the relationship of mother and anima. It is after the 1944 experience and in total opposition to his 1937 stance:

> She is not an invention of the unconscious, but a spontaneous product of the unconscious. Nor is she a substitute figure for the mother. On the contrary, there is every likelihood that the numinous qualities which make the mother-image so dangerously powerful derive from the collective archetype of the anima, which is incarnated anew in every male child. (Jung 1951, par. 26)

In 1952, Jung returns to his first book, the "Psychology of the Unconscious," and makes many changes but probably most importantly deletes the idea that the hero is reborn from a hierosgamos with the spiritualized mother. In the place of the mother, he puts the anima, of course. I do not think he realized that the correction was an error insofar as it is a misinterpretation and a misrepresentation of his own original experience. In 1912, it was, indeed, the mother as the symbol of the unconscious that still ruled him. His first coniunctio which he called "hierosgamos" was with her. It took all of the thirty-two years to 1944, age sixty-nine, to finally displace the mother and enthrone the anima as the uncompromised symbol of the unconscious and thereby signal the culmination of Jung's individuation and his experience of himself as a fully distinct monad. Only after his experience in 1944 can he say:

> The objectivity which I experience in this dream [of Emma Jung, in 1955] and in the visions [of 1944] is part of a completed individuation. It signifies detachment from valuations and from what we call emotional ties. In general, emotional ties are very important to human beings. But they still contain projections, and it is essential to withdraw these projections in order to attain to oneself and to objectivity. Emotional relationships are relationships of desire, tainted by coercion and constraint; something is expected from the other person, and that makes him and ourselves unfree. (quoted in Hannah 1976, pp. 281–282)

This was a transient state rather than a continuous way of being for Jung; however, it signalled that the immaturity of the mother-tie, the continuing pull toward dependence and unconsciousness which made yielding to anima and woman threatening to Jung, was largely dissolved. Paradoxically, only after this "objective" experience was Jung able to write passionately of love (Jung 1963, pp. 353–354). These years from midlife to about age seventy and their preoccupation with the confrontation and the conflict of opposites had come to an end.

Thus, for Jung, there were two significant transformations in his adult life. The first dated from about 1913, actually:

[I]t was not for a year and six months after the publication of "Psychology of the Unconscious" . . . that I began to be acquainted with my own unconscious. The interval was a sort of incubation period, a preparation for a whole new period of life. A new wind was blowing, for — a very important fact — a new period of life was coming on. (McGuire and Hull 1932, p. 56)

The second transformation was in 1944. The years in between were heroic years, although Jung equated the end of his heroism with the death of Siegfried in his dream of 1913:

The dream showed that the attitude embodied by Siegfried, the hero, no longer suited me. Therefore, it had to be killed. . . . This identity and my heroic idealism had to be abandoned, for there are higher things than the ego's will, and to these one must bow. (1963, p. 180–181)

Who would have known it was going to take Siegfried so long to die? Even when he writes this account in *Memories, Dreams, Reflections* when he is eighty-three years old, Jung does not seem aware that Siegfried did not die in that original ambush. Jung's mother complex remained alive for years, and his hero dared not retire prematurely.

To look back now, it seems clear that Jung was not on the best of terms with his anima and unconscious over these intermediary years and that he could not further develop the concept of anima as long as his continuous *auseinandersetzung* with her was one long coherent phase. On many occasions, he refers to the four stages of the anima (e.g., Eve, Helen, Mary, Sophia) that come from Goethe, from the gnostics, and probably from Nietzsche as well, but he truly does nothing of consequence with this paradigm and actually seems confused by some of its implications (e.g., Adler 1973, p. 264–265). With regard to his development, it seems to me that Jung's path was collectively determined to some extent in that his individual anima was a scintilla, a piece, of the *anima mundi*, the world soul, and what Jung was doing internally was what the world was also doing, that is, enduring two world wars and the excesses of the interbellum during which no one escaped the exacerbated problem of opposites, especially the problem of good and evil. In his psychology, Jung was truly, as Vanderpost put it, "the story of our time." May our subsequent times be gentler, although this hardly seems likely. In another way also, Jung was a man of his times, for he set his masculine ego the ongoing task of subduing and dominating the anima, thus reflecting the male and patriarchal bias of Western temperate-zone culture for over two millenia. This masculine bias not only represented the general situation between men and women but also that between logos and eros.

Regarding the analyst's anima, for that is what this account is about, let us ask who among the several anima figures that peopled Jung's psyche in those thirty-two years—Preiswerk, Spielrein, the artistic voice, Toni Wolff, Miss Miller, Salome, Galla Placidia—who of these most poignantly played the counterpoint to Jung's conscious attitudes and especially to his massive conceptualizing intellect? My choice is clear: it was Salome, Jung's most often cited and most frequently maligned anima, who dates back to his first confrontation with the unconscious after his break with Freud. In April of 1931, Jung delivered a lecture in Dresden, Germany. He later spoke to Dr. Joseph Henderson about the talk:

> It was a high-level audience of high-level people, full of gehiemrats, etc. . . ., very important people, much persona. Jung suddenly began to let his anima talk out of himself very spontaneously. They were delighted. They giggled and swayed. They just loved it. Jung said he could not have done it if a woman had been present. She wouldn't have liked it. He said they would never invite me back. When they get home they will say, "Who was this man who made me feel that way." They would be ashamed of themselves for having such a good time. Their scholarly personas would object to their having enjoyed themselves. (Personal communication, Joseph Henderson)

Barbara Hannah chided Jung in 1939 about the success of a lecture he gave at the Royal College of Medicine in England. She asked if his anima had danced on his forehead again as she had in 1931 in Germany. He became angry at her but apologized the next day. She thought she understood why he had been chagrined, but I do not think she did. Of this lecture in 1931, the same one to which Dr. Henderson refers, Barbara Hannah says:

> [Jung] had lectured in Germany and had come home *very* dissatisfied with the wild success he had had. He said to me, at this time: "I positively felt my anima dancing on my forehead and fascinating the audience on her own!" (Hannah 1976, p. 259)

And who was it who was dancing on Jung's forehead but Salome. Salome of the seven veils, Salome the amoral, who would dance for the Germans, for the English, for Herod, for whomever pleased her. Jung says she was blind because she contained his inferior feeling (Jung 1989, p. 92). Indeed, she was full of blind instinctual feeling, but she was blind like Justice is blind, for she had absolutely no discrimination. She was something of a whore. So much for morality. She had John the Baptist's head cut off because he spurned her; so much for her respect for the religious man. And so much for the mighty intellect. But she inspired Jung also. It was she in a dream who gave him the god Aion (Jung 1989, pp. 92–99), a complex chthonic pagan deity whom she could worship. With regard to Salome and the mother, consider what Jung has to say:

> The overwhelming majority of men on the present cultural level never advance beyond the maternal significance of woman, and this is the reason why the anima seldom develops beyond the infantile, primitive level of the prostitute. (Jung 1931, par. 76)

Was Jung to develop beyond Salome or is it more like he says in a letter to a cousin, dated July 31, 1935:

> You are not responsible for your constitution but you are stuck with it, and so it is with the anima, which is likewise a constitutional factor one is stuck with. (Adler 1973)

Actually, Salome does evolve after 1944, but when she does reappear, she is merged with another figure and no longer herself. I will speak to this in the next section.

Although Jung did not trust his anima figures, at least not Salome, Dr. Henderson points out that Jung, in private and especially in his seminars, appeared to have a good relationship to anima. In these settings, Jung seemed quick of wit, full of joy, vigorous, and very related. These qualities come through clearly in the readings and in many personal testimonies and interviews (e.g., McGuire and Hull 1932, p. 50ff). How to understand this? To my thinking, it was the mother-anima playing the bass line to the other anima figures. The mother-anima manifested as function (i.e., atmosphere) and not as form and her enduring and loving external representations were the two women forever about him during those years: Emma Jung and Toni Wolff (about the latter Jung sculpted in stone in Chinese characters after her death: "lotus, nun, mysterious") (Joseph Henderson, personal communication). After all, Jung had come together with Toni Wolff the same year he had formulated his hierosgamos of the hero with the spiritualized mother. With regard to Jung's positive mother complex, it seems true from many personal accounts that he provided an extraordinarily powerful and reassuring holding environment in a Winnicottian sense and that he was capable of unbounded, although discriminating, good cheer and caring.

Clinically, during his mid years, Jung exhorted the use of will regarding anima problems (e.g., Adler 1973, pp. 72–73, 84, 213, 246, 463). As an analyst, he seems by various accounts like a seer, who, as with his own anima, kept a certain distance clinically. What I think of as the archetypal clinical stance is one in which a positive archetypal transference is presumed and is not the subject of extended investigation and interpretation. The analyst brings instead relevant commentary and amplification from the intellect and the nonmaternal anima while simultaneously holding the patient with deep good will and positive regard that flows from the relatively unconscious maternal.

With his illness and the accompanying visions of 1944, Jung comes to the direct emotional experience of the coniunctio, which is a new kind of anima experience. What does he tell us of this new way, and in what ways does he fail to inform us?

IV

In 1944, after his nearly fatal heart attack, Jung experienced three weeks of nightly visions about which he said:

> It is impossible to convey the beauty and intensity of emotion during those visions. They were the most tremendous things I have ever experienced. (Jung 1963, p. 295)

The content of the visions were coniunctios in Jewish, Christian, and Greek metaphor. For Jung, two aspects of this experience were new to him. The first was that he experienced a total submission to his seemingly immanent death before having had the visions, for he was ready to die and was disappointed at having to return to life. Second, he had a direct and immediate experience of beauty unmediated by his intellect. Only after these experiences did Jung make such statements as:

> rational understanding or intellectual formulation adds nothing to the experience of wholeness, and at best only facilitates its repetition. The experience itself is the important thing, not its intellectual representation or clarification, which proves meaningful and helpful only when the road to original experience is blocked. (1955–1956, par. 777)

> I falter before the task of finding the language which might adequately express the incalculable paradoxes of love. Eros is a "kosmogonos," a creator and father-mother of all higher consciousness. (Jung 1963, p. 353)

It was, we presume, because he had been severely abased by his illness that Jung was able to write of the importance of direct experience and also "Answer to Job," which, Barbara Hannah says:

> is totally different from all of Jung's other books, in that he did not write as usual in a "cooly objective manner" but gave a free rein for once [!] to his "emotional subjectivity." (Hannah 1976, p. 301–302)

In Job, of course, Jung discerned the human being who had been devastated for no understandable reason and perforce had totally and completely submitted to the greater power of fate or god or what-have-you. This is the lesson that Jung learned for himself in 1944. Before that, his submission to life and the unconscious, even including his ordeal of the years around 1916, had been relative. Notwithstanding his fear of and respect for the unconscious, Jung had used his intellect to negotiate and traffic with these forces, but his illusion of personal power came to an end in 1944, at least for a while. With his heart attack and near death, Jung tasted full defeat. To my knowledge, he never waxed on in print or in person about the negative and onerous aspects of his ordeal, but he did tell Aniela Jaffe: "It was then that life busted me, as sometimes it busts everyone!" (Jaffe 1984, p. 99) Also, in *Memories, Dreams, Reflections*, Jung says that, in addition to "the deepest bliss" of the visions, "there was a darkness too, and a strange cessation of human warmth" (Jung 1963, p. 321).

The quintessential natural law of anima came trenchantly clear to Jung at this time. The anima is purely and irremediably irrational. It is illusory to think that she is necessarily constrained by logic or that her form and function are derivative from the mother and can be shaped and influenced by intellect and psychological insight. Anima, the archetype of life, is as direct, awesome, and immutable as death. Para-doxically, it seems to take great suffering and/or loss of what we cherish most in order to defeat the last vestiges of ego and to connect us most deeply with the ultimate mysteries of anima; namely love, beauty, and wisdom. Strangely, it is suffering that allows us to experience life most fully, and it is the anima as the ultimate other that mediates passion in its dual aspects of suffering and ecstasy. What the Rabbi said to God we might say as well to the anima: "Please take your illness and your lesson. I don't want either of them." Or as an analyst friend said, "We work in analysis for years in hopes that we can survive when something finally happens."

This is not to say that with new humility and direct access to experience Jung lost his bearings or his intellect and became ethereal and otherworldly like the music teacher in Herman Hesse's *Magister Ludi or the Glass Bead Game*. To the contrary, according to Aniela Jaffe, Jung retained his power and charisma, his good nature and profundity, but also his unromantic crustiness:

> He could speak with biting scorn of the "ideal of harmony" that hovers before many people—they are often "feeling-types"—because it is not in accord with the truth of life and the truth of man. In the long run it cannot be kept up; sooner or later it comes to a disappointing end, turns into disharmony. (Jaffe 1984, p. 112)

So much for "having arrived."

Actually, although Jung lauded "the experience itself" after 1944, he never sacrificed or even subjugated his intellect which remained his most salient feature until his death seventeen years later in 1961. As soon as he was out of his one-year convalescence, Jung was writing and formulating more vigorously than ever before: "and one problem after another revealed itself to me and took shape" (Hannah 1976, p. 288). His Sophia, his penultimate anima figure, suited Jung ideally in this regard. This is what he said about her in 1935: "In the end, inasmuch as the anima transforms into Sophia, there is no longer the wise old man or the anima because they become one" (Jung 1988, p. 533). Thus, Jung's Sophia incorporated the detached intellect of the wise old man, and Jung remained ever thinking. Although Jung postulates Sophia as Job's salvation, Jungian students of "Answer to Job" continue to find the book's most compelling feature to be the deity's use of man in its quest for consciousness. This formulation is a rational theodicy and a continuation of Jung's intellectual *tour de force*. The feminine as healing balm for the inconsolable is evident more as a premise than a felt fact. Otherwise said, in the amalgam that is Sophia, Salome has yielded to Philemon.

Even after 1944, Jung's particular configuration of strengths leaves largely unexplored and unchampioned the aspect of the anima that deals with direct experience not mediated or conveyed by intellect. One may discern two kinds of direct emotional experiencing at the archetypal level, numinous and aesthetic. Jung knows the numinous well. It pertains to experiences of the Self, or some might say of god, either transcendent or immanent, and Sophia is the anima correlate of these numinous events. There are, in turn, two kinds of aesthetic experience. The first is of animate things or rather of the animating essence of animate things, the spirit and the soul of them, the Self that is not *the* Self but some one particular person's Self. The aesthetic experience of a particular Self is love or variations thereof. Psyche is the anima in this realm. The second kind of aesthetic experience is of inanimate things but specifically of the phenomenological qualities of things, including those phenomenal aspects of animate things. For example, one may be taken with the color, line, or composition of a painting, or the texture, tone, or rhythm of a musical piece, or the sculptural form, movements, or smell of a person or animal. The aesthetic experience of these qualities is perceived as beauty and is under the sway of Aphrodite.

Let me expand on this last kind of direct experience because it is exactly where Jung is weakest and where we must seek our own direction. This is from Hillman:

> By beauty we do not mean beautifying, adornments, decorations. We do not mean aesthetics as a minor branch of philosophy concerned with taste, form and art criticism.

> Beauty is . . . the very sensibility of the cosmos, that it has textures, tones, tastes, that it is attractive.

> Beauty is an epistemological necessity; it is the way in which the Gods touch our senses, reach the heart and attract us into life. (Hillman 1981, pp. 27–29)

Although Jung knows the numinous well, he knows the direct emotional experience of love less, and he knows beauty least. In fact, he is woefully ignorant of it. It is his wont and ours also as traditional Jungians to explain the experience of love and beauty by labeling them as numinous experiences, by saying that a loved person or object carries the Self (or more likely, that we, as analysts, carry the Self of and for patients). In the latter 1930s, Jung began to modify this stance, in effect, through his espousal of alchemy which presumes an ensoulment of matter. Nonetheless, Jung's own sense of beauty, articulated as early as 1908 in a letter to Karl Abraham, remained largely true for him for his entire life.

> So far the analysis is going ahead splendidly. Seldom in my analytical work have I been so struck by the "beauty" of neurosis as with this patient. The construction and the course of the dreams are of a rare aesthetic beauty. (Adler 1973, p. 5)

Even at the end of his life, it is the understanding that is of the essence, not the experience itself:

> Objective cognition lies hidden behind the attraction of the emotional relationship; it seems to be the central secret. Only through objective cognition is the real coniunctio possible. (Jung 1963, p. 297)

The beauty that many people find in the world in all kinds of art and nature, Jung depreciated in 1922 and never revalued: "Aestheticism . . . lacks all moral force, because 'au fond' it is still only a refined hedonism." (Jung 1921, par. 194) Untouched by the beauty of the sensate and by the immediate experience of it, Jung had little use for the persona except as a necessary piece of psychological furniture in the service of adaptation and homeostasis. Persona still carries a rather negative valence in Jungian circles; it remains synonymous with superficial. The problem is one of differentiating between materiality and show, which has no soul, and beauty, which does.

There is a vignette that imparts a sense of the state of development of Jung's aesthetics in the last part of his life. Margaret Tilly, a concert pianist and music therapist from San Francisco, visited Jung in 1956 when he was eighty-one years old and was invited to demonstrate music therapy to him. First she asked him if he knew anything about music. He told her, to her surprise, that his mother was a fine singer and so was her sister and that his daughter was a fine pianist. He said he knew the whole literature. When she began to play for him, however, Jung was absolutely overwhelmed. According to Tilly, he said: "I don't know what is happening to me—what are you doing?" (Jensen 1982, p. 126–127). He then talked to her excitedly about her work with patients:

> This opens up whole new avenues of research I'd never even dreamed of. Because of what you've shown me this afternoon—not just what you've said, but what I have actually felt and experienced—I feel that from now on music should be an essential part of every analysis. (Ibid.)

Dr. Henderson says that Jung often attended concerts but had not been touched, had not "gotten it" (personal communication). There is abundant evidence also of Jung's inability to appreciate much poetry and especially modern art, both of which actually infuriated him at times. If he could not comprehend it with his intellect, it seemed difficult for him to appreciate it. He felt he understood the Wotanic excesses of Germany of the latter 1920s and early 1930s, but he did not "get it," did not feel the full impact of the events, and did not express the outrage he was able to express toward modern art (Adler 1973, vol. 2, pp. 81, 82). Irrespective of when he straightened out his thinking around Nazism, Jung's failure to register and communicate an immediate experience of outrage made his deficiencies apparent to the world. I can only conjecture that in his individuation a world-class figure must endure a world-class corrective for his blind sides.

This interaction with Margaret Tilly illustrates a final point regarding direct experience, which is that each kind of direct experience does have a moral concomitant, a "moral force," quite in contradiction to Jung's statement of 1922 that it does not. With regard first to the numinous, thoughts and problems "revealed" (Hannah 1976, p. 288) themselves to Jung, and Jung's moral obligation, which he accepted, was to open to these ideas, take them seriously, study them, write them down, and communicate them. (In this particular way, he was akin to Moses who, alone of all the prophets, received his revelations in words rather than images (Kaplan 1990).) With regard to love, there are also moral concomitants. To see into a person deeply, especially if that person knows that he or she has been seen, obligates the seer, according to my own code, to treat that person with special care and consideration. With regard to my first patient in this paper, the one who threw the geraniums, I recall a very brief eye encounter during her early hospitalization in which I saw something alive, bright, and beautiful in her, and thought for an instance that I was the one doctor who could help her. I also recall that she saw me regard her in this way for that very instant. I dismissed the moment as inconsequential, so brief and fleeting was it. Afraid and callow, I did not recognize the importance of that instantaneous contact and did not know how to respect that direct experience. Without knowing why, I was relieved that she still had that twinkle in her eye at our last meeting on the street.

Finally, with regard to beauty, the categorical moral imperative is to live the life that is felt, to let nature run through us. There was a primitive conception, Hillman informs us, that the beautiful and the good, the aesthetic and the moral, were synonymous (1984, p. 33) and Aphrodite ruled over those times when to experience beauty for its own sake was good. Jung immediately wanted to subvert his experience of Tilly's music to research, to intellectual paths, but what he really wanted, it seemed, was to share the experience with many people, with patients. Perhaps he should have arranged special small concerts for special friends, instead. Irreverently, I think he should have taken up the penny whistle or waxpaper and comb, for perhaps, in some small way, he could have generated his own aesthetic experience for himself from out of himself, for what is creativity but that.

In the myth "Amor and Psyche," Psyche is ultimately taken by Eros to live with him and his mother Aphrodite. The story ends at this point and Neumann does not explore the implications of this threeway household which seems to be the new order of things in that recognition of the human psyche and love for it is added to the beautiful and the good. It is well beyond the bounds of this paper to explore much further these aspects of anima, but what seems needed is the pursuit of a moral aesthetic in which direct experience of love and beauty demands deep consideration and respect, not only by the one who has the experience, but by informed others who know what it feels like when gods speak, even when it is to others. If I know that you love something or someone or that you are truly taken by a certain beauty, it is important that I respect and even, if possible, protect you, your world, your love, and your beauty. It is an abomination to presume to tell you that what you love is wrong or that what you experience deeply and directly as beautiful has no real value. Certainly, it is the worse kind of violation to destroy others' loved objects willfully. Those who do this to others are without the capacity to know love or beauty themselves.

I was well along in this paper, spurred by my own frustrations and untended needs in Jung's psychology, piecing together the meaning of my anima experiences over the years, and looking for enfranchisement for other parts of myself, when I discovered James Hillman's Eranos lectures of 1979 (Hillman 1984) in which he has spelled out his own theses regarding aesthetics in his own way and using his own lines of Jung's development. Hillman's work is stunning to me in the beauty of its constructions and formulations, thereby illustrating the very answer to what is being sought: an embodied and ensouled intellect. I am humbled by his scholarship and have especially learned from his treatment of Aphrodite, portions of which I have quoted earlier in this paper. Odajnyk (1984) criticizes Hillman, suggesting that he is simply an artist *manqué*, that "one can write in the vein of Hillman and his imitators without ever really having had a relationship with the unconscious," that "with full immersion [in the unconscious], one stops talking so much. Words and images aren't that important any more." All of these rejoinders may be true in the short view and in terms of particulars, but in the long view, I think that Odajnyk has misunderstood what Hillman has tried to do.

This is not to say that Hillman has succeeded in all ways. As the person given to preoccupation with the numinous may slop over into sanctimoniousness or asceticism and as the lover may become the seducer or satyr, so, too, those given to beauty may err in the direction of dandyism or dilettantism. It seems wrong to define a deep and earnest pursuit by its excesses alone. Although, at times, it seems that Hillman skirts about some kind of Jungian High Culture and approaches an artfulness more akin to traditions of literary criticism than psychology, the mix of these two disciplines, for me, feels particularly fertile and generative. Both disciplines seek the ground of being, at least, in their present pursuits, and both occupy themselves with its forms and possibilities of expression. On the other hand, accused of being overly aesthetic, Hillman, in his turn, criticizes the patriarchalism and the hierarchical mind of those who are taken with the *numinosum* of a monotheistic god. Monotheism, at root, is the belief that all is One, but the assumption that monotheism aims to negate or subsume all autonomous expressions of that One is not a necessary concomitant. "There shall be no other gods before me" may be read as a disavowal of derivation by the deity, in other words, as a claim to being the first and only source of all, as opposed to the more limited claims of mythological figures that always have a genealogy, are themselves contingent on, at least, time and fate, and vie for power with near equals (Kaufmann 1960). Monotheism is not patriarchalism. The aesthetic may be equally authoritarian in its excesses; so may eros. May this not be a fight among anima aspects, between Sophia, Aphrodite, and Psyche, about which of them can promise the richer life. We know that Jung had his favorite.

Jung's ultimate anima figure appears to him in a dream in 1955 in which he experienced for the last time the same extraordinary beauty he experienced during his visions of 1944. Shortly after her death, Emma Jung appeared to him in the prime of her life wearing a dress that was "the most beautiful thing she had ever had" and that was made for her by Jung's cousin, the medium, Helene Preiswerk:

> Her expression was neither joyful nor sad, but rather objectively wise and understanding, without the slightest emotional reaction, as though she were beyond the mist of affects. I knew it was not she, but a portrait she had made or commissioned for me. It contained the beginning of our relationship, the events of fifty-three years of marriage, and the end of her life also. Face to face with such wholeness one remains speechless, for it can scarcely be comprehended. (Jung 1963, p. 269)

In this dream portrait of his wife, there is for Jung a coming together of the aesthetic and the real, the beautiful and the beloved, the anima and the mother, the manifest and the symbolic. And wisdom, too. Here, I think, at long last was an anima with whom Jung could feel perfectly at home. Of course, her affect had to remain a little muted.

References

Adler, G. 1973. *C. G. Jung Letters 1906–1961*. 2 vols. Princeton, N.J.: Princeton University Press.

Beebe, J. 1984. The father's anima as a clinical and as a symbolic problem. *Journal of Analytical Psychology* 29:277–287.

Carotenuto, A. 1980. Sabina Spielrein and C. G. Jung. *Spring*, pp. 128–145.

———. 1982. *A Secret Symmetry: Sabina Spielrein Between Jung and Freud*. New York: Pantheon Books.

Corbin, H. 1972. *Mundus imaginalis* or the imaginary and the imaginal. *Spring*, pp. 1–19.

Goodheart, W. 1984. C. G. Jung's first "patient." *Journal of Analytical Psychology* 29:1–34.

Gordon, R. 1984. Comment on "The Father's Anima as a Clinical and as a Symbolic Problem." *Journal of Analytical Psychology* 29:289–290.

Hannah, B. 1976. *Jung: His Life and Work*. New York: Capricorn Books.

Henderson, J. 1967. *Thresholds of Initiation*. Middletown, Conn.: Wesllyan University Press.

Hillman, J. 1985. *Anima*. Dallas: Spring Publications.

———. 1981. *Eranos Lectures 2. The Thought of the Heart*. Dallas: Spring Publications.

Jaffe, A. 1984. *Jung's Last Years*. Dallas: Spring Publications.

Jensen, F., ed. 1982. *C. G. Jung, Emma Jung, and Toni Wolff*. San Francisco: Analytical Psychology Club of San Francisco.

Jung, C. G. 1920. *Symbols of Transformation*. Princeton, N.J.: Princeton University Press.

———. 1921. *Psychological Types*. *CW*, vol. 6. Princeton, N.J.: Princeton University Press, 1971.

———. 1928. The relations between the ego and the unconscious. In *CW* 7:123–304. Princeton, N.J.: Princeton University Press, 1953.

———. 1931. Mind and earth. In *CW* 10:29–49. Princeton, N.J.: Princeton University Press, 1964.

———. 1931. The stages of life. In *CW* 8:387–403. Princeton, N.J.: Princeton University Press, 1960.

———. 1939. Conscious, unconscious, and individuation. In *CW* 9i:275–289. Princeton, N.J.: Princeton University Press, 1959.

———. 1946. The psychology of the transference. In *CW* 16:163–326. Princeton, N.J.: Princeton University Press, 1954.

———. 1951. The psychological aspects of the Kore. In *CW* 9i:182–205. Princeton, N.J.: Princeton University Press, 1959.

———. 1951. *Aion*. *CW*, vol. 9ii. Princeton, N.J.: Princeton University Press, 1959.

———. 1954. Concerning the archetypes, with special reference to the anima concept. In *CW* 9i:54–73. Princeton, N.J.: Princeton University Press, 1959.

———. 1955. The theory of psychoanalysis. In *CW* 4:83–226. Princeton, N.J.: Princeton University Press, 1961.

———. 1955–1956. *Mysterium Coniunctionis*. *CW*, vol. 14. Princeton, N.J.: Princeton University Press, 1963.

———. 1963. *Memories, Dreams, Reflections*. New York: Pantheon Books.

———. 1976. *The Vision Seminars*. Princeton, N.J.: Princeton University Press.

———. 1984. *Seminar on Dream Analysis*. Princeton, N.J.: Princeton University Press.

———. 1988. *Nietzsche's Zarathustra*. 2 vols. J. L. Jarrett, ed. Princeton, N.J.: Princeton University Press.

———. 1989. *Analytical Psychology*. Princeton, N.J.: Princeton University Press.

Kaplan, A. 1990. *Innerspace*. Brooklyn, N.Y.: Moznaim Publishing Corp.

Kaufmann, Y. 1960. *The Religion of Israel*. New York: Schocken Books.

Kirsch, T. 1983. Book review of *A Secret Symmetry* by A. Carotenuto *Quadrant* 16:89–92.

Long, C. E. 1917. *Collected Papers of Analytical Psychology*. London: Balliere, Tindall, and Cox.

McGuire, W., ed. 1989. *Analytical Psychology. Notes of the Seminar Given in 1925*. Princeton, N.J.: Princeton University Press.

McGuire and Hull, eds. 1932. *C. G. Jung Speaking*. Princeton, N.J.: Princeton University Press.

Meltzer, D. 1988. *Apprehension of Beauty*. Strath Tay, Scotland: Clunie Press.

Schwartz-Salant, N. 1982. *Narcissism and Character Transformation*. Toronto: Inner City Books.

Stein, M. 1983. *In Midlife*. Dallas: Spring Publications.

Anima and Animus:
An Interpersonal View

Louis Zinkin

Prelude

This paper falls into two parts, the first theoretical, the second practical. This is because it is not clear that the anima and animus as described by Jung are primarily to be thought of as clinical concepts, although he certainly thought they have clinical implications. The practicing analyst has to make a distinction between a way of working with patients and the theory which underlies this way of working, even though while actually working, this distinction tends to disappear. It seems to me particularly important to make it when *thinking* about concepts, particularly when considering what place they may have in clinical practice. In my own thinking, I have found that it is much easier to be clear about what I think than about what I do. It is important to respond naturally rather than artificially to patients and only afterward can I really look at the theoretical basis of what I am doing. The words *anima* or *animus* may simply not cross my mind while with the patient but afterward I might realize that had they not

Louis Zinkin is Hon. Consultant Psychotherapist and senior lecturer at St. George's Hospital, London, and a training analyst of the Society of Analytical Psychology and graduate and training analyst of the Institute of Group Analysis, London. Recent papers include "The Grail Quest and the Analytic Setting," "The Group as Container and Contained," and "The Grail and the Group." He conducts a private practice as an analytical psychologist, group analyst, and marital therapist.

been in the back of my mind, I would not have said or even thought what I did. So my theory in part one may seem relatively clear-cut, easier to argue against or agree with, than my clinical illustrations in part two. I do try to indicate how I think when I am with the patient but this may seem somewhat idiosyncratic until I try to apply concepts such as the anima and animus. I leave it to the reader to judge whether these concepts enhance or detract from my descriptions.

Part One: Some Theoretical Reflections

The Difficulties

The anima and animus are archetypes. They are also names for that part of any person which belongs more properly to the opposite gender. These two statements are not easily compatible. How can an archetype be part of a person, even an unconscious part? This is the first question one must ask of Jung before one can consider how these concepts can be fruitfully used in clinical practice. This is not restricted to the anima and animus; it can be asked of all the archetypes described by Jung. But with anima and animus one has, in addition, to ask what is meant by gender. If nothing else divides Jungian practitioners, surely this will. It is no longer a question on which any two people can readily agree. On the other hand, Jung's thinking lends itself readily to reinterpretation, partly due to the difficulty of his writing.

Nobody could call Jung easy to read. Some of the difficulty is due to his style and some to the complexity of his subject matter but there is, as well, a certain confusion in his thinking and his manner of reasoning. Particularly vexing is his way of making loose connections and associations which lead him to inconsistency and self-contradiction. Yet, on first acquaintance, many of his ideas seem quite simple and straightforward. In the "Two Essays" (Jung 1943), the definitions in *Psychological Types* (Jung 1921), and in his contribution to *Man and His Symbols* (Jung 1964), even in the Tavistock lectures (Jung 1935), he is relatively clear and simple. One may agree or disagree with what he says but not feel bewildered by what he is saying. In his more difficult texts, such as *The Psychology of the Unconscious* (Jung 1911–1912), particularly before its revision and republication as *Symbols of Transformation* (Jung 1952) or *Psychology of the Transference* (Jung 1946), one can rapidly find oneself bemused by the way these apparently simple ideas become so complicated, so ambiguous, and create so many contradictions that the reader is tempted to give up the concepts themselves. One might easily come to the conclusion that one was initially misled by the apparent simplicity of a concept which breaks down under Jung's own scrutiny of it.

The anima and animus are prime examples of this problem. Nothing seems easier than to recognize that a man has an unconscious female part of himself which, because he disavows it, is liable to be projected, as some kind of female figure, onto women. A woman on whom he has projected this female figure might then become mysteriously fascinating to him, so that he might fall in love with her, or, if the anima takes a negative form, he might fear or reject or avoid or despise her until, perhaps with the help of analysis, he becomes sufficiently individuated to have integrated this female part and to take back the projections, so that he will then see the woman more as she truly is. He will then not only be more complete but better able to relate satisfactorily to women. It is easy, too, to grasp the idea that women have a similarly unconscious male part, with its own positive and negative features, which also requires integration. So far, so good. There are a hundred elementary accounts of Jung which give this apparently simple outline of his views. Even so, the reader might have a problem with the names Jung chooses for these parts and ask why the female part should be called "anima," which means "soul," and the male part "animus," which means "spirit," and a man might encounter some difficulty if he tries to hold a conversation with his anima, as Jung did.

Even this account, although easy to follow, will not easily satisfy the modern reader who knows that we cannot take for granted that we know what men and women *really* are, in the way that Jung assumes. The reader, even if she or he is not a feminist, is now fully aware that no easy generalization about what are now often pointedly called "women and men" can be made without putting at risk the author's claim to impartiality. Can we even speak of feminine or masculine psychology in the way Jung did so freely?

Thus the very basis of the appeal to simplicity with which Jung started, that men and women, who were obviously not the same, must have basic differences in their psychologies, can no longer be assumed. This does not mean that the basis is untrue, and even if Jung's ideas are thought to be the highly biased overgeneralizations of a typically chauvinistic man of his day, it may still be the case that there are, indeed, fixed characteristics which will always differentiate the psychologies of men and women, even if the differences are not exactly what Jung thought they were.

Unfortunately, the revolution in thinking about sex and gender has been so rapid that, like all revolutions, it has produced some radical new solutions, some of which are discovered to be, in their turn, naive over-simplifications, which either propose new differences as stereotyped as the old or deny differences altogether. In either case, these new proposi-tions can provide an easy target for a reactionary backlash. In the field of analytical psychology, they may provoke the demand for a return to orthodoxy, to the word of Jung as he inscribed it in his writings.

Orthodoxy has a positive aspect, too, in the wish to respect Jung or at least not to do violence to his genius, but this can be frustrated by a number of difficulties. The truly orthodox, the fundamentalists, will soon encounter Jung's own unorthodoxy, his own rebellion toward his own attempt to simplify and to classify when his fertile imagination took over. Others who see this as a weakness in Jung and try to correct it may run into the danger of a different kind of violation. In their attempt to be good thinkers and to be clear, concise, and logical, they may destroy much of the work of Jung's imagination which gave so much subtlety to his ideas as they developed.

Then there is the influence of particular schools of thought associ-ated with regional differences in analysis and training, the insidious influence of a group effect, usually inspired by one or two leading figures. These, while paying homage to Jung, may introduce modifica-tions that alter the emphasis or "flavor" of all his concepts. Such move-ments form subgroups in the Jungian community which may fight bitter battles.

Finally, each individual is free to differ from Jung as well as from his or her training group on any point of theory or practice without following up the consequences. Theories are like buildings: only certain bricks can be removed without the whole edifice collapsing.

In composing this paper, I found my self facing each of these problems and continually had to ask myself not only whether I still agreed with Jung but, at times, whether the extent of my disagreement constituted a sort of heresy. Even the most basic ideas, such as the archetypes or the collective unconscious, which might be considered cornerstones of the building, did not escape an agonizing rescrutiny.

Contrasexuality and the Impossibility of Objectivity

It will become apparent that, in one respect at least, I have remained orthodox. I continue to regard the anima and animus as being contrasexual archetypes. This is because even though I can see that both genders may share the same images of the archetype in its male or female form, it also seems clear to me that the anima refers to an image of women derived from a male view of women and femininity while the animus is derived from a feminine view of men and masculinity. In other words, although I take Jung's descriptions as revealing a biased view of the opposite gender, I do not see how anyone can be totally unbiased in this respect and this bias reflects an irreducible restriction of viewpoint based on essential male-female differences. This irreducible problem is one that characterizes psychology as a study of people, in that we are always looking at ourselves. By dividing ourselves into groups, we may imagine we are looking at *other* people. Who are the most objective about women? Other women or men? Perhaps we can never get beyond a point of view and can never avoid bias.

When speaking of a view or viewpoint, I am using the visual modality as a figure of speech but I mean to include all the ways a man can experience femininity. I certainly do not mean to restrict this experience to observation. Pure observation, rather than participation, if such a thing were possible, would lead to pure fantasy, probably perversely voyeuristic or psychopathic, rather than reaching the desired objectivity of science. It is in relating to girls and women and getting some idea of what it is like to be one that a man can develop the feminine potentiality in himself and thus develop a mature rather than primitive anima (and, of course, vice versa for women and the animus). If the bias resulting from each person remaining either a man or a woman is inescapable, however, this may not be wholly undesirable. The meeting of points of view is what makes dialogue possible. In fostering dialogue, the objective is not to be objective: men cannot be objective about women without treating them as objects, and to this, women will rightly object.

I shall come back to this point later and develop it. As I do, it should be borne in mind that although my subject is the anima and animus, the same considerations apply to all the archetypes. Although they are often said to be "personalized," I prefer to regard them as embodied by persons and therefore not conceivable in the absence of persons. Knowing the archetypes by relating to them means, in practice, relating to persons who embody them. But before developing my own views, I should like to draw attention to the great division of opinion on the notions of anima and animus in the literature on analytical psychology, forming what could loosely be called revisionist and orthodox schools of thought.

Two Schools of Thought, Six Authors in Search of a Character

I shall take three well-known authors from each school, orthodox and revisionist, and draw attention to the kind of evidence they use to support their arguments. I can only give here the briefest summary of their views. My three revisionist authors are Whitmont, Hillman, and Samuels.

Whitmont (1969, Chapters 11, 12, and 13), basing his argument on empirical clinical observation, proposes that we often in analysis meet the moody woman who is anima-possessed as well as the opinionated man who is animus-possessed. He therefore does not question Jung's descriptions, which led Jung to posit the idea of anima and animus, but questions only whether they could be differentiated between men and women.

Hillman (1985) argues from his position as an archetypal psychologist that the archetypes are not parts of us and that, therefore, they cannot possibly be said to belong to us. Rather, they lie neither within nor without but they form us and all our ideas about them. He sees the archetypes within a framework of polytheism, rejecting the Judeo-Christian tradition much more thoroughly than Jung ever did. Anima and animus are for him archetypes with the status of a Greek god and goddess so that anima, like soul or psyche, can be talked of as "she" rather than "it" and used without the definite article. His rejection of contrasexuality is logical and consistent with his overall picture of a revisioned psychology.

Samuels (1989), who belongs to a younger generation of Jungians or, as he would say, post-Jungians, takes a more extreme position. Reviewing the evidence, he concludes that there is no such thing as a feminine principle. His evidence is not confined to a study of the nature of the psyche but to a consideration of whether the anatomical and physiological differences between men and women need form the basis of thinking of characteristically feminine or masculine psychology. His questioning of feminine psychology is consistent with his questioning whether there is a specifically Jewish psychology. The argument, difficult to prove or to refute, is that there are no innate differences in the *psychology* of any group of individuals and that whatever differences might be found are attributable to culture, with the important consequence that they can be modified.

All three of these views are unorthodox in that they have in common a rejection of the contrasexuality of the anima and animus but retain Jung's idea that they are archetypes. Each must be taken up in the light of the evidence they provide, which is of three different kinds: clinical observation in the case of Whitmont, mythological reflection for Hillman, and biological study for Samuels. I have taken these three simply as three among many views that can be called dissident.

A detailed discussion of the positions taken up by these three authors is not in place here, but I should like, at this point, to say that although I find much that is persuasive in the arguments of all three, I am not finally convinced by their evidence that we should make the fundamental change from Jung's views that each requires. Although their revisions are consonant with the widespread reevaluation of the way men and women see themselves, I see this reevaluation better expressed in the view that there are specifically different male and female psychologies, that is to say, that men and women are constitutionally profoundly different psychologically, even though Jung's ideas of what these differences are need to be reconsidered. His own descriptions now sometimes seem stereotyped to the point of caricature.

I should now like to cite briefly three authors who espouse the more orthodox viewpoint on contrasexuality. Again, my choice out of so many is somewhat arbitrary, but each is one who has impressed me deeply.

The first is Grinnel (1973), an eminently orthodox Zurich analyst with an extraordinary grasp of alchemical symbolism. His book appeared as recently as 1971. Although he dwells on the alchemical phenomenology of male and female figures, he has no hesitation, when discussing their clinical application, in speaking of "feminine psychology," meaning the true nature of his female patients, however much they may appear to have departed from it.

Penelope Shuttle and Peter Redgrove (1986) base the idea of feminine psychology very firmly on biological differences. Women, having periods, understand periodicity in a way that men cannot. Women are not therefore merely suitable screens for male projections, for example, giving rise to the notion of the dark goddess. They are actually closer, through the experience of their own bodies, including the rotting smell of their own menses, to the cyclical nature of birth and death than man can be.

The third is Dunne (1989) who, approaching the same question through her own dream as well as through theology, reaches similar conclusions. She draws on myth a great deal for her evidence, particularly on the myths of Semele, Eros and Psyche, and Beauty and the Beast, which she sees as variants of the same myth. She makes it clear that these myths are not just patterns of archetypal imagery coming from the collective unconscious but that they are expressions of the real differences between male and female psychology which are dependent on their bodily differences.

Again, we have here three outstanding examples of writers who draw their evidence respectively from clinical observation, biology, and mythology. Again, any evaluation of their work properly requires confirmation or denial based on a study of the evidence they offer. Each, from a particular perspective, is arguing for contrasexuality as Jung did.

As can be seen, all six of these authors, whether orthodox or not, have added something to Jung from their own fields of knowledge. Unfortunately, although each argues persuasively from a specialized standpoint, they do not reach the same conclusion and the controversy is not settled. My own position may turn out to be equally controversial. However, my wish to add my own voice to that of so many others in this debate is based on three considerations that I think are inherent in Jung's writings but are often overlooked. These three can be placed in a logical sequence as follows:

1) Man is essentially a self-defining animal. He can virtually be whatever he wants to be. Therefore, psychology always has to be based on a group definition of Man. As for Man, so for Woman. This hardly needs saying but saying it brings out the problem that there are these two great subgroups and that they are not, in all respects, the same.

2) No science is possible without making generalizations, and in psychology, to generalize about Man is to set limits on the plasticity of self-definition implied in (1).

3) To avoid contradiction between the above two observations, a hierarchic order of presentation is required, e.g., Humankind, with Man and Woman as subgroups where there are also larger and smaller subgroups, as well as the individual person, have to be placed in a serial order of priority, which cannot be done without an implied system of values.

Self-Definition and Its Limits

John Shotter, in his *Images of Man in Psychological Research* (1975), argues that how psychologists behave should be more clearly linked with the way Man is defined and stresses the enormous plasticity that is possible in definition. As a kind of guiding myth, he uses Pico della Mirandola who, in a way that might seem extreme to our modern thinking, sees Man as having no "natural" nature. In Pico's creation myth, God had more or less created the universe but then had the problem of wanting to create Man because He "desired that there should be someone to reckon up the reason for such a big work, to love its beauty and to wonder at its greatness" (Shotter 1975, p. 12). The problem was that he had nowhere to put him and, interestingly from our point of view, "there was nothing in his archetypes from which he could mould him" (ibid.). He therefore decided to place him in the midpoint of the world and leave to him to mould himself and choose whether to go upwards or downwards. So God says to Man: "Thou . . . art the moulder and maker of thyself; thou mayst sculpt thyself into whatever shape thou mayst prefer. Thou canst grow downwards into the lower natures which are brutes. Thou canst again grow upward from thy soul's reason into higher natures which are divine."

This humanistic picture of Man at the center, with the archetypes already used up, so to speak, of Man capable of infinite transformation but subject to a preexisting order, a hierarchically ordered arrangement in which "higher" = divine and "lower" = brutes, is similar to Jung's picture of Man as a sort of individuating animal. But Jung, no more than Pico, meant the myth to be taken literally. The transformation required imagination, which for Jung needed to be active, but imagination is required only if there are limits to what can be realized without it. One of these limits, or constraints, lies in our biology, our "animal nature." another lies in such matters as our race, our age (or stage of life), and, most importantly for our present preoccupation, our gender. Here biology does seem to play a decisive, although as yet not clearly understood, part.

Biological Basis for Sex Differences

There is a substantial and growing body of evidence supporting the notion that there is no easy division to be made between sex and gender. Such a division is commonly made by feminists. In its extreme form, sex differences are thought to be confined to a few indisputable physical differences, such as the presence of the primary and secondary anatomical and physiological features of the grossest kind: penis or vagina, distribution of body fat and body hair, etc., and none of the differences listed under "sex" are thought to be responsible for gender. These are considered to be entirely the manifestations of cultural expectations. I think this point of view is similar to that espoused by dynamic psychiatry when it wishes to dispute "organic" or "genetic" explanations for mental illness. Analysts tend to overargue the case for environmental origins because what is caused by the environment can be more easily changed by the environment in the form of analysis (although Jung himself believed that a toxin was responsible for schizophrenia). Now it is true that there is an enormous amount of prejudice about the sexes and perhaps most of the commonly held views on the differences between them are the result of culturally bound stereotypes. But not all. We should look carefully at both sides of the debate. We should beware of lowering the level of argument to a battle between those who say it's all in our genes and those who say it's all due to culture. Culture is at least in part the expression of our biology and also constrains our attempts to liberate ourselves from it. We are unique among the animals in our development of culture but this can be seen as a very slow evolutionary development of our species, as animals competing for survival. We know also that genes do not exert the influence only at the beginning of life, with the environment then taking over, but that there is a continuous interchange between the two throughout life.

Males differ genetically from females through the presence of the Y chromosome, which like the penis, women do not have. It is in the early stage of fetal development that the Y chromosome brings about the production of testosterone, which brings the distinctively male primary and sexual characteristics and their changes throughout the life cycle, producing differences of a physical nature between the sexes. So far there is no disagreement. The problem arises when it is suggested that psychological differences may have the same origin through the hormonal expression of the different chromosomes. The main opposition has been from intersexual cases of boys mistakenly being brought up as girls and vice versa. But many of these cases have, on close examination, been found to support the idea that masculinity results from testosterone rather than cultural expectations. Not only does testosterone production have psychological effects throughout life, but it seems that about two months after conception, the genetically male fetus produces testosterone which influences the actual brain structure. For example, there is the famous and often quoted case of the American male identical twins born in the early 1960s. One of the twins had his penis accidentally severed during circumcision at seven months. One year later, it was decided to alter him surgically into a girl, so his testes were removed and a vagina constructed, and he was brought up as a girl. It was thought that she then developed with a comfortable female identity. However, it was later found that she had severe psychological difficulty after puberty in adjusting to a female role. One case proves nothing either way, of course, but this case had been much cited as dramatic proof of the conventional wisdom that nurture, not nature, was responsible for gender. It may well be, however, that in this case it was the difference in brain structure that produced the psychological difficulties (Diamond 1982).

There are also cases of families such as the Dominican one studied by Julianne Imperato-McGinley (in Durden-Smith and de Simone 1983). A genetic abnormality transmitted through seven generations has produced no less than thirty-seven cases of babies born and brought up as girls with a strong female identity who changed into boys, with penis, testicles, and strongly marked secondary sexual characteristics at puberty. These seem to have made the transition from female to male quite comfortably. Again, it seems highly likely that these children's brains were primed in utero to be male, which found natural expression with the onrush of testosterone production at puberty when hidden testes descended and the clitoris grew into a penis.

If it is true that male and female brains show statistically signifi- cant differences, it is hard to argue that there are no fundamental psychological differences. Such brain differences have been shown con- vincingly in animals, both in rats and in primates, and while it is less easy to demonstrate, there is considerable evidence that this is also true for humans (Durden-Smith and de Simone 1983). These anatomical differences reside in the much greater thickness of the corpus callosum, the fibers connecting the two hemispheres, in the female. There is also a different distribution in the language centers in males and females, demonstrated by stimulation during neurosurgery. This was originally done not to establish sexual differences but to avoid damaging lan- guage skills. It was found, and confirmed by many different observers, that the language centers are more widely dispersed in women than in men, in whom there seems to be a greater specialization of functions between the two hemispheres. There is also evidence of front-back differentiation of brain structure so that in cross section, the caudal end of the corpus callosum is thicker in males than females, not only in adults but in the fetus. This difference is so striking that the sex can be determined with one hundred percent accuracy. A large number of papers, going into great detail, are focussed in seminal ones by Jean- nette McGlone (in Durden-Smith and de Simone 1983).

In a series of influential papers, Pierre Flor-Henry has developed a theory which, although drawn from biological, i.e., neurological and biochemical sources, should be of interest to Jungians (particularly when considering the anima-possessed man) (1978, 1979). He believes that the superiority in men in the coarse visual-motor skills (as compared with women's superiority in language skills) is associated with mood, with movement, and with sexual fulfillment. This combination is organized by the right hemisphere, and, in the male, it is only later that it comes under the control of the left (verbal). This would mean the left-sided hemisphere verbal control is more precarious than in women. This, he believes, is the reason for the much greater preponderance in men of aggressive sociopathy and deviant sexual acting-out. There seem to be exaggeratedly "right-sided" men who commit crimes that are practically unknown in women. It would certainly confirm Jung's idea that when males become dominated by their moods, they are under the possession of the anima.

The differences, which are considered in great deal in Durden-Smith and de Simone (1983) can be summarized as follows. Men seem to be more specialized than women; they are better at activities requiring not only greater muscular strength but greater visual-motor skills, such as locating objects in space; they are better at abstraction and mathematical ability. Women are not only better at mothering and nurturing but are more verbal; better at fine visual-motor skills, which make them not only better at needlework but also more sensitive in intimate relationships; they have been shown to be more responsive, for example, to changes in the expression of the human face and they speak differently in that they use much more nonverbal expressive gestures in conversation. Much of the differences observed can be attributed to the long evolutionary period in which men were hunters and women gatherers. This is far greater than the period in which agriculture developed, let alone the tiny period of industrial society. Even today, in spite of the numerous demonstrations of the different roles of men and women in different societies, which purport to show that culture is more important than nature, there are no known societies in which women hunt, although in a minority of cases, they assist men in hunting. There are no societies run by a group of women (even Mrs. Thatcher surrounds herself with men). Although there are patrilineal societies, there are not and probably never have been any truly matrilineal ones, and the Amazons exist only in myth (for a more detailed argument of this position, see Lionel Tiger and Robin Fox 1972).

No doubt there is some scope for the differences to change in the future, even the biological ones. Humankind is self-defining, and the differences are only statistical and do not therefore apply to *all* men and *all* women. But what I want to insist on here is that there are obstacles, limits, and constraints which have to be taken into consideration and that these are not simply due to prejudicial stereotyping but have a foundation in nature. Sex and gender should be distinguished but the distinction is not a crude or simple one. Furthermore, none of the differences I have mentioned should be thought of as *inequalities* or in any way justifying one gender dominating the other. They do help us to establish the ways in which men and women can be complementary to each other while retaining their respective autonomy and equality in the social power structure.

Part Two: Anima and Animus in Clinical Practice

Clinical Orientation

Jungian analysts do not all practice in the same way. The variations in technique are so great that the usefulness of Jungian concepts cannot easily be compared among practitioners unless full allowance is made for the conditions in which analysis is taking place as well as the aims and interests of the analyst. These factors will determine what it is that the analyst is looking for and is most likely to discern, indeed in what it is that the analyst will be regarding as the clinical "material." It seems to me to be most important that any hostility that one analyst has toward the orientation of another should be at least held in check by these considerations.

As I am a member of the London school, it will come as no surprise that I am interested in development, in infantile origins, in the details of personal history, in seeing patients four or five times a week, in the use of the couch, in psychoanalytic contributions, especially of the British object-relations approach, and consequently in the subtle vicissitudes of the transference and the countertransference. This does not mean that I am not a Jungian, and although I am deeply interested in religion, mythology, and alchemy, these are not in the forefront of my mind while I am with patients. They are, nevertheless, in the background and, at times, become very illuminating and then enter the foreground. I am sure that, conversely, other Jungians, who seem to be actively looking for impersonal archetypal material, must equally be struck, at times, by the emergence of personal historical factors and that most of the differences between rival schools can be seen as matters of relative emphasis.

In the last decade, in addition to intensive analysis, part of my own clinical work, having had a training in group analysis, has been with groups and also with couples seen conjointly and in couples groups. There seem to be a rapidly increasing number of Jungian analysts now extending their work to these areas. As others are finding, too, working with more than one person at a time, with a Jungian theoretical framework, opens up new questions about that framework. One begins to question not only the rather introverted bias of Jung's interests, which led to an overemphasis on inner- rather than outer-world phenomena, but also his great insistence on the individual, which colored his view of individuation. These considerations have gradually come to have a marked influence on my individual work, and although I have written more extensively elsewhere on this subject (Zinkin 1989), this paper will be more comprehensible if I summarize here some of the implications for the study of the manifestations of anima and animus in a clinical setting.

Inner and outer events were, at least in theory, given equal prominence by Jung in his great division between introversion and extraversion. In his diagrams of the psyche, used in his seminars, Jung arranged inner and outer hierarchically, although either the ego or the collective unconscious (or Self) might be at the top or bottom of the hierarchy. These diagrams can be studied in Jacobi, *The Psychology of C. G. Jung* (1939).

Working with groups and couples, one has to pay special attention to a third area, the interpersonal, and one cannot but be struck by the fact that it is in this area that so much of psychic life is lived and psychological development takes place. One is further drawn to the view that the phenomena being observed are simply indescribable except in interpersonal terms. In the U.S.A., the great pioneer of this whole mode of thinking was Harry Stack Sullivan, and in Britain, a similar pioneer has been S. H. Foulkes who has developed the notion of group analysis based on the idea that "Man's social nature is an irreducible basic fact" (Foulkes 1964, p. 109).

A further influence has been infant research, which places a similar emphasis on the interpersonal and on intersubjectivity in the first social exchanges between the mother and her baby. This in turn has altered my notions of reductive analysis and reconstruction of infancy (Zinkin 1991).

Clinical work, by its very nature, demands of its practitioners that they distinguish between health and illness, normality and pathology, but although every therapist explicitly or implicitly has to make such distinctions, it is rare for them to be spelled out in a clinical presentation. In marital work, especially as one sees distressed couples, one is compelled to address questions like: "What is marriage?" "Is it a good idea?" "How should a man and woman try to live happily together?"

"What roles should they play?" "What distribution of work and play should they try to agree on?" There is a tendency in our pluralistic age to say there are no rules and no universal answers to questions like these. Nevertheless, one is being addressed as a consultant who is expected to know what is healthy and therefore desirable and what is unhealthy and needs to change. Working with couples as a Jungian leads one to ask questions about anima and animus projections, one onto the other. But this means having to make judgments about what is contrasexual and split-off and what is contrasexual and integrated in each partner, and what each partner can reasonably expect in the way of change from the other. The problems raised are not easily solved. Working with my wife as a co-therapist, I find that we by no means always agree about these judgments, and we certainly find it difficult to get agreement with the two partners. What we work for is, of course, agreement between all four of us but even when we have achieved this quarternio, this wholeness, who is to say that we have "got it right"? Nevertheless it is essential to have at least a provisional working model of healthy male/female relations.

In this paper, I have chosen to concentrate on individual analysis, which is still the main clinical model for analytical psychology, and in my two clinical examples, I will be trying to show how these questions are just as valid in the analytic dyad as in the treatment of couples. In both examples, there is a constant struggle to achieve agreement about what is male and what female, what is part and what whole, what is projected and what really belongs to the other. The struggle involves both partners in the analysis and is not just a question of the analyst analyzing his patient while processing his countertransference or "irrational" reactions to his patient.

I have chosen to present two very short extracts from long and intensive analyses from my clinical practice. It will be noticed that in both examples the analyst, being myself, is male and the patient female. This is quite deliberate. My view of females is necessarily limited by me being male, while the females' perception of me is similarly limited. The gender of the analyst has often been thought to be irrelevant in the long run because both male and female figures can so readily be projected onto the same analyst. I think that this common assertion, although it has some truth in it, overlooks some very real and important differences. I have many limitations as a therapist, and although I can go a long way to overcoming them, I can never be a female one and this has consequences for both my men and women patients. With men, we can only deal with our perceptions or fantasies about the absent women, while with women, neither of us can be sure that we understand each other in the way we would if our bodies did not have significant differences. What I do believe and hope to illustrate in my two examples is that anima and animus problems can be most fruitfully worked with where the genders are different and where both partners are faced with the gender barrier, uncrossable except in the imagination. If the genders are the same, fantasies about the opposite one can never be properly tested out, whereas a woman's fantasies about men can at least be subjected in the here-and-now to my own perceptions of myself, as can fantasies about women where a female therapist is working with a man.

Clinical Example 1: Anna

For my first example, I should like to describe the beginning of just one session. I opened the door of my consulting room to admit Anna. As I stood there, expecting her as usual to leave her coat on a nearby chair and walk silently to the couch without looking at me or speaking, in a ritual which has taken place a hundred times before, she surprised me by bending down to pick up a glove, saying, "Here's a glove" and then placing it on the piano which stands nearby. I said and did nothing and she went to the couch and lay down. As she reflected on what had just taken place, it emerged that she had not at all liked what had happened at the beginning and particularly was critical of herself and the way she had behaved on coming into the room. Reflecting on her entry and trying to understand her difficulty, I thought of an actress who has not made a good entrance onto the stage. I think of Stanislavsky, who might have said to an actress: "Go onto the stage. You will see a glove on the floor. Pick it up!" It is the kind of thing which sounds perfectly simple but is, in fact, a difficult exercise. Like an actress (and Anna, I knew, was very interested in acting), Anna was acutely aware of being observed and this contributed to her inability to act spontaneously. She was then faced with the problem of trying to reconstruct the action leading up to the scene she had to play and how it might have been quite different. She reported her thoughts as follows: when she saw the glove, she noticed that it was an old one and this gave her pleasure. She thought of running out and pursuing the previous patient, who had just left, and also of handing it to me, but this she could not do. Looking at me and handing the glove to me would have been a dangerous testing out of a fantasy. Our hands might have touched—and then? It was not difficult for me to imagine the possible sequels. I could now see that my idea of the actress performing in front of the great director was not quite accurate. The exercise would be even more difficult. She would find another actor on the stage, a man, but would be given no idea as to what her relationship with him was supposed to be. She could, for example, imagine they were lovers but she could not know whether the actor would have the same or a different idea of their relationship. In other words, her spontaneity could not exist except in a context provided by the other. To give meaning to their actions, the two actors would have to express a common understanding of what their past relationship had been.

Anna's difficulty was that although a great deal of intimacy had been built up during the analysis, she could not at that moment rely on this and I had become (and indeed was acting) the formal analyst rather distantly recognizing a patient coming into a consulting room, thus perhaps this was the scene in which she was acting (or trying to). In this scene, she might have thought I had not remembered her and myself as having been any closer than we now seemed to be, or that even though I had remembered, I was not expecting her to have remembered. Or perhaps she remembered only after she had come in and then it was too late. On such occasions, it is tempting to ask the patient what has been going on in her mind but to ask is to show that one has already not understood and the exercise has failed.

This is the kind of incident which brings to my attention the archetypal background against which it occurs. The problem that emerged was that Anna had behaved in a dull, muted, mechanical way which was acutely painful to her because she longed to be remembered and to be recognized by someone she loved and who loved her. I am not calling this "transference," which, strictly speaking, would suggest that such an expectation was based on an illusory or possibly delusional projection, although it undoubtedly had certain transference elements that might be analyzable. It would be truer to say that it was not her fantasy but her actual behavior which was an acting-out of transference. The fantasy was that she meant nothing at all to me. She was just another patient, possibly an interesting case, but certainly not one for whom I would have any special feeling. This was certainly not the reality. Her behavior then and for most of the ensuing session had a quality of lifelessness.

If one sees, as I do, the archetypal level as a backdrop to the relationship, then the operative myth is the one I find myself thinking about when trying to understand what is going on in the relationship. Usually I find that the myth which comes to mind is one that reflects the genders of the patient and myself. I cannot easily be Demeter to Persephone but I can quite easily be Orpheus to Eurydice. In this particular instance, my archetypal backdrop was not one of the great world myths but a fairy tale, "The Little Mermaid." This came to my mind because she had once told me that this story had made her cry.

In this story, the little mermaid makes the mistake of falling in love with a drowning prince, and so, instead of drawing him down to his death, she saves his life and he returns to dry land. From then on, she wants to become human and to have a soul. Before she can go onto dry land herself, she needs legs (and presumably genitals, although these are politely not mentioned), and the condition imposed on her by the Sea Witch is that she has to have her tongue cut out. She willingly submits to this brutal mutilation. When on the land, she not only finds that her every step is agony but the prince does not recognize her and there is no way in which she can remind him who she is. Looking at it from the prince's point of view, which Hans Christian Andersen does not, one is reminded that it is often difficult to recognize someone in an unfamiliar context and in any case, she has made a dramatic change: she is no longer a mermaid, no longer at home in her environment. She is now a human but a mute and crippled one. Nevertheless he is drawn to her and she becomes his constant companion. When he later meets another girl, he wants to marry her because she reminds him of the one who rescued him. The little mermaid has to endure the agony of mutely witnessing this new relationship and thus cannot gain the soul she craves.

Part of Anna's agonizing dilemma when she entered my room was that she could not speak. She, of course, was not really mute, and indeed she was able to say a few words but she could not truly speak to me. She could not remind me who she was. If she had to remind me, it meant that I had not remembered. It was as though what had really happened to her, or what she hoped had really happened to *us*, belonged to another existence, another realm. No action was possible unless I could remember who she was in this other realm. I was not giving any sign that I recognized her other than as my patient, who had arrived as she always did for yet another session of analysis. Like the little mermaid, she might also be expected to be jealous of the other woman but this would not be the primary problem, which was existential and concerned with more basic problems of identity, the nature of reality and fantasy, of change and the meanings of discontinuities in time and space, in socially constructed roles, in intimacy, and in forbidden love. As an analyst, it was difficult to know what might be in her mind at this moment and she, being mute, was relying on my ability to understand. So now I knew she could not know what I knew, and she, for all I knew, might think I was cruelly testing her or might, on the other hand, not realize she was not behaving perfectly normally. I should add, too, that she knew I had a visual defect which might have prevented me from seeing the glove until she had drawn my attention to it but she could not be sure that this was so. As when reading the story, one feels there should be a simple solution which would avert the tragedy. Surely, one thinks, the prince should have been able to recognize the little mermaid without her tail. Why could he not see with his own eyes this girl who loved him? Alas, in the story, he never does and there is no happy ending.

What is curious about the story is that a mermaid, an obvious anima figure, should want a soul. One might think that she *is* a soul and that what she needed was a body. Perhaps Andersen has made a mistake. I do not think so. One does not need to think so logically when making up a story, or rather, there might be a right-brained logic taking over from a left-brained one. This must be the case when an archetype appears in a story that seems to be about people. Mermaids are not exactly people. They may be half-people, or it may always be ambiguous, never clear whether they are or not. They do not usually fall in love themselves, and when the little mermaid does this, she begins a process of departing from her mermaid nature. Having fallen for a mortal man, at the point when his mortality is evident, she, too, has to become fully human if she wants to see him again. For this, she has to pay a terrible price. The lose of her tongue is not the loss of human speech but of her mermaid song, which, sirenlike, draws men to their deaths. As a watery underworld being, she might act as, or stand in for, the man's soul but she cannot herself have one. In fact, she has no real existence but is merely a fantasy figure for the man, who could then be said to have projected his anima or lost his soul. Once she loses her mermaid powers, she ceases to be the anima or soul but begins to have a real existence for herself. Then she experiences the pain of a lack that can only be made good by another, by the man she has saved. She has to face the ordeal that the man, who no longer needs saving, can exist without her, is no longer drawn to her, and cannot appreciate that, out of her love, she did not use her powers of attraction, which for him would have meant death. Later, she has a chance to kill him and save herself, but once again, she lets him go and even this he does not know.

The patient who gets the love of the analyst through seduction always knows that his love is not given freely but that he has fallen captive to her powers of fascination and then can no longer function as an analyst even if he escapes the professional "death" of being struck off the register. She knows this only if she is no longer innocent, no longer without insight or consciousness of the power of sexual difference to elicit the projection of men's animas. Anna had considerable anima power but she could not use it. If the true business of analysis is what Hillman has called "soul-making," then a woman can only make soul for a man by *not* being his anima. If she is this, she loses her true self. She helps the man's soul-making only by retaining her true femininity, which men can appreciate when they are not projecting but perceiving truly.

I have put forth this explanation in a way that may seem odd. It might be objected that it is not necessary or desirable for a woman to make soul for a man. She only needs to do it for herself. But this disregards what I believe to be crucial. A man cannot know what it is to be a woman. He can imagine it but only because women exist. He cannot relate to a female part of himself other than by recognizing in himself what he imagines to be in a woman's consciousness of being a woman. If this is so, a woman cannot fulfill his longings for a soul by being an anima projection screen. This would only trick him and might destroy him. It is only through her own actual femininity that a woman can provide a man with a soul, and if she does so, she makes soul for herself in the relationship, because she, in her turn, cannot understand her feminine nature without the different nature of men. In the case of Anna, I have made the point that a fantasy was not what was wanted to make our relationship come alive. It was not that what was remembered was only a dream, something not "really" true, but that what was happening now was the dream, a bad one, in which reality had been forgotten. The reality could only find existence within our relationship. It is true that my task was the very difficult one of helping her to internalize the relationship that belonged uniquely to us, and by "internalise" I mean recall it and anticipate it in my absence. But what I do not mean is that there might be some independent possibility of her understanding this outside the context of our relationship, however much she might enjoy or resonate with myths, fairy tales, or alchemical texts.

In my analysis of Anna, it was important to work on her personal history, especially her very traumatic early childhood in which there were separations of which she could make no sense. The anima archetype, as portrayed by the little mermaid, is inseparable from this but does not itself deal with it. No amount of amplification could help her if her individual history was left out. But the story had a linking function. First, it placed the archetype in a setting where an individuation process is taking place as the mermaid becomes a real girl. Then the plight of the mermaid can be linked to the patient's actual childhood, and it can also be seen to be reenacted in the here-and-now of the analyst-analysand relationship including its unconscious elements in both participants in the form of transference and countertransference. The archetype itself plays only a limited role in this process. From a therapeutic point of view, its significance was that it had not remained outside awareness but turned up as an image expressing what was missing in our relationship. If this is made good, it will disappear into the background again. The anima as "soul image" then disappears and soul takes its place.

In the light of these observations, the earlier theoretical problems can be readdressed. Sometimes the archetypal realm is given a more basic position, notably in "archetypal psychology." This viewpoint could lead to the suggestion that our notions of male and female are themselves derived from the archetypes. This would imply that the sense of mystery attached to them was derived from the essentially unknowableness of the archetypes and therefore can only be apprehended through images. Men and women might then be regarded as convenient pegs on which to hang the archetypal clothes, equally convenient pegs being the sun and moon or gold and silver or umbrellas and purses. Quite logically, Jung's notions of the contrasexuality of the anima and animus then have to be discarded.

Such a view can easily be derived from a particular way of working. If the analyst is seen purely as one accompanying the patient on the journey of individuation, if the patient, for example, has been having dreams indicating that a *coniunctio* is taking place, with the analyst drawing the patient's attention to alchemical or mythical parallels to the dream material, it is perfectly possible to conclude that the patient has both an anima and an animus because both appear in the dream. Not only the sex of the patient but also that of the analyst would be immaterial. This might easily seem to be the case where the analyst is following Jung's procedure of minimizing the transference through infrequent sessions in the face-to-face position. On the other hand, the same claim is made by some analysts who work with the transference all the time and see all the material in terms of projections onto the analyst. These analysts claim that the actual sex of the analyst makes no difference because, in the long run, the patient's fantasies may take a male or female form. If the focus is neither on the psyche and the collective unconscious nor on the transference as the intrapsychic peculiarity of the patient but on the interaction seen as the joint production of the participants, then the gender of the participants (as well as other unalterable facts about them) play an all-important part.

In my clinical example, which cannot be separated from the way I work, it is evident that the nature of the experience that Anna and I had together would not have been the same if I had been a woman or she a man. It is true that a homosexual attraction would have seemed similar in some ways. But imagining homosexual intercourse would have introduced many factors not present in the heterosexual relationship and these would have completely altered the tone of the encounter. In my imagined exercise, Stanislavsky would have had to ask a man to pick up the glove or if he had asked a woman the other person on the stage would have had to be a woman. It is not difficult to see that the resulting performance would not be the same. It might still be argued that the differences would reflect only the social or personal reality but not the archetypal or transpersonal level. There seems no end to this form of argument, which would include the idea that the archetypes are, by definition, quite impersonal and that it is only we who personify them or that they can only appear to us in the guise of persons. Although these arguments are often used by Jung himself, they do not do justice to my own clinical experience. Social or personal reality is not, for me, a lower-level distortion, through archetypal projection, of a purer, higher but essentially unknowable impersonal truth; on the contrary, it seems to me that impersonal abstract patterns often referred to as archetypes are the distortions of the living relationships in which the true archetypes have their existence. The emergence of the mermaid, in my example, is not of an archetypal image transcending my actual feeling for Anna. In spite of its universality and numinous qualities, the image is a partially impersonal distortion of men's perceptions of women. Although called a "soul image," it is a false one. A true soul can be acquired only if the mermaid sheds her tail and changes her habitat.

What I have said here applies also to the other archetypes. There can be no child archetype without children, no trickster without tricksters, no senex without old men. The archetype is a backdrop that universalizes our experience of the particular and thus deepens our experience. But there is no substitute for relationships with others which put the archetypes into perspective. My view is that there is a social reality not solely determined by the archetypes. that it is largely constructed by people in relationship does not make it less real. It is at a different level from the reality of the archetypes, and while they enrich it, it also enriches them.

Jung's personal history, particularly as related in *Memories, Dreams, Reflections* (1963), tends to give the misleading impression that he was able to individuate in isolation from others, particularly because of his social isolation as an intelligent but withdrawn country boy, with his depressed father, his remote, "medieval" mother, and his sister, who is hardly mentioned. I think it is true that these early experiences, leading to a split between his number one and number two personalities, were mostly in existence in his private, inner world but that what saved him was his development as a public figure in his outer world experiences, in that he met others in the wider world who shared his experiences, so that he could develop them as part of a generalized psychology. These other real people were often remote figures in time and space, although it is important not to under-estimate the presence of the actual women in his life, particularly his wife, Emma.

Although Jung was very interested in psychic reality, he still needed to understand it in relation to everyday reality. It would not have been possible for Jung to achieve individuation through his dreams and visions until he had discovered others who had similar ones. In "The Psychology of the Transference," Jung diagrammatically represents the situation where there is both anima and animus (1946, par. 422). The relationship of the adept to the *soror mystica* (his female helper) is used as the analogue of the transference. "Now the adept," says Jung, "is conscious of himself as a man, consequently his masculin-ity cannot be projected, since this only happens to unconscious con-tents" (1946, par. 421). He says this in a passage where he is discussing the possibility that the male figure of the King (in the second picture of the Rosarium) represents the anima and the Queen is the animus. If the *coniunctio* represents the transference-countertransference relationship as Jung suggests, then he is taking the Rosarium pictures as represent-ing the unconscious relationship between the analyst and patient, assuming that one is conscious of himself as being male and the other of herself as female, e.g., where the doctor is male like the adept and the patient female like the *soror*. Only in this way can his diagram, where the anima of one relates to the animus of the other, fit the analytic situation. What happens in the frequent cases where the ana-lyst and analysand are of the same sex is not clear in this account. Despite the title, "The Psychology of the Transference," Jung is not primarily concerned in this essay with describing the intricacies of the transference as illustrated with actual patients, only with the intricacies of the alchemical series, which for him illustrate the complexity of the unconscious relationship of the analytic dyad. What the reader makes of the analogy depends on his or her own clinical experience. Nevertheless, it provides a background for what Schwartz-Salant calls the "interactive field" in which in addition to the couple of persons in the room, there is also the unconscious couple (1989). For me, this notion of the interactive field enables us to describe phenomena that exist only as the result of the interaction of two or more people.

There is therefore an intermingling of individual psyches, each of which is unable to individuate without the other, and the archetypal figures that arise do so not within the individual, nor wholly outside, but within the relationship they have with each other. I do not, like Winnicott (1971), regard this as a transitional area, but an area on a higher level of reality than that of the single individual. In the early parent-child interaction, I believe that the two-person experience is the primary reality for the child, taking place in the patterns of the synchronized nonverbal exchanges between the two participants (Stern 1985). These take the form of certain universally found communication patterns, equivalent to "the patterns that connect," to use Gregory Bateson's phrase (1979). These may well be the earliest manifestations of the archetypes. I think it would be quite possible to use the Rosarium pictures for illustrating what goes on in the mother-infant dyad in the same way that Jung does for the transference, and it is significant that Jung never regarded the transference as unique to the analytic situation. This leads me to a conclusion quite different from Jung's: that the analytic situation provides the ideal setting in which the mother-infant relationship can be relived, and so I deliberately cultivate and explore the transference-countertransference interaction in my clinical work because I consider this early interaction influential to all subsequent relationships. While it is not my special aim to demonstrate the clinical value of this way of working in this paper, I do want to reiterate the point that the anima and animus as a pair of archetypes do not have their existence in the individual psyche but that they come to life in the dyad, the interactive field formed by a group of two.

Clinical Example 2: Felicity

My second example is another female patient, Felicity. In this case, I will focus not on my anima as elicited by her for me but on her animus as elicited by me for her. In this case, the animus was not only projected onto me but also experienced by her as a part of herself.

Felicity was very enthusiastic about her analysis with me. Her enthusiasm was so great that she created misgivings in me as to whether I could fulfill her expectations of it. She came from a great distance for her sessions, and the long journeys there and back were filled with thoughts of the analysis and with her endeavors to understand her own inner world. She recorded her dreams in great detail and had done so for herself long before she began analysis with me. The sheer volume and richness of the material, whether it was dreams, fantasies, thoughts about her family or her work, or memories of childhood, often made it difficult for her to talk without providing an endless commentary on what she was saying. For instance, if she brought a dream, she also had to provide all the meanings it already had for her and all the associations that had occurred to her, before and during the telling of it. As this might go on for a long time before I actually knew what the dream was, let alone felt ready to interpret it, and because while she was doing all this, she was also having more thoughts, fantasies, and memories which made her want not to talk about the dream at all, it was often a long time before I said anything at all. It was not as chaotic as it might sound, and I did not usually feel swamped, nor did I feel a strong desire to talk myself. She was coherent and articulate, and I was interested in what she was saying and not in a hurry to intervene. She, on the other hand, did not feel the same. She got fed up with having so much to say, so much to comment on, and with not being able to say something simply and spontaneously and then see how I responded. At times, she would become exasperated and say something like: "Oh, shut up, Felicity!" Curiously, she regarded this talker and commenter, including her critical efforts to shut herself up, as a masculine part of herself and by contrast could see the feminine part as a shape, which she outlined with her hands as being like a single vertical eye, which she said was looking both inward and outward. My own contribution was to say that the shape she described seemed like a vulva and she instantly agreed. This led to reflections on the vulva being an opening to an interior self as well as to the outside world. She then reported the following dream, which had two parts:

Dream: *She wanted to have a holiday by herself and rented a cottage in a very beautiful part of the countryside. But when she got to the cottage, she found that there was a man already there. He was down-at-heel and "slobbery" and she did not much care for his appearance. He claimed that he, too, had booked the cottage. Although she did not welcome his presence, she agreed to let him stay there, too.*

In the second part she was again in a holiday cottage. This time she was inside and was sharing it with two other girls. They had all just arrived, were unpacking, and the atmosphere was one of "girlish fun." They were being giggly and light-hearted. Then a man, whom she immediately recognized as the man in the first part of the dream, arrived at the door. He demanded entry, once again claiming a double booking. But she was not going to be fooled a second time and indignantly refused, whereupon he begged and pleaded to be allowed to stay, assuring her that he would be no trouble. The other two girls were quite amused and said: "Let him stay." But she got very angry and said: "Either he goes or I go!" The dream ended and she had no idea what the outcome was.

The man was undoubtedly an animus figure. He could also be regarded as the shadow but what was striking was his maleness, although not in an attractive or exciting form. The situation is reminiscent of certain fairy tales, such as "Beauty and the Beast" or "The Frog Prince," in that she was required to accept his presence, although in the dream this was not in return for any help he had given. Also, he had tricksterlike qualities, although this became apparent only in the second part, when she could see through his crudely attempted deception. But he is still mainly the animus.

In discussion, the dream was closely associated with the previous material on the vulva as an entrance to her private interior space and with the memory of an older man who had romped with her when she was about thirteen. She thought she could remember feeling his erect penis but she could certainly remember her mother coming in, angry at what was going on.

In another session soon after this, going over the same material, she found herself wanting to stay after the end of the session. She wanted to ask me if she could stay for another session even though she knew that I had another patient to see then. She became quite upset at her difficulty in actually asking me this, and she both let me know what the question was and explained at the same time that I must not answer. As the session neared its end and she went on being upset, I gently said that of course I could understand her need to stay. Although I did not answer the question itself (and in any case she already knew the answer), I did not hurry her out but waited till she had recovered herself sufficiently to be able to leave. I did not know how long this would take but she got up to go only a few minutes over the ending time.

Although there is a great deal in this material which could be discussed, what was very striking was how her behavior, following the dream, repeated the idea of the double booking. This time it was she who was wanting to stay, even though she knew she could not claim the right to do so. It happened because she had to stay in London for an evening event and had nothing to do and nowhere to go in the meantime. Her regressed self, which could not bear to leave and could not bear the thought of her place being taken by another, was being expressed, not by being a seductive anima figure but by a male part of herself which she did not act out but which she could nevertheless communicate to me.

In her experience of herself, the masculine part of Felicity was much larger than her femininity. She come across to me as quite a feminine personality, albeit with certain masculine traits, but her own experience of herself was of the little eye (I?) that could be quite overwhelmed by the masculine part or animus which didn't stop talking and arguing. It was only gradually that she could acknowledge the power of the eye either to refuse or to grant admission to her inner chamber, as she is able to do in the second part of her dream, and to recognize it therefore as private (analogic, female) rather than secret or forbidden (digital, male).

In a later session, the penultimate one before a holiday break, Felicity talked about how contented she felt lying on the couch, knowing I was sitting so close that it would be possible to reach out with her hand and touch me. It felt safe and peaceful. I asked her whether she now felt that she had let me in. Her response was to feel surprised that I should ask such a question. Surely I knew. She was not only surprised, she was upset and no longer felt safe. This reaction made me feel that I had made an insensitive mistake in asking her the question.

In the next session, the last before the break, she said she had quickly felt all right again after leaving the day before. This happened because she was able to recall what it had felt like being safe with me and knowing she was going to come again the next day. But in the course of the session, it happened again. She was saying that lying on the couch felt like lying in my arms. I said, "That sounds like mother's arms." Then, thinking this didn't seem quite right, I added, "Is it mother or perhaps a lover?" She tried to think about my question and said "a lover," but I went on to reflect that this would be exciting rather than restful and she said that talking about it was exciting but perhaps it had been more like the way one feels after making love. She immediately had some critical thoughts about this idea by realizing that she had not had an experience like having sex. As she tried to deal with these thoughts, her mind became active in a way that reminded her of her mother who talked endlessly, "yakking away." This talk got in the way of any genuine communication with her mother. "She just doesn't relate to you," she said. She recognized that the way she herself talked often had this same quality of "yak yak yak," which got in the way, not only of relating to me but of relating to herself. Not only did it go into a great deal of detail but it had a note of hostile criticism in it. This again seemed to her to be a distinctly masculine part of herself. The feminine part had no voice, or perhaps it had a very soft voice that got completely drowned by the masculine talk. It is easy to recognize in Felicity's self-description the animus, which is not truly masculine but corresponds to her image of masculinity when it manifests itself both in her mother and in herself. It could be said that what she thought of as masculine was a stereotypically distorted version of assertiveness which she associated with men, expressing her opinions in a female imitation of the way men talk. One of the analytic tasks would be to integrate both talking and asserting herself with her shy and quiet femininity, which not only did not want to talk or ask questions but did not want me to either. Talk concealed another kind of speech associated with "relating" and with intimacy.

Although my account of the animus, based on my patient's insights, is not quite the same as Jung's description of the opinionated animus-ridden woman, it is still very close to it. The need for another kind of speech associated with femininity is experienced as a need for silence or an inability to speak, very similar to what Anna had experienced. My own view is that it is not really silence as such that is required, only the silencing of the alienating talking. Silence may be a failure to communicate. Although it is impossible not to communicate at all, the message sent in silence may not be received or may be received as a false message. *King Lear* provides a wonderful example of what I mean. "Nothing will come of nothing: speak again," says King Lear to the silent Cordelia at the beginning of the play, a "nothing" which is echoed again and again in the play. At the end, in the moving reconciliation scene (V.3), Lear, expecting to end his days in prison with his daughter, says:

> . . . so we'll live,
> And pray, and sing, and tell old tales, and laugh
> At gilded butterflies, and hear poor rogues
> Talk of court news; and we'll talk with them too

Who loses and who wins; who's in, who's out;
And take upon's the mystery of things,
As if we were God's spies. . . .

Lear now understands something he had no conception of at the beginning of the play, when he wanted speeches from his daughters. He
understands now the value of a different kind of talk, seemingly mere
gossip, but whose content has little importance while it eloquently
expresses *relationship*. Words are used but the exchange is nonverbal.
This is similar to the "exchange of sweet nothings" between lovers but,
again, I think it derives originally from the first exchanges between
mother and baby. It is this maternal behavior which, I believe, is
responsible for the association of eros and of relationship with femininity. It is a gentle voice not really requiring words, and it may take the
form of singing (a right-brain activity which can remain intact after a
stroke when the left-brained speech center is destroyed). The mermaids
sing "each to each" and it is the sirens' song which can distract the
sailors to their death.

The conversation, using words but also expressing the relationship, that Felicity sought with me was a combination of male and
female corresponding to logos and eros, based on actual rather than
metaphorical male-female differences.

Conclusions

There has never been a time when our notions of male and female
have been more often in the melting pot and, because of the way Jung
has set out his ideas of the anima and animus, this has thrown the
Jungian world into some disarray. It is now possible to discern a wide
variety of conflicting views on the anima and the animus. In this spectrum of views, my own has tended to support the idea that we should
retain both terms of Jung's concept, namely that they are (1) *contrasexual* (2) *archetypes*. On the other hand, because of the great plasticity of
the human psyche, our ability to define and redefine ourselves, a great
deal of modification takes place in the culture, especially as mediated
by the mother in the early months of life. It is this plasticity that gives
rise to gender-confusion and to homosexuality seen in the clinical situation and supports the idea that everyone has both an anima and an
animus. What has concerned me here has been the limitations of this
plasticity. We can redefine ourselves in the imagination or we can set
about becoming what we have imagined. Having periods or having a
baby or having an erection is not the same as imagining what it feels

like to have them. For both men and women, and thus for every individual, there is always a lack, which requires relationship, and my main clinical emphasis has been on the achievement of agreement or consensus between analyst and analysand on how they are relating to each other, without any certainty that by doing so, they are reaching any final conclusion about absolute truth. In turn, this means placing more emphasis than usual on interpersonal rather than intrapsychic happenings.

Working with couples and with groups has also helped me to be aware of certain limitations in dyadic analysis, particularly in working with the animus and anima. I referred earlier to the limitations of gender but would like here to make one further observation. It concerns the well-recognized problem of the deleterious effect analysis may have on the patient's partner. This is usually attributed to the difficulty she or he has in coping with the progressive effects of the analysis. This cannot be the only explanation and I am not satisfied, either, that separate analysis for the partner is the answer. If we believe that our patients are reaching greater maturity but that unfortunately this is leading to the breakdown of their marriages, there may be something wrong with our theories and our values. If we believe that seeing the partner will spoil the analysis, there may be something wrong with our notion of preserving the analysis. If we do see the partner, there are certainly technical difficulties but the outcome for the continuing analysis can be profoundly richer.

My plea throughout has been for holding onto Jung's assumption that male and female psychologies are in a nontrivial sense different and that these differences are not reducible to culture but have deeper, ultimately biological roots. Acknowledging these fundamental differences does not, however, mean holding onto Jung's own rather dated descriptions, which do now seem to have a cultural bias.

This means that each individual has to acknowledge a permanent lack of whatever is characteristic of the opposite gender. Analysts play an important part in helping men and women to live happily with each other, and this means each gender group has to acknowledge a psychological lack which they can find only in the other. This standpoint, as I hope to have demonstrated, makes a difference to the clinical handling of the anima and animus.

This brings me to a more general conclusion that goes beyond gender issues and which I can set out only tentatively here. Because we live in social interaction with others, we do not have to look solely within ourselves to attain the sense of completeness, which Jung saw as the goal of individuation. Although Jung recognized this by distinguishing the extravert from the introvert ways of individuating, he does give the overwhelming impression of the priority of the inner to the outer world. In my emphasis on relationships with others, I have tried to avoid the dichotomy between inner and outer events because each person is relating outwardly to the inner world of the other as well as to his or her outer reality. This consideration does not apply only to male and female questions but is most easily grasped in this area. Even if it is true that we all have some degree of bisexuality, a woman can never fully "realize" her maleness in the way a man can by *being* a man. But if she can live happily with men (not necessarily literally living with one, although this helps, but living in enjoyable relations with them), she can realize her maleness in another way because her imaginative capacity to know what being a man feels like is necessary for these relationships. Needless to say, the converse applies for men. The human being is above all not only a social but an imaginative being, and despite our seemingly infinite capacity to redefine ourselves, it is through our imagination, our ability to imagine what it is like to be the other and to be part of the relationship with the other, that we attain a sense of being more than we are. In this way, our very limitations are also our strength.

Afterthoughts

This is not meant to be another paper, but I would like to use this opportunity not just to repeat what I said before but to try to put things more clearly now that I know what everybody else at [the Ghost Ranch] conference is saying about a topic which we are all finding to be bristling with difficulties.

My main preoccupation has been: how much can we tinker with what Jung wrote? We don't know what he would be saying if he were alive and could be here today; we only know what he did say. We are not short of texts but they were composed at different times and for different audiences over a long lifetime. Do we consider, as the best guide to his thought, his more carefully thought-out *Collected Works*, his *Red Book* which was meant to be private, or his seminars, which are so lively and spontaneous but were certainly not meant to be studied by scholars more than half a century later pondering over his every word?

There seem now to be two main camps. One holds that men have an anima and women an animus. That is what Jung said. The other, perhaps now the majority, holds that both sexes have both, or that they

exist as a pair but are not part of the individual psyche, being archetypes. Jung never said that both have both, but it might still be
inferred or it might be regarded as a justifiable extension of his ideas.

Much is being made here of a change of direction after 1944, when
Jung spoke less of the anima and animus as contrasexual and more of
the syzygy. This may be true, but what are we to make of it? The fact is
that Jung never actually said he had changed his mind and no longer
thought his earlier formulations were right.

That might be because nobody likes to admit he was wrong or it
may be that Jung did not realize that his new position was incompatible
with his old, but it may also be that it is we who are eager to find this
change of mind, because we simply can't stomach any longer what he
said about women, and perhaps we are not very happy with what he
said about men either. Personally I doubt whether he did change his
mind about men and women very much, and I think it more likely that
the change we do see was more a change of interest than a change of
mind. My most convincing documentary evidence for this is *Man and
His Symbols*, where Jung, about one year before his death, wrote, "It is
this female element in every male that I have called the 'anima' " and to
illustrate this he refers to a patient whose "female side was not nice"
(1964, p. 31). But what would this book be called if it came out today?
"Man and Woman and Their Symbols"? "Human Being and His or Her
Symbols"? I suppose we might settle on "The Symbols of Humanity,"
but these evasive tactics would not conceal what Jung actually had
written in the text.

This, of course, does not mean that *we* cannot modify his concepts
in the light of advances in knowledge, but to do so in this case raises for
me enormous problems which I compared, in my paper, to removing
bricks from a building without being sure we were not removing a
cornerstone. When I began thinking about my paper, I took as my
starting point a definition of anima and animus as contrasexual archetypes. It was only in the course of writing it and reading around it that I
realized how precarious this definition was, both words of it. The word
archetype has a very long history, although Jung used it in quite a
special way, but the word *contrasexual* does not appear to exist! I could
not find it in the *Oxford English Dictionary*, not even in the largest
version, not even in the Supplement. So presumably it was coined by
Jung. Should we keep it a secret or should we inform the OED? The
neologism was necessary purely for the anima and animus. It has
become increasingly an embarrassment to us, although we need have
no worries if it is divorced from the word *archetype*. It is the conjunc-

tion which we find difficult. Another possibility. is to dispense altogether with the anima and animus as being archetypes. That would be
the opposite of Hillman's view but solves the same problem. I think we
will find that whatever reasons we give for doing so will turn out to
apply just as much to the other archetypes that Jung described and that
will lead in turn to us abandoning the archetypes or what Jung meant
by them and what would become then of analytical psychology?

The reason the other archetypes are in danger is that the problem
is not posed solely by a revolution on sex and gender instigated by
feminists. It is not just that Jung based his ideas on a view of men and
women which the feminists, quite rightly, say we should not hold. The
feminist protest is part of a larger and more fundamental protest than
the political one directed at the domination of women by men. This is
but one example of the dangers that result from a certain type of
thinking to which Jung was prone. What is at stake now are all claims to
universality based on observed differences of any kind (and, of course,
Jung has been accused of racism as well as sexism). The protest is
particularly against generalizations about people after they have been
divided into groups. Can we refer to universals and call them archetypes when, as soon as we try to describe them or differentiate them in
any way, they so rapidly become stereotypes? The present intellectual
climate is particularly against any ideology that rests on group differences being institutionalized. It is strongly resistant to claims that differences are grounded on objective facts.

With this goes a questioning of the notion of objectivity itself. We
are, we are told, no longer in the Renaissance, which placed Man at the
center, nor in the Age of Enlightenment, where there are comfortable
certainties, and no longer in the modern age of Einstein, where we can
take into account a world of relativity. We are instead faced with a
bewildering succession of challenges. They are mostly "isms" which
Jung did not much care for. They come and they go. Even existential-
ism, which brought out the choice each of us has to act authentically,
here and now, is "out." So, too, is phenomenology, which placed all
the value on how we experience the world. Structuralism, which, while
it lived, was welcomed by Jungians because it at least recognized certain
structures that could be seen as cross-cultural and cross-disciplinary and
seemed so much like archetypes, is no longer very much alive. No, we
now add the prefix "post" before the "isms." This means that we come
after something. We are post-Jungians, for example. We come after,
but what are we? Well now we are *post*-structuralist and indeed post-
modernist, which means we do not know any longer what a text is, who

is its author, and who has the authority to say what it means. This, of course, has a profound bearing on the practice of Freudian psychoanalysis, because psychoanalysis relies on the authority of the analyst to decipher the hidden text which the patient provides. Jung, just as much as Freud, believed in the ultimate objectivity of this text, and its objectivity could be established through its collectivity.

Then there is the question of the subject. The notion of the individual which Jung prized so much is no longer acceptable and has been replaced by "the subject," which is now deconstructed and "decentered" and forever alienated. It certainly bears little relation to Jung's "Ego," which he thought was the center of consciousness. The subject is not the center of anything. So we have problems not only with Jung dividing people into groups but with his notions of the individual and therefore with individuation, which rests on a reconciliation of the individual with the collective.

Freud, who was less concerned with such problems, spoke of the "bedrock" of biology and although he gave up his project, which would have reduced everything to biology, he built his theory on a *foundation* of basic identifiable instinctual urges originally due to our animal nature. Although Jung rejected Freud's mechanistic, deterministic, and reductionist stance, he needed a bedrock, too. How could he found a new psychology without foundations?

Having released the libido from Freud's instinctual straitjacket as well as questioning Freud's simplistic notion of reality as a restraint on the instincts, Jung still had to find what it was that limited and ordered and thus gave shape to the psyche. There had to be some notion of ultimate reality that was not relative to anything else. He needed this because without it, it is not possible to talk of the psyche at all, and he, not unnaturally, regarded the psyche in its totality as the subject matter of psychology: no psyche — no psychology. So for Jung and for us, the bedrock is the archetypes. These, as we know, have a multiplicity of images but an underlying *structure* which can be apprehended but not known directly. How then can they become the foundations for the psyche and for psychology? Over and over again, Jung answered this question in the same way. You find the same image in widely different cultures, so there must, according to Jung, be universal structures which lie beyond the individual, beyond the way in which any particular society is organized, beyond any spatial constraint, and beyond history itself. Our gods were therefore, for Jung, really archetypes, and although symbols become outmoded and stale, the underlying realities do not. They could not, because they were not to be located in time or space. Surely none of us would disagree that this is what Jung thought until the day of his death? And surely it is our agreement with these ideas which makes us all Jungians in spite of our differences? We may be post, but not as post as all that — not past the post. So, like all the other contributors to this conference, I have found myself engaged in a kind of salvage operation. And, like all the other contributors, I have been forced to consider both the differences between men and women and then go on to contemplate the nature of difference itself.

Throughout all Jung's thought are oppositions of this kind. The way to deal with opposites is to unite them, but having done that, what becomes of the opposition? Were the differences which made them opposed a mistaken difference, now subsumed in the new unity? Or do they continue to exist within this unity, continuing to relate to each other in a tension of unremitting opposition which is an integral part of the unity? Here it is worth noting that deconstruction, as understood by Derrida, does not seek to abolish the opposition. By reversing and displacing the opposition, it extends the meaning of the sign, the relationship of signifier to signified, and the relationship of signifiers to other signifiers in a structure that resembles that of language itself. The male-female opposition is but one example of such oppositions and one that is of great interest to feminists, especially in France. They are conscious of the fact that females are not only defined in a derogatory way by males (all feminists are aware of that) but that men are in charge of the symbolic order itself and it is this that makes women into objects, such as objects of exchange, as Lévi-Strauss thinks.

It does seem undeniable that Jung was restricted in his thinking by seeing the problem from a male point of view, but women have gradually come to realize that they are themselves trapped if they can only oppose this point of view by a mode of argument learned from men, thereby entering the very patriarchy they oppose and thus betraying themselves. In this respect, the work of Irigiray is interesting in that she considers that women can only overcome this problem by developing a dialogue, not with men, but with other women, and she looks particularly to the mother-daughter relationship, pointing out that, historically, this has disappeared from mythology since Demeter and Persephone. We cannot find it very easily in alchemical studies and it cannot be symbolized in the alchemical images of the *coniunctio*.

To return to the question of how we can salvage the idea of contrasexuality: what I am looking for is some way of recognizing that men and women are profoundly different, but equal, and this requires some form of essentialism. I have suggested that there are *essential* differ-

ences between man and woman and have taken sides in the complicated debate of culture vs. nature by concluding that there are innate
psychological differences between the two sexes and this is the reason
why we can talk of male and female archetypes and a male and female
principle. It is not just that men and women can both have notions of
goddesses as well as gods, but that this is possible because each sex *is
restricted* to a limited point of view. However much men understand
women, or women men, they can never escape a certain restriction in
their viewpoint. A man cannot know what it is to be a woman; he
always confronts Woman as the Other and she likewise confronts Man.
The question of innate differences requires evidence, of course, and
although there are many feminists who quote long lists of studies to
show that we tend to be influenced by culturally determined stereotypes, they may themselves have a vested interest in promoting this
view, because their interest is political rather than scientific. What I go
on to consider relies on statistics, and we should be duly cautious, but
so do all the studies on *beliefs* about sex and gender. Science, of course,
has its limitations and is regarded by feminists as a patriarchal enter-
prise that is antifemale because it seeks to dominate nature, which it
sees in the despised female gender, but leaving this argument aside,
what happens when we look more closely at anatomical differences is
that they are by no means restricted to the obvious primary and secondary sexual characteristics, but that there are uniformly found differences between the male and the female brain. If brains are different,
surely this is of interest to psychology? If looking at the brain can
enable an observer to say whether its owner is male or female, the
implications must be different than those resulting from inspection of
the genitals, whether or not this inspection is restricted to ascertaining
whether a penis is present or absent.

The differences are by no means crude ones and do not lead to
crude conclusions. It is not that one hemisphere is male and the other
female, but there are nevertheless differences in the two sides, and
particularly significant are the differences in their connections and
these differences make a difference.

There is a great deal of evidence that these different brains are
formed under the influence of hormones in the first few weeks of
intrauterine life. What has fascinated me in this research is that one
cannot say: "So what?" because the observed differences are manifested
by different ways of thinking and feeling in the two sexes and these
correspond not just to our current stereotypes, but also to the very
ancient ideas of "the male and female principle," and are far more

ancient than that, before the birth of language. They can be seen to be the result of evolutionary pressures that have adapted men for hunting and women for mothering. Men are therefore not just physically stronger than women, but have better gross visual-motor coordination, are better, that is, at locating objects in space, better at abstraction, and therefore at abstract reasoning, and therefore at generalizing, which requires abstraction. Women seem to be better at very fine visual-motor coordination, better at reading the fine changes of expression on the human face, better at language, better at taking in particulars and looking more at the immediate context of the concrete situation. These are, of course, only statistical differences, but they are very striking. In general, men are far more specialized than women, which gives them some advantages but deprives them of others. This is found in hemispheric specialization so that language centers are found to be more localized in the male than in the female brain. None of these repeatedly observed differences can be accounted for by culture; they are laid down according to whether there are Y chromosomes present before the sex of the fetus is known. This means that although we are all potentially bisexual, we are all female to begin with and it is the male hormone that then adds maleness to the embryo.

I think that Jungians should rejoice at these findings because they justify Jung's bedrock as being anterior to cultural differentiation. This is not to say that culture does not play an enormous part as well, and that we should not attend to the problems of exploitation which are potentially correctable. Nor does any of this work suggest any inequality between the sexes. It does support the idea of equality in complementarity, which I think Jung really did think was right. If you look at the opposites of extraversion and introversion, you find the same thing. Theoretically they were equal, but there is no doubt which Jung thought it was better to be! Nevertheless he recognized that his bias was a result of his own typology.

I have devoted this summary to basic principles because the question of clinical usefulness depends on it. This I have tried to show, in my paper, with two clinical vignettes illustrating the rather limited view I take of thinking about any of the archetypes in day-to-day clinical work. I do not look all the time for archetypal images as I think some Jungians do. They are, of course, always to be found, but they are not, for me, to be placed in the foreground. The anima and animus are therefore only very occasionally in my mind when I'm with a patient and my two examples represent the exception rather than the rule.

In conclusion, I'd like to stress something I meant to say in my paper and did originally say, but either my unconscious or my word processor saw to it that it got left out. That is that I don't think we are in the business of training mystics, and although there is a mystical approach which brings together and transcends all these problems, it is not one which many patients can adopt. I think Jung was a mystic, however much he disclaimed it. I am not one, although I have always been deeply interested in mysticism. I think this means that I do not look for completeness as the goal in quite the same way as Jung did. I rely for a sense of completeness more on the realization that each individual is permanently incomplete but can nevertheless enjoy his or her partness.

A man will always be a man and never a woman. His womanly side can best be realized not only by developing *his* femaleness, but by enjoying and living as fully as possible with women, and this applies also vice versa to women. The anima as a female part of a man is a male image which may or may not be a distorted image of what is embodied in a woman. In the clinical situation of analysis, the aim is to see that the image can change from a distorted to a true image of what the Other actually is. It remains a restricted and limited point of view but is no longer a false one. I therefore think it should still be possible to say with Maurice Chevalier, although not with the same sexist bias with which he said it: "Vive la difference!" I hope it will be understood that I am taking not a sexist but an interpersonal view.

References

Bateson, G. 1979. *Mind and Nature*. London: Wildwood.

Diamond, M. 1982. Sexual identity, monozygotic twins reared in discordant sex roles and the B.B.C. follow-up. *Archives of Sexual Behaviour* 2/2.

Dunne, C. 1989. *Behold Woman: A Jungian Approach to Feminist Theology*. Wilmette, Ill.: Chiron Publications.

Durden-Smith, J., and de Simone, D. 1983. *Sex and the Brain*. London: Pan.

Flor-Henry, P. 1978. Gender, hemisphere, specialization and psychopathology. *Society, Science and Medicine* 12B.

Flor-Henry, P. 1979. On certain aspects of the localization of the cerebral systems regulating and determining emotion. *Biological Psychiatry* 14/4.

Foulkes, S. H. 1964. *Therapeutic Group Analysis*. London: Geo. Allen and Unwin.

Grinnell, R. 1973. *Alchemy in a Modern Woman: A Study in the Contrasexual Archetype*. Dallas: Spring.

Hillman, J. 1985. *Anima: An Anatomy of a Personified Notion*. Dallas: Spring.

Jacobi, J. 1939. *The Psychology of C. G. Jung*. London: Routledge, Kegan Paul, 1942.

Jung, C. G. 1943. *Two Essays in Analytical Psychology*. *CW*, vol. 7. London: Routledge Kegan Paul, 1953.

———. 1921. *Psychological Types*. *CW*, vol. 6. Princeton, N.J.: Princeton University Press, 1971.

_____. 1964. *Man and His Symbols*. London: Aldus Books.

_____. 1935. *The Tavistock Lectures: Analytical Psychology—Its Theory and Practice*. In *CW* 18:1–145. London: Routledge Kegan Paul, 1968.

_____. 1946. *Psychology of the Transference*. In *CW* 16:129–340. London: Routledge Kegan Paul, 1954.

_____. 1911–1912. *The Psychology of the Unconscious. CW*, vol. 5. London: Routledge Kegan Paul.

_____. 1952. *Symbols of Transformation. CW*, vol. 5. London: Routledge Kegan Paul.

_____. 1963. *Memories, Dreams, Reflections*. London: Routledge, Kegan Paul.

Mirandola, Pico della. 1487. *The Dignity of Man*. Wallis, trans. New York: Bobbs-Merrill, 1965.

Samuels, A. 1989. *The Plural Psyche*. London: Routledge, Kegan Paul.

Schwartz-Salant, N. 1989. *The Borderline Personality: Vision and Healing*. Wilmette, Ill.: Chiron Publications.

Shotter, J. 1975. *Images of Man in Psychological Research*. London: Methuen.

Shuttle, P., and Redgrove, P. 1986. *The Wise Wound: Menstruation and Everyman*. London: Paladin.

Stern, D. N. 1985. *The Interpersonal World of the Infant*. New York: Basic Books.

Tiger, L., and Fox, R. 1972. *The Imperial Animal*. London: Secker and Warburg.

Whitmont, E. C. 1969. *The Symbolic Quest*. New York: Putnams.

Winnicott, D. W. 1971. *Playing and Reality*. London: Tavistock.

Zinkin, L. 1991. The Klein Connection. *Journal of Analytical Psychology* 36:1.

Gender, Animus, and Related Topics

Polly Young-Eisendrath

> *To be human is to be subjected to a law which decentres and divides: sexuality is created in a division, the subject is split; but an ideological world conceals this from the conscious subject who is supposed to feel whole and certain of a sexual identity.*
>
> Juliet Mitchell, "Introduction" to
> Jacques Lacan, *Feminine Sexuality*

In this paper, I am working from a strong conviction that the concepts of anima and animus are most useful clinically when they refer to psychological complexes of contrasexuality.[1] The division into two genders, inscribed by culture with different power and status meanings, marks each of us from birth onward, leaving us always as outsiders to the others. The nature of gender difference, arising in culture and designated through a form of embodiment, marks us with a culturally inscribed meaning and makes the contrasexual other a perpetual outsider, an unconscious complex of not-I.

I define anima and animus as gendered complexes of not-I, as emotionally charged collections of images, habits, thoughts, actions, and meanings of contrasexuality that limit and define self. Obviously,

Polly Young-Eisendrath, Ph.D., is chief psychologist and Jungian analyst at Clinical Associates West in Bala Cynwyd, Pennsylvania, and senior research psychologist at the Institute of Pennsylvania Hospital where she teaches, supervises, and conducts research projects. Her fourth book, *Jung's Self Psychology: A Constructivist Perspective*, is forthcoming.

contrasexual complexes are not the only complexes of not-I that structure unconscious material, nor do they exclusively generate images of sex or gender. Mother and father complexes may dominate the contrasexuality of a particular person, but these complexes may be differentiated from anima and animus in another person. Images of women and images of men may be highly charged with emotional meaning and connected with something other than contrasexuality (such as goddess images that arise in women). What marks contrasexuality is the unique relationship with the self. The contrasexual other constrains and defines the self, so to speak. The way I imagine myself as a woman carries with it a tandem meaning of what I imagine to be human but not woman. (Anything I imagine to be human *and* female, I could potentially be.)

As a woman, I am limited in my subjectivity — in constituting myself as a subject or agent — by my gender and its designations within culture. I am also absolutely limited by my form of embodiment (any effort to change that form necessarily results in something other than a male body; I cannot become male). How I imagine this limit, the images I hold to be male and masculine, and my own intersubjectivity with male people is a central psychological aspect of female selfhood, in my view. Contrasexual complexes are uniquely meaningful because all known cultures (with only a few exceptions) divide people into two genders. These are inscribed differently, especially in regard to power, status, and authority.

I would like to restrict the use of anima and animus to a gendered psychology in which the anima is a product of the imaginal and relational life of male people, and the animus, a product of female people. Without this restriction, I believe we are confronted with a plethora of definitions that confusedly overlap with other concepts such as soul, spirit, animation, enthusiasm, transcendence, symbolic bridging to the unconscious, and many other highly significant psychological concepts whose meaning may be arbitrarily skewed by association with gender or sex differences. When I say "arbitrarily skewed," I mean that gender and sex are such powerful signifiers that association with them leads to certain designations within any discourse. These designations are likely to turn principally on the significance of gender. Designating anima as soul, referring to the soul as female, and then assuming that men and women *both* have anima / soul experiences creates, in my view, a condition that psychoanalyst Jacques Lacan calls "mystification." Mystification is any effort to deny or cover over the difficulty of the absolute division between the sexes. (Obviously, men and women *have* soul

experiences. These can be called "soul experiences." Breaking the connection between soul and men's animas moves discourse about soul
outside the realm of sex differences and gender.) By restricting anima
and animus to contrasexual complexes, one must return always to the
gendered subjectivity of the person who is inscribing experience with
meaning.

Anima, in the account I am offering then, is the expression of
male people imagining what it means to be female, to give birth, to
nurture, and to be embodied in a female form, as well as all else they
experience as the female other. For male people, anima seems to
include both idealized and feared "powers" that are connected to birth,
sustenance, beauty, and the life force. Projections of anima onto
women may result in men fearing and idealizing women, their bodies
and appearances, and their capacities. In patriarchy, the power of the
female as other is woven intricately into many levels of discourse in a
way that has guaranteed the unity and privilege of the male speaker.
Necessarily, anima images and symbols *for* woman (generated by men)
have become images and symbols used *by* women to represent their
own sexuality and experiences. These images of positive and negative
power often confuse women who may exclude both legitimate and
other power from themselves. Additionally, female people throughout
the world live in societies that marginalize them and assume their
inferiority to govern their own and others' lives. Without a gendered
concept of anima, we tend to deny or mystify the power differences
between male and female people and to forget the centrality of "man-
made" language in constituting all that woman is supposed to be. A
gendered concept of anima also problematizes male fears and fantasies
of women by making these distinctly a product of a complex psychology, rather than facts of biology or child-rearing practices.

Animus, according to my view, is a product of the female psyche,
and female people imagining what it means to be male, to have dominant positions in culture making, to have decision-making power and
status, and to be embodied in a male form, as well as all else they
experience as male otherness. Projections of animus onto men may
result in women idealizing and fearing men, envying their imagined
intelligence and dominance, their freedom, and their power. Women
projecting power, objectivity, and intellect onto men is such a common
cultural practice that its analysis has become a major cultural movement
within feminism and psychoanalysis. Taking back these projections
appears to lead to a profound psychological change, especially in a
male-dominated society such as ours in which female people have only

begun to go on record and become culture makers. Power differentials between the genders have so far prevented women's accounts of men (animus images) from being primary representations of male experience and sexuality used *by* men, although this is perhaps changing. (Maintaining the gendered distinction between contrasexual complexes encourages an analysis of difference in the ways women's images of men, and men's images of women enter into discourse.) Perhaps because women have had little access to images of a strong and complete female self, the animus has been theorized in other depth psychologies as women's desire for masculine status or strength (e.g., castration complex or penis/phallus envy), and this has often taken a narrow biological or political form. The concept of animus in analytical psychology is a distinctly psychological treatment of female masculinity.

Contrasexual complexes may appear in either positive, idealized forms or in negative, feared, and devalued forms. The essence of their clinical usefulness, for me, lies in their stimulating psychotherapists to make maps through which we come to understand the constituting (and defense) of a self through projection, projective identification, and counterprojection of these essential images of difference of sex and gender.

How these images affect us in our daily lives and over the course of our development is not well understood. In order for us to investigate gender meanings in a clinical setting or in a research endeavor, we must keep in mind power and status differences, differences of embodiment, and the relative newness of understanding these. It is only through contributions from both male and female people that these differences can be investigated and understood. Until very recently we have had only male accounts of these differences. Often these accounts have ignored men's location in culture and their gender biases about what it means to be male or female.

Understanding gender to be a psychological and cultural experience of self/other, I recommend the elimination of archetypal feminine and masculine principles from our theorizing about gender and contrasexuality. As Jungians, we have often assumed that feminine and masculine principles exist universally as archetypes emanating from nature and/or human embodiment. At this point, I do not see any persuasive evidence that universal categories of gender exist across cultures which translate sex differences of embodiment into consistent gender meanings. Moreover, any naming of dichotomous and absolute differences between the genders (such as masculine Logos and feminine Eros) tends to deny the psychological difficulties of gender/sex differences by relegating them to stereotypical categories that function to maintain a social order. As Lacanian theorist Jacqueline Rose says,

> Sexuality belongs in this area of instability played out in the register of demand and desire, each sex coming to stand, mythically and exclusively, for that which could satisfy and complete the other. It is when the categories "male" and "female" are seen to represent an absolute and complementary division that they fall prey to a mystification in which the difficulty of sexuality instantly disappears. (Lacan 1982, p. 33)

If we ignore gender differences and assume, for example, that both men and women have anima and animus, then we have lost the perspective of *difference* in a cultural context where genders have profoundly different privileges and status. If we assume, on the other hand, that we *know* already what is "natural" for each gender, then we will tend to perpetuate patriarchal and Jungian stereotypes. Denying and stereotyping gender differences are pitfalls I would like to avoid.

My overall purpose here is to revise and clarify the theory of animus/self and put it into line with my understanding of contemporary gender theory and research. I also intend to advocate the definition of animus as a psychological complex in girls and women, to be used as a lens for understanding the development or differentiation of the female self. I say girls and women because my topic is mostly animus and female psychology, not gender overall. I will touch on the theme of envy in regard to gender and present some clinical concerns involving animus development.

At this moment, we all are still influenced by gender stereotypes in everyday conversations that limit and shape our expressions and expectations of self/other. We necessarily participate in expectations that female people are less adequate than male people, and that male people possess the knowledge and resources on which we all depend. In order to account for these hardcore beliefs, we must be alert to the projections of psychological complexes that are powerfully organized by gender meanings.

Locating Myself

What I say below arises in certain contexts that influence my thinking in a way I would like to make explicit. I am a Jungian analyst, a clinical-developmental psychologist, a teacher, a psychological researcher, and a feminist. In all of these contexts, I consider myself primarily a psychologist — a practitioner of a science or critical theory of *personal being*. As a psychologist, I am most interested in change and stability of personality (personal being) over the lifespan.

As a developmental psychologist (in my teaching and research as well as my practice of Jungian analysis), I am most influenced by discourse about pattern and metaphor. "Pattern explanation" (Overton 1990) is the explanatory form that has been developed particularly in Piagetian and neo-Piagetian structural psychology; it uses noncausal or acausal models that are integrative (but not linear) to trace the process or sequence of development. Development is understood as a sequence of patterns (e.g., biological, relational, sociocultural) that are periodically reintegrated.

Discourse in developmental psychology includes certain metaphors of "structure" such as *stage* or *position* or *frame of reference* to signify stable organizations of experience. Descriptions of stages are researched and presented in comprehensive models that depict progressive or directional development of these organizational forms. The Jungian model of individuation — depending as it does on the differentiation and integration of psychological complexes — can be understood as a structural developmental model.

Such models are not linear because the stages are not additive. A useful way to understand structural reintegration is to visualize concentric nested spheres; each sphere represents an organization of reality (a *Weltanschauung*) or a depiction of patterns of expectations or beliefs. Each new stage (each outermost sphere) is a new organization or paradigm of meaning that accounts for all organizations that have already occurred, but reorganizes these in a new and comprehensive way. At any developmental moment, a person may use any stage or organization that has already been structured. In other words, a person may "regress" and use "old" images or patterns or beliefs. Every person is limited, however, by the properties of the most "recent" or complex organization achieved. No one can "skip" a stage. We can only rely on structures that we have already organized.

My practice of analytical psychology is also strongly influenced by an epistemological perspective: constructivism. Constructivism is a presupposition that all experience is "constructed" by people and not primarily "given" by the world or embodiment. I do not deny the importance of embodiment and "affordances" of the perceptual world in limiting our possible experiences. In fact, the limitations or constraints of our embodiment and emotional life provide the basis for a psychology of universals, and hence for a theory of archetypes and complexes. As a constructivist, though, I want to give primary status to belief or interpretation in understanding any "object" of awareness. People construct their worlds, but neither nature nor biology constructs people, from my point of view. Nature and biology limit the worlds we can construct, but we have barely begun to understand how the limitations work.

To say this yet another way, we do not discover some reality that is "out there," but rather we invent our reality from our beliefs. Our knowledge is primarily *pattern-matching* and we all search for the best fit with the patterns or expectations we hold. For this reason, I believe that it is incumbent on psychologists and psychotherapists to make descriptive maps, and hence to become conscious of the patterns of image and belief that people (including therapists) predictably bring to their experiences. These maps can be partly standardized because we are universally embodied, emotional, relational, and agentic creatures who develop in some uniform ways and because we are shaped by certain tribes and cultures whose meanings we can discern.

In this regard, feminism has been an especially important context for me in the ways it has illuminated the cultures of gender. I define feminism as a civil rights movement that promotes a discipline of egalitarian values and ideals for relationships among people. Feminism has problematized gender, making us conscious of gender as a pervasive signifier and determiner of experience. As a feminist, I have made an ethical commitment to enhanced mutuality, trust, and reciprocity among people; I oppose all forms of dominance–submission among adults. Feminism has assisted me in understanding how power and status contribute to the meanings of gender, and how gender functions in our creations of self and other. Advocating, as I do, a contrasexual theory of gendered self, I am enabled to make psychological maps of the split subjectivity of gendered persons. This allows me to be especially alert to how gendered meanings enter into the domain of women and men on all levels of experience, from the subjective productions of dreams to the intersubjective projections and projective identifications of complexes, to the nuances and patterns of conversational speech. More than any other single psychological concept, the concept of contrasexuality has afforded me opportunities to explore the projected and introjected meanings of anima and animus in terms of the unity of male subjectivity and the marginality of female meanings within patriarchy.

My final epistemological context is relativism. I assume that an interpretation is relative to its place in a context, rather than independent of such consideration. I am a rational relativist, guided by certain principles of logical explanation (e.g., noncontradiction) in terms of the way in which I might favor one interpretation over another. I tend to agree with philosopher Hilary Putnam when he says, "truth is idealized rational acceptability" and "truth and rational acceptability are *interdependent* notions" (1989, p. 9). He means that a situation does not itself legislate how words are used. No objects exist independently of conceptual schemes precisely because there are no standards for the use of even logical notions apart from conceptual choices. This does not mean that everything is simply a matter of language, but to talk of facts without specifying the context in which the discourse occurs is to talk of nothing, as Putnam says. The word *fact* has no fixed use apart from the conceptual scheme in which it is embedded.

As a relativist, I realize that I choose to interpret anima and animus as contrasexual complexes (that is, anima and animus are not "facts" — given in the nature of the human psyche). As I mentioned earlier, others have chosen to interpret animus as penis envy or castration anxiety. I choose the concept of contrasexuality because it opens up explanatory categories of gender that I cannot access through any other psychological model. I want neither to reduce the fantasies and fears of contrasexuality to biological differences (such as penis or womb envy) nor to child-rearing practices (such as identification with a female caregiver). I want to acknowledge the division of the sexes as a major psychological marker for human subjectivity (just as Freud, Lacan, Klein, Horney, and Jung did in their own ways), but I want to keep the content open for research (both clinical and empirical). When it comes to understanding any particular image produced by an analysand, I often entertain several competing interpretations that are logically consistent and contextually relevant. I know that context allows meaning to fluctuate and that I may not be able to access the best context at a particular therapeutic moment.

This brings me to a common criticism of Jung's theories. Jung is criticized for being a "foundationalist" or "essentialist" in the way that his psychology is thought to be a pursuit of first premises or self-evident givens, of facts that lie somehow "beyond" experience. Jung has sometimes presented his ideas about archetype and universal principles as though they were ahistorical and acultural, existing outside any context whatsoever. Jung's theories about gender differences and contrasexuality are particularly apt to be construed as foundationalist or essentialist when he offers an account of archetypes of masculine and feminine that supposedly structure men and women in a "natural" or self-evident manner.

I believe that Jung's theory of a psychological complex, organized around an archetypal core of emotional arousal, is primarily a constructivist theory of psychological functioning in which emotion and image are the underlying forms for the construction of the world. Moreover, by linking anima and animus to the theory of complex, I can present a culturally relative account of a Jungian psychology of gender. Both one's own and the other gender are constructed within a family, society, and culture. They are relative to these contexts.

I assume that gender has no ahistorical, universal meanings. This means that I do not privilege either the structure or function of the human reproductive organs as grounds for self-evident gender meanings. No matter the case or person that may be the object of my study, I assume that there is no neutral overarching measure or model that might conclusively determine the "real truth" or the normative personal meaning for gender outside of a particular sociocultural context.

Gender, Difference, and Androcentrism

Like many other (but not all) feminist theorists, I draw a strong distinction between sex and gender. *Sex* is the anatomical structure and functional properties of the human body that *signal* that a person should be placed in one gender group or the other. In most cases, sex is definite and inflexible and indicates certain expectable differences between the functions of male and female bodies. Breasts, vagina, vulva, smaller body size, menstruation, pregnancy, lactation, menopause, and greater longevity are expected for the female. Penis, greater body size, greater physical strength, impregnation, and lesser longevity are expected for the male. What these biological constraints might actually *mean* within any society or family varies by *gender categories* or expectations. Gender is the cultural or familial meaning assigned to sex differences. Gender is flexible and contextual, dependent on the particular practices of the family or society in which a person develops. Sex is concrete and definite. The psychological identification with one's sex — role expectations and meaning — is obviously the development of *gender* identity.

Assignment into a gender group is not flexible in any major organized society. Sex is typically established at birth from the features of the infant's body; they are "read" in order to place the infant in a gender group. When the sex of an infant is ambiguous or anomalous, parents and doctors organize quickly to assign a gender and *change the body* if necessary. Gender serves many cultural and social purposes, and we are anxious to have it assigned. Membership in one of two groups is exclusive. In essence, each of us is assigned at birth to one of two clubs, and we must practice by the rules of our club for the rest of our lives. We look in at the others as outsiders. This condition of being identified with one gender and constructing the other as an outsider has important psychological implications.

What about the meaning of gender in our North American societies? Research conducted by Broverman, Clarkson, et al. in the 1970s and replicated thereafter, has shown clear evidence of the collective prejudices we share in our expectations of gender. From a broad spectrum of the United States population, surveyed using a paper-and-pencil questionnaire, these sociologists discovered that American women are expected to be weaker, less competent, and more emotionally expressive than their male counterparts. Men are expected to be more intelligent and objective than women. Perhaps most surprising, these researchers have shown that an *ideal* woman is expected to be more passive and less competent than a healthy adult. Personal responsibility and self-determination, cornerstones of American ideals for adulthood, are in conflict with social role expectations for adult women.

Other research on gender stereotypes and expectations (e.g., Bem 1974, Deaux and Lewis 1983, Gilligan 1982, and Ruble 1983) amplifies the Brovermans' early studies and provides a clear profile of the expectations held for male and female people in North America. Psychologist Alice Eagly (1983) summarizes these expectations in two categories: communal and agentic. Female people are expected to be more *communal*, characterized as follows: showing concern for the welfare of others; displaying nurturant qualities, interpersonal sensitivity, emotional expressiveness, and a desire to be at one with others. The *agentic* category is associated with male people and the following: showing asserting and controlling tendencies; displaying independence from other people, self-confidence, self-sufficiency, self-expansion, and the urge to master. These are gender stereotypes or expectations that function to assign people to certain kinds of tasks and attitudes, to limit people to certain roles and possibilities. As Jungian analysts and candidates, we need to be alert to the influence of gender stereotypes on our theories.

In *Deceptive Distinctions*, sociologist Cynthia Epstein surveys a range of contemporary cultures in regard to the "dichotomous thinking" of gender differences. She is wary of this thinking, whether it is the product of traditionalists who declare that basic differences between the sexes determine responses to the world or of feminists who declare that women and men live in different worlds, almost as two species. She says,

> Dichotomous distinctions rarely avoid creating ranked comparisons, and, in the case of female–male, whatever characteristics are ascribed to each gender, those associated with men rank higher. How does this happen? We shall never know. When classification occurs in human society, some win out because they are more intelligent, some because they are bullies, and many because they got there first and set up the rules. (Epstein 1988, p. 233)

She claims that dichotomous categories are especially effective for preserving power advantages. They serve the existing power structures in becoming versions of "we" and "not-we." This advantage, from her point of view, serves to keep women doing more work of lower social status than men. She asserts that "women's work" is both poorly valued and frequently repetitive and that it is "rejected by men for good reason when they are able to assign it to others. The skills attached to women's work are rarely transferrable or are regarded as so" (ibid., p. 234). Unless women are privileged, they have, as a group, more work to do than men, moving between paid and unpaid labor, from workplace to home.

Is this a matter of gender or power differences? No one can say because the two cannot be separated in our current system. Provocatively, Epstein says,

> No society rewards or honors the people assigned to do its most essential work — the mundane labor that keeps it going on a day-to-day basis, providing food and shelter, cleansing the wastes, burying the dead. It gives them *some* reward (so they will keep at their tasks) and . . . it may coerce them to continue. (Ibid., p. 235)

Let us look briefly at a few of the psychological implications of the dichotomous gender distinctions we have been discussing. Among the social roles that appear to exemplify the traditionally female attributes of care and concern for others, the roles of wife and mother are most prominent. Studies whose results speak *for* (e.g., Vergrugge 1982) and *against* (e.g., Bernard 1972a, Baruch and Barnett 1986) the psychological advantages of marriage for women have been reviewed by psychologists Rosalind Barnett and Grace Baruch and published in a book they edited on the topic of gender and stress (Barnett, Biener, and Baruch 1987). From their own and others' surveys of thousands of actual women, it appears that being a wife may (if happily married) increase experiences of *pleasure* in a woman's life, but is unrelated to self-esteem or even life satisfaction. In other words, married women do not report feeling better about themselves or more satisfied with their lives than single women, although they may report greater pleasure or comfort in relationship. On the other hand, employment status and decision-making power in the workplace are significantly related to life satisfaction for *both* married and unmarried women and for men (ibid., pp. 132–133). The role of wife, in and of itself, does not appear to increase a woman's sense of power or life satisfaction, although paid work does.

How about being a mother?

> [B]eing a mother is rarely associated with psychological well-being and is often associated with psychological distress. Findings from recent studies, for example, indicate that being in the role of mother did not predict any of three well-being indicators—that is, self-esteem, pleasure, or low levels of depressive symptomatology. (Ibid., p. 132)

These authors point out that many studies now indicate that the role of mother is often women's primary source of stress, because the demands are high and the control of outcomes is low. Moreover, assumptions of self-blame and responsibility are likely to be a part of this nurturant role. In spite of the reality that one has little actual control over the welfare or happiness of another, mothers usually blame themselves when their children show signs of distress. Psychological theories that reinforce the blaming of mothers, as I have illustrated elsewhere (Young-Eisendrath 1984), may increase self-blame until it becomes a version of self-hatred. Moreover, if women are expected to be "just naturally" more nurturant or more effective in the parenting role, their distress is even greater.

Many gender stereotypes in psychological theories arise from *androcentrism*. Androcentrism is the tendency to see things from a male point of view, to accept the male version of experience as true and valid for "mankind" (meaning humankind) in general. In my training and development as a Jungian analyst, I was sometimes faced with theories of female inadequacy—theories like penis envy, the animus-possessed woman, or the inferiority of women as makers of culture (see, for example, Stevens 1982). These theories are based on an assumption that the female person is inherently *lacking* something—penis, money, intellect, objectivity, or sometimes education, husband, house, whatever. Once the female person is seen as lacking, one can reason that she is just "naturally" depressed, enraged, or compensating for her inadequacy. Florence Wiedemann and I (1987) have called this form of psychological androcentrism "Pandora psychology" from the Greek story of the first woman, who was beautiful but empty. In this andro-centric version of female psychology, a female person is fundamentally inadequate (always beginning with this premise) and can be under-stood only in light of her reaction to this inadequacy. Instead of being a woman unto herself, she is not-man.

We have been reviewing some of the consequences of female gen-der expectations and androcentrism for psychological theorizing and women's lives. Before I turn to the animus *per se*, I would like to review one more feature of how we treat the idea of difference in our psycho-logical theorizing about gender. I will use some terminology I have found to be helpful; it comes from psychologists Rachel Hare-Mustin and Jeanne Marecek (1988) in a thoughtful paper on post-modernism and gender. They describe two types of "errors" that are made fre-quently in psychological theories about gender, especially theories used in psychotherapy.

The first type they call an "alpha bias" after the statistical error of inference. This is a view that *exaggerates* difference. The idea that men and women embody archetypal masculine and feminine principles is an example of this view. Some contemporary feminist theories of gender differences also have an alpha bias. Chodorow (1978), Gilligan (1982), Miller (1976), Belenky et al. (1986), and Young-Eisendrath (1984) all present assumptions about gender differences that exhibit the alpha bias. In these psychologies, female people are characterized as more connected, relational, empathic, and caring than male people. Male people are more separate, rational, and dominance-oriented than female people. The underlying argument is generally that female people remain identified with their mothers and have less anxiety about their gender identity and more ease in close relationship than male people (who must disidentify with the early caregiver).

The other bias is called "beta bias," and it is the tendency to deny that gender differences exist. Beta bias runs the other side of the gamut: both sexes are essentially androgynous or equally capable of the same abilities, once we account for the structure and function of sexual organs. Beta bias occurs in most theories of family therapy and healthy androgyny. In structural family therapy (e.g., Minuchin 1974) and strategic family therapy (e.g., Haley 1976), no distinct differences are presented regarding the roles played by male and female people in the family or the power differences between them. Theories of healthy androgyny (e.g., Bem, Martyna, and Watson 1976 and Singer 1977) hold that male and female people are capable of the same traits if given appropriate contexts. Beta bias theorists, in general, ignore the power and status differences between the genders and the implications of role expectations for gender identity and social meanings.

The alternative to ignoring or stereotyping is to study patterns of subjectivities, to attempt to "read" the narratives presented by female and male persons of their gendered identities and their contrasexuality. Disavowing universal principles of masculinity and femininity means that I refuse to *stereotype* gender differences according to presumed natural differences between the sexes. It does not mean that I dismiss the division into two genders as a fundamental signifier of difference in human life. I am obviously interested in the psychological consequences of the ubiquitous presence of two genders and in studying imaginal and other psychological features of the contrasexual complexes of men and women. To reiterate, I assume that gender and contrasexuality carry important distinctions that infuse and constrain selfhood. I am enthusiastic about collecting and studying both dream and fantasy narratives of contrasexuality from actual people; these clarify the images and meanings at the boundaries of a gendered self. Narratives of women, of both self and animus, are especially interesting to me because they are still largely missing from our mindsets.

Demaris Wehr (1987), Andrew Samuels (1989), and Caroline Stevens (pp. 00–00) are other Jungian theorists who share with me the desire to understand sexual and gender differences in terms of lives and narratives of people within a context, rather than as universal or foundational categories of ahistorical opposites. There are two major problems with the notion that masculine and feminine constitute universal principles of acultural gender difference: (1) that it is self-evident and natural for men and women to fit into certain roles and attitudinal types because of their sexual structures or functions; and (2) that the anima complex of the male personality is subsumed under the same category as actual women and, conversely, that the animus of the female personality is related to descriptions of actual men. These assumptions not only presume to determine for everyone what is right, natural, and healthy, but also create a psychologically dangerous confusion. This is the confusion between male *images* of female people and the *subjectivity* (actual experiences) of female people, and female *images* of male people and their subjectivity.

When men's anima images are fused with the lives of actual women, we are lost in androcentrism — already a widespread problem in our society. Our cultural records are still lacking in female voices and narratives. Movies, magazines, plays, television, and novels are full of men's anima images portrayed as accounts of female lives. We all suffer from aspects of this confusion. On the other hand, when female people confuse their animus images with male people, there are troublesome relational consequences for both women and men (see "identity relationship" in Young-Eisendrath and Wiedemann 1987, pp. 169–175). When our psychological theory reinforces the confusion between contrasexual images and actual people, we may find ourselves faced with problematic countertransferential situations. To state this from a female perspective, if my male therapist imagines me to fit his seductive or highly sexualized anima—which he has seen depicted in countless movies—*and* he has a theory to support the blurring of fantasy with actual women, then I had better be prepared to bear some heavy assumptions and interpretations, if not more.

By differentiating the contrasexual complex of each gender from the subjectivity of the other gender, both clinical and cross-gender relational issues are vastly clarified. Differentiation of male femininity (anima) from women and female masculinity (animus) from men seems to me to be the precious nugget of effective marital psychotherapy with male–female couples, in removing the barriers of projective identification and psychological deadness in marriage. A valuable humility ensues from the serious recognition that one has constructed a coherent image of the other (from one's own experiences) that may present a barrier to receiving the validity of another's subjectivity. Differentiation and understanding of the psychological complex of one's own repressed gender enhances one's ability to listen, clarify, and respond to the subjectivity of another person.

Complex and Archetype

A psychological complex is a collection of associated bits of experience (e.g., ideas, habits, sensations) around an archetypal core. A complex is characterized by an emotional state that emanates from a core archetypal image. An archetype is a universal tendency to form a coherent image in an emotionally aroused state. (By "coherent image," I mean a representation in visual, aural, or kinesthetic form that can be evoked again.) Theoretically, a complex becomes a subpersonality of associated bits of experience organized around an emotionally infused image. The image cohered originally in a situation of emotional arousal (i.e., a situational pattern or set of stimuli) and the reexperiencing of the image and/or the situation or the emotional state may evoke the complex. Every complex "lives" or develops historically, accruing more associations through each reenactment, but the archetypal core remains the same.

The above account of archetype and complex is constructivist and relative and entirely consistent with Jung's later (1944–1961) work. Note that this account eliminates the distinction between a collective unconscious and a personal unconscious. The metaphor of layers of the unconscious is an archeological one. It tends to invite essentialism by spatializing the mind and assuming that "greater depth" has a concrete meaning (i.e., the collective unconscious). The collective unconscious is then thought to exist outside of experience or context. If all psychological complexes are organized around archetypal cores, then we do not need a metapsychology of a deeper or separate unconscious that exists outside of any context. A constructivist reading of Jung emphasizes that a psychological complex is *both* personal (originally formed and reevoked in personal experience) and archetypal (universal in terms of ahistorical, acultural expressions/images of human emotions).

This model is consistent with contemporary object-relations theories such as those of Sullivan (1953), Bowlby (1986), Stern (1985), Lichtenberg (1983), and others (e.g., Sroufe and Fleeson 1986), which describe the evolution of an "inner representational" world through the progressive internalization and differentiation of attachment figures.

Most of these theorists assume that the capacity for "emotional object constancy" (Mahler, Pine, and Bergman 1975) is the first developmental achievement of a subjectively organized psyche. This idea refers to the ability to "conserve" (to maintain and keep in mind) models or images of self and other as continuous and differentiated, as well as ambivalent (both good and bad). The idea of conservation is originally Piagetian (exemplified in his famous experiments with children and volume conservation). Conserving an image of self initially and always occurs in tandem with conserving an image of other.

Jung's model of a subjectively organized psyche is one of a dialectical relationship among psychological complexes that exemplify ambivalence: they have both positive (idealized) and negative (feared and devalued) elements. The ego complex of individuality (the I) is one among many; there are many complexes of not-I (e.g., mother/father) that organize the remainder of the personality. Although Jung clearly recognizes the importance of ego development for individuation, he does not assume the ego has the capacity to unify the personality around consciousness. He does not privilege the ego as the dominant complex; instead he offers a "dissociation" model of the psyche. He problematizes the unity of the individual subject: unity is a difficult achievement. Consciousness does not "provide" unity for a personality with multiple organizations, multiple voices.

The goal of individuation (successive integrations of psychological complexes into consciousness) is unity of the personality. Jung assumed that unity could be achieved either through a conscious dialectical awareness (insight and self-reflexivity) or through accumulated transcendental experiences (transcending the ordinary limitations of self). The dissociation model of psyche can speak to such diverse clinical phenomena as hypnotic trance, borderline states, creative inspirations, psychotic states, multiple personality, symbolic connections, and neurotic conflicts.

Self, Animus, Envy

Aion (1951) is, in my opinion, Jung's attempt to set forth a constructivist program for the study and understanding of self/other representations. Although Jung conceives of a constructivist program in which image is the ground of psyche and experiences are organized through emotional arousal, he violates his own objectives. His most conspicuous mistakes are made in describing gender and other differences as though they were acultural and ahistorical. For example, about animus he says:

> I have called the projection-making factor in women the animus, which means mind or spirit. The animus corresponds to the paternal Logos just as the anima corresponds to the maternal Eros. But I do not wish or intend to give these two intuitive concepts too specific a definition. I use Eros and Logos merely as conceptual aids to describe the fact that woman's consciousness is characterized more by the connective quality of Eros than by the discrimination and cognition associated with Logos. (Jung 1951, par. 29)

Jung's intention here seems to be to identify anima/animus as "projection-making" factors. His assumption of ahistorical gender differences, however, leads to the universal "fact" that women are inferior in their discrimination and logos. Emerging only a few lines further on is a notorious description of an "animus-possessed" woman for whom "Logos is often only a regrettable accident" (ibid., par. 29). Jung is describing a woman's style of argumentation when she is unconsciously influenced by her animus:

> it consists of *opinions* instead of reflections, and by opinions I mean *a priori* assumptions that lay claim to absolute truth. Such assumptions, as everyone knows, can be extremely irritating. As the animus is partial to argument, he can best be seen at work in disputes where both parties know they are right. Men can argue in a very womanish way, too, when they are anima-possessed

and have thus been transformed into the animus of their own anima. . . . No matter how friendly and obliging a woman's Eros may be, no logic on earth can shake her if she is ridden by the animus. Often the man has the feeling — and he is not altogether wrong — that only seduction or a beating or rape would have the necessary power of persuasion. (Ibid., par. 29)

Jung has eliminated the legitimacy of the woman's subjective experience with his "opinions" about her irritating qualities. *He* carries his own projections about the woman (based on a model of universal differences between the sexes) into what appears to be a sanctioning ("he is not altogether wrong") of potential abuse by a man against a woman. If a male therapist were to read this and take it seriously, he could easily imagine that his own anima responses to an argumentative woman were justified in terms of *her* behavior alone, not at all his responsibility.

There are several ways to correct Jung's misplaced foundationalism while retaining the clinically useful distinction of a contrasexual complex. The first, as I have suggested, is to assume that gender is a construction based on family, society, and culture. The second is to keep in mind that power and gender are blended in our cultural roles and habits. Third is to conceive of animus and anima as psychological *complexes* that must be analyzed in a personal, historical manner. To understand them as complexes means to eliminate the foundationalism of universal archetypes of gender differences. As complexes, they can be seen as organized around the archetype of not-I (intrapsychic other) after gender differentiation has been completed. Although there are many other complexes of not-I, as I said before, the complex of contrasexuality is a boundary complex for the self because of the universal division into two gender groups. This division creates both a split subjectivity (I/countrasexual not-I) and an intersubjectivity (self/other) of gender and sexual differences that are relative, contextualized, and culturally embedded. A relative, contextualized theory of contrasexuality ultimately rests on a constructivist reading of Jung's theory of self (archetype of self), but that discussion cannot be taken up here.[2] Instead, let us look in greater detail at the process of early gender differentiation as it may affect female self identity.

If early attachment relationships and action patterns develop smoothly in roughly the first eighteen months of life, we find the emergence of *intersubjective* organization (self/other) in the second half of the second year. Subjective individuality (the I) comes into being with intersubjectivity as the distinction between oneself and other(s) is clarified. Self-recognition occurs reliably with the emergence of self-conscious emotions (see Lewis et al. 1989), secondary to the primary emotions observable at birth (e.g., sadness, fear, disgust, joy). Self-conscious emotions are envy, shame, pride, embarrassment, and guilt. Self-conscious emotions apparently infuse the core arousal state for what I would like to call the "self complex" but is called the "ego complex" within existing Jungian theory.

Although everyone is predisposed to form a unified image of self, clearly observable by roughly the second half of the second year, the particulars of anyone's self-images are imbued with the *meanings* of individuality of a specific family, tribe, or society. Our society highly values personal responsibility, individual achievement, and independence; North American selves are assumed to be individual and separate.

Beliefs about self serve critical functions in the ways people relate to each other and the environment. As philosopher Rom Harré says, "A person is a being who has learned a theory, in terms of which his or her experience is ordered" (1984, p. 20). Our society offers a theory of female self as *less than* or inferior to male self.

Gradually from birth to the age of five or six years, children differentiate the "three great classes of being" — persons, animals, and inanimate objects. It is only after they have achieved an understanding of both *person*-ality and self/other that we can talk about gender as wholly meaningful.

The psychological meaning associated with the contrasexual complex begins at about eighteen months with self/other differentiation and takes on its full colors by the age of five or six years. Although children can label gender differences rather early in life, at or around two years, it appears that they do not understand the exclusive nature of gender until around school age. In a comprehensive review of sex-role differences in development, psychologist Diane Ruble (1983) distinguishes between the early labeling of differences and "gender constancy," the consistent labeling of oneself and others as male and female despite superficial transformations. Being able to "conserve" gender — to understand that gender is constant although the surface changes — (e.g., hairstyle) — is not accomplished until five or six years of age, even seven years in some studies. This means that children do not fully recognize their confinement to the same gender club until they are in elementary school. Gender constancy seems to be critical to children's motivation to learn same-sex models for behaviors and attitudes:

> According to Kohlberg [1966], once children develop a conception of a constant, categorical gender identity, they become motivated to learn what behavior is appropriate for their gender and to act accordingly. (Ruble 1983, p. 444)

Attending to same-sex toys and role models is one element of this achievement that most children demonstrate. Also by school age, most children recognize that girls' games and toys are inferior to boys' and that boys' activities include greater freedom and movement. For example, girls will often include a boy who wants to play with them, but boys generally exclude girls and disdain any boys who play girls' games.

The normative psychological theories about gender differences have been based on the idea that female people lack something. The theory of penis envy is certainly one of these. In most of its forms, it stresses the recognition and desire for the penis in little girls from eighteen months to three years of age. From the discussion above, we can see that it is likely that boys and girls actually believe they *can* (and probably will) accrue the privileges of the other gender at some point in the lifespan. When little girls want a penis or little boys want to have babies, adults quickly tell them they cannot have these because these belong to the others. But small children cannot yet wholly understand the exclusive nature of gender. Such exclusivity seems profoundly "unfair." Young children may not then be operating out of envy as much as pure desire.

Although current research on self-recognition (e.g., Lewis et al. 1989) indicates that Melanie Klein places envy much too early developmentally (around six months of age), she seems accurate to regard envy as a difficult self-conscious emotion, directly connected with self–other configurations. She suggests that envy is a particularly malignant form of aggression because it is a desire to destroy what is good in the other rather than to possess it for oneself (jealousy). Because the other is seen as controlling resources and richness without sharing these with the self, and the self feels no possibility of possessing them, the self wants to destroy the resources of the other. The developmental position of envy actually emerges from a sense of emptiness in the self. If the self feels resourceful and able, the self will not feel envious, perhaps jealous or hateful, but not specifically envious.

I believe that envy becomes connected with female gender especially through socialization processes that "empty" the female self of authority, power, or competence. The achievement of gender constancy means the absolute recognition of being closed off from the resources of the other gender group, no matter what. At about the time that gender constancy sets in firmly, children are just beginning to understand the theory of the inadequacy of the female self. This theory is a hardcore belief in patriarchy. It is inescapable. When girls and women consume this belief—as they must in order to enter the culture—they are ripe for envy.

Theories of penis envy and phallus envy are inadequate because they assume the *real* primacy and fullness of male advantages. They do not problematize or theorize the notion of male advantage. All theories that assume that males have greater resources and advantages as "fact" will increase feelings of female inadequacy.

The psychological theory of an animus complex offers advantages in terms of organizing the images and narratives of female masculinity. First, it supplies us with a model to be filled with the subjective accounts of female people, their experiences of maleness and masculinity (which may or may not include body parts and privileges of men). Second, it avoids the "adultomorphizing" of many Freudian configurations of penis or phallus envy that appear to be inconsistent with a lot of current research on child development. Third, it provides a model that is psychological in nature and is not determined primarily by biology or another fixed category.

When Florence Wiedemann and I began working on *Female Authority* (1987), we collected thousands of dreams and transferential accounts from our clients, young and older women. We looked for schematic patterns in the images and emotions of masculine themes and male people. From our study of these accounts, we formulated a general model of self-animus that can be schematized as two psychological complexes that interface in experiences of intersubjectivity. One is the ego complex of female self and the other is the animus complex of masculine other. The animus may be projected onto male people or institutions or even animals. It may be identified with in dreams and in complex-specific states of waking life.

By the time gender constancy has clarified the exclusive nature of gender, many other emotions have entered into the configuration of animus, although self-conscious emotions are often the constellating emotions on a daily basis. Many aspects of experience—language, culture, male people, ideals, abuse, etc.—become parts of the historical and narrative aspects of the complex.

When Wiedemann and I examined our clinical data (especially transferential material from therapy), we discovered that images of self reside in the animus complex and that images of animus also reside in the ego complex. This means simply that emotions/images in either complex can evoke both subjective and objective configurations.

Using the model of individuation, Wiedemann and I constructed a developmental continuum from the image configurations we found, a continuum that followed clinical evidence of kind of psychopathology, ego development, etc. Each new configuration of animus is assumed to encapsulate and reorganize those that have come before. As I said earlier, a new "stage" or paradigm of meaning reorganizes all that has come before, and yet a person can revert to *any* already organized paradigm at any moment. No developmental achievement is ever final nor is any framework of meaning ever completely stable. Life is a fluctuating configuration of different meaning systems, arising within particular emotional environments. Still, for each person there is apparently a limit to the ability to configure self/other and to feel more or less able to act.

Some Clinical Notes on Animus Development

Obviously, the first organizations of psychological complexes of not-I are not gendered. Experiences of inanimate objects, animals, and the "giant" others (the powerful caregivers) are probably the first variety of not-I complexes.

The ability to cohere and continue as a unified subjectivity — as an I who is embodied — is a difficult task that is never wholly achieved. Alien complexes, such as animus or shadow, are also images of subjectivity, images of the not-I that compete with the I, both within and outside ourselves.

The occasion for a gendered organization of not-I is hypothesized by Wiedemann and myself (1987) — and others in gender studies — to be a product of gender differentiation and conservation. The animus as Alien Outsider, the first stage of animus development, is probably a diffuse psychological complex that collects together the otherness of masculinity with many images that arise from inanimate and animal worlds. The "intruder" into the mother–daughter union, the awkward interloper in the self-same fabric of female relationship, and the aggressive, hostile, incestuous attacker are common forms of the animus as alien outsider.[3] This form of animus is a common occurrence both in the transferential field of therapy and in dreams of analysands and clients.

I would like to describe briefly the typical holding environments and transferential fields connected with each stage of animus development. In order to present a brief overview of the model, I have named and given a few features of each stage, as well as the story we chose to capture the emotional meaning of each stage. There are five stages:

(1) *Animus as Alien Outsider* (Killer, Rapist): containment of self in maternal world; mistrust, fear, rage; *Rape of Persephone*

(2) *Animus as Patriarch* (Father, King, God): sacrifice of self; shame, envy, pride; *Pandora*

(3) *Animus as Youth, Hero, Lover*: surrender of self; guilt, initiative, love; *Amor and Psyche*

(4) *Animus as Partner Within*: recovery of self; anger, aggression, gratitude, interest; *Ariadne and Dionysus*

(5) *Animus as Androgyne* (full range of human potential): integration of self; primary emotions and gratitude, satisfaction; no story plot available

These stages, names, and stories represent the images and patterns we saw in our clients' complexes (as inferred from our models of differentiation and individuation), with the exception of the last stage which we took more from developmental research. We chose stories from patriarchy to remind us of the conflicts for women living in patriarchy. These are not ideal or edifying stories, but maps or emotional accounts that seem to fit what we gleaned from the women themselves.

As I said above, the Alien Outsider form of the complex links together aggressive, intrusive, feared images of males and other "aliens." Accompanying the alien animus, we find a powerful idealized or devalued Mother complex. The interactive field of therapy is highly charged and "dangerous" — filled with abandonment depression, fears, envy, separation anxiety, desires for mergers, and fears of mergers. The therapist must provide "good-enough" mothering in a holding environment of accurate mirroring and clear, able differentiation of the figurative from the literal, of the imaginal from the relational. Safety and differentiation (as well as integration) are key themes in the transitional space. If therapy succeeds, the client is able to assimilate some of the "reality" of living — in her culture which marginalizes her and in her life which frightens her.

The second form of animus, the Patriarchal complex, links the powerful good/bad Father with the empty, depressed, enraged Mother complex. Sometimes the Mother's animus, who is often characterized as the "sensitive man" (the one whom I call the "underground genius" and find represented in the figure of Hephaestus in the Pandora story), replaces the good/bad Father as the powerful male image. At the Patriarchal stage, the therapeutic field is charged with doubt, ambivalence, power struggles, oppositions, and refusals. The *appearance* of the therapist is critically important for an effective holding environment; somehow the therapist must appear to be competent, healthy enough, attractive, and/or "successful." The appearance of the therapist generally cannot be openly interpreted (because the client cannot distinguish between appearances and other aspects of a person), but is a central issue in the transference, no matter the sex of the therapist. The therapist must be able to contain the therapeutic process through interventions that enhance the development of personal responsibility in the client — responsibility for her own subjectivity, her emotional life, decisions, the expectations and images she brings to experience. The therapist must be able to offer hope without gratifying or patronizing and to be idealized without flinching (or becoming inflated). Often the effective therapist will be seen as the powerful Father-God-King who is demanding and self-serving. Typically, a client at this stage will show very little gratitude and much envy during the middle phase of treatment. She may be seen as an unsatisfying client who is resistant and hypercritical.

The Lover-Hero animus complex links to mystery and desire to know the other and to idealization and hope. Images of partnership and a desire to share the responsibility and the intimacy of treatment make a client at this stage seductively attractive to the therapist, male or female. The client fears a reliving of abandonment and her own rage at the limitations of her female identity. She confronts the negative Mother complex in terms of rage, grief, and loss due to the powerlessness of women. The holding environment is grounded in authenticity, abiding reflective attention, humor, empathy, and collaborative meaning-making.

The Partner Within stage is rare in therapy or elsewhere, but demands the complete authenticity and creative talent of the therapist. All emotions are engaged and many complexes are constellated, but a reflective consciousness is present on the part of the client when necessary.

I have found the stages of animus development to be rich and useful in forming a diagnostic picture and an expectation of the transferential field. The whole model, as a map of individuation, is still a hypothetical one. The model needs to be further investigated, with a wider number of cases, to see if it holds up as a form of content analysis. On an immediate basis, however, these configurations or maps of complexes permit me (in the heat of a moment) to step back and get a perspective and to do this gracefully.

As I understand it, there are three kinds of relationship necessary for transformative therapy: the "real" relationship or kinship libido, the transferential relationship, and the therapeutic relationship (in which I am the protector of the therapeutic process, know the terrain, and carry the maps). It is in this third area that I make most use of the concept of contrasexual complexes. The clinical techniques or methods (e.g., interpretation, silence, reflection, etc.) that might be brought to bear in doing therapeutic work are a thing apart from the map.

At the time we were researching and writing our book, another group of women was researching and writing a book on forms of epistemological development in girls and women. I believe their work is an important adjunct to ours because knowledge, competence, and confidence as a knower are aspects of animus development in our society. Mary Belenky et al. (1986) gathered their data for *Women's Ways of Knowing: The Development of Self, Voice, and Mind* from hundreds of interviews with women they found in various educational settings. Their work provides a strong foundation for our hypothesis of stages of development of animus because they reached beyond any particular context and talked to women from different classes and backgrounds. They also inferred five stages that comprise a developmental continuum, matching well with ours:

(1) Silence
(2) Received Knowledge
(3) Subjective Knowledge
(4) Procedural Knowledge
(5) Constructed Knowledge

I look forward to other therapists and researchers collecting imaginal material and searching for women's experiences of animus in dreams and relationships. I consider the study of contrasexuality to be a cornerstone for new relationships between women and men and for knowledge about the effects of gender exclusivity.

Concluding Remarks

I hope I have illustrated the clinical usefulness of the theory of animus as a psychological complex arising out of the differentiation of self and other. I appreciate our theory of contrasexuality because it invites a psychological analysis of the other arising in one's own subjectivity. This is extremely useful in clarifying gender differences and opening up the possibility of mutual self-revelation with a person of the opposite sex, provided we revise our theory of gender so that it is relative and contextualized. If we continue to use acultural, ahistorical assumptions of universal masculine and feminine principles, we will continue to be at risk of simply projecting our own Jungian versions of male and female onto the entire world. As I mentioned earlier, a valuable humility ensues from the serious recognition that we construct coherent images of the other that may present a barrier to receiving the validity of another's subjectivity. I hope my paper has clarified some of the issues surrounding this recognition.

Notes

1. This paper greatly benefited from the generous and detailed comments of Demaris Wehr, and the insightful advice and perspectives of Jolé McCurdy and Jane Lewis. I thank you for your help.

2. For a complete account of a constructivist treatment of Jung's self psychology, see Young-Eisendrath and Hall, *Jung's Self Psychology: A Constructivist Perspective* (New York: Guilford, in press).

3. Erich Neumann's (1959) paper, entitled (in English) "The Psychological Stages of Feminine Development," published in *Spring*, had a great deal of influence on my early thinking about self/animus development. Over time, as I stated in *Female Authority* (1987), I came to disagree with his position of the female advantage in relationship (resting on the "natural" greater closeness of the female infant to the mother). Neumann's work on the development of the feminine is inspiring and fruitful for thinking about any developmental model of female identity, but it is limited by foundationalism and acultural theorizing about universal meanings that have not been substantiated by archeological and anthropological evidence.

References

Barnett, R., Biener, L., and Baruch, G., eds. 1987. *Gender and Stress.* New York: Free Press.

Baruch, G., and Barnett, R. 1986. Role quality, multiple role involvement, and psychological well-being in midlife women. *Journal of Personality and Social Psychology* 51:578-585.

Belenky, M. F., Clinchy, B. M., Goldberger, N. R., and Tarule, J. M. 1986. *Women's Ways of Knowing: The Development of Self, Voice, and Mind.* New York: Basic Books.

Bem, S. L. 1974. The measurement of psychological androgyny. *Journal of Consulting and Clinical Psychology* 42:155-162.

Bem, S. L., Martyna, W., and Watson, C. 1976. Sex typing and androgyny: further explorations of the expressive domain. *Journal of Personality and Social Psychology* 34:1016-1023.

Bernard, J. 1972a. *The Future of Marriage.* New York: World.

Bernard, J. 1972b. *The Sex Game: Communication Between the Sexes.* New York: Atheneum.

Bowlby, J. 1986. Developmental psychiatry comes of age. *The 1986 Adolf Meyer Lecture.* London: Tavistock Clinic.

Broverman, I. K., Broverman, D. M., Clarkson, F. E., and Rosenkrantz, P. S., and Vogel,

S. R. 1970. Sex-role stereotypes and clinical judgments of mental health. *Journal of Consulting and Clinical Psychology* 34:1–7.

Broverman, I. K., Vogel, S. R., Broverman, D. M., Clarkson, and F. E., and Rosenkrantz, P. S. 1972. Sex-role stereotypes: a current appraisal. *Journal of Social Issues* 28:59–78.

Chodorow, N. 1978. *The Reproduction of Mothering: Psychoanalysis and the Sociology of Gender.* Berkeley, Calif.: University of California Press.

Deaux, K., and Lewis, L. L. 1983. Components of gender stereotypes. *Psychological Documents* 13:25.

Eagly, A. 1983. Gender and social influences: a social psychological analysis. *American Psychologist* 38:971–981.

Epstein, C. 1988. *Deceptive Distinctions.* New Haven, Conn.: Yale University Press.

Gilligan, C. 1982. *In a Different Voice: Psychological Theory and Women's Development.* Cambridge, Mass.: Harvard University Press.

Haley. 1976. *Problem-Solving Therapy.* San Francisco: Jossey-Bass.

Hare-Mustin, R. T., and Marecek, J. 1988. The meaning of difference: gender theory, postmodernism, and psychology. *The American Psychologist* 43, 6:455–464.

Harré, R. 1984. *Personal Being.* Cambridge, Mass.: Harvard University Press.

Jung, C. G. 1951. *Aion. CW*, vol. 9ii. Princeton, N.J.: Princeton University Press, 1959.

Kohlberg. 1966. A cognitive-developmental analysis of children's sex-role concepts and attitudes. In E. E. Maccoby, ed., *The Development of Sex Differences.* Stanford, Calif.: Stanford University Press.

Lacan, J. 1982. *Feminine Sexuality.* J. Mitchell, ed. J. Rose, trans. and ed. New York: W. W. Norton.

Lewis, M., Sullivan, M. W., Stanger, C., and Weiss, M. 1989. Self-development and self-conscious emtoions. *Child Development* 60, 146–156.

Lichtenberg. 1983. *Psychoanalysis and Infant Research.* Hillsdale, N.J.: Analytic Press.

Mahler, M., Pine, F., and Bergman, A. 1975. *The Psychological Birth of the Human Infant: Symbiosis and Individuation.* New York: Basic Books.

Miller, J. B. 1976. *Toward a New Psychology of Women.* Boston: Beacon Press.

Minuchin, S. 1974. *Families and Family Therapy.* Cambridge, Mass.: Harvard University Press.

Overton, W. 1990. The structure of developmental theory. In P. van Geert and L. P. Mos, eds., *Annals of Theoretical Psychology.* New York: Plenum.

Putnam, H. 1989. *Representations and Reality.* Cambridge, Mass.: MIT Press.

Ruble, D. 1983. Sex-role development. In M. H. Bornstein and M. E. Lamb, eds., *Developmental Psychology: An Advanced Textbook*, 2nd ed. Hillsdale, N.J.: Lawrence Erlbaum.

Samuels, A. 1989. *The Plural Psyche.* New York: Routledge.

Singer, J. 1977. *Androgyny: Towards a New Theory of Sexuality.* New York: Harper and Row.

Sroufe, A., and Fleeson, J. 1986. Attachment and the construction of relationships. In W. Hartup and Z. Rubin, eds. *Relationships and Development.* Hillsdale, N.J.: Erlbaum.

Stern, D. 1985. *The Interpersonal World of the Infant.* New York: Basic Books.

Stevens, A. 1982. *Archetypes: A Natural History of the Self.* New York: Morrow.

Sullivan, H. S. 1953. *The Interpersonal Theory of Psychiatry.* New York: Norton.

Vergrugge, L. M. 1982. Women's social roles and health. In P. Berman and E. Ramey, eds., *Women: A Developmental Perspective.* Washington, D.C.: U.S. Government Printing Office.

Wehr, D. 1987. *Jung and Feminism: Liberating the Archetypes.* Boston: Beacon Press.

Young-Eisendrath, P. 1984. *Hags and Heroes: A Feminist Approach to Jungian Psychotherapy with Couples.* Toronto: Inner City Books.

Young-Eisendrath, P., and Wiedemann, F. 1987. *Female Authority: Empowering Women Through Psychotherapy.* New York: Guilford Press.

The Gender Archetypes

Edward C. Whitmont

The concepts of anima and animus as they apply to consciousness and gender are in need of revision. A good deal of rethinking has been stimulated by clinical experience as well as by the impact of feminist criticism. In the following I shall propose a reformulation that is at variance with classical Jungian theory.

Jung's original formulation limited animus and anima to a contra-sexual dynamic only: animus pertaining to women, anima to men, as projection-making factors which give to the unconscious of men and women a contrasexual imprint. On the strength of accumulated clinical experience this limitation does not seem to be justified. The man's unconscious contains unassimilated archetypal and personal male components just as the woman's contains unassimilated archetypal and personal female components.

According to Jung's definition, "woman's consciousness is charac-terized more by the connective quality of Eros than by the discrimina-tion and cognition associated with Logos," and "in women . . . Eros is the expression of their true nature, while their Logos is often only a

Edward C. Whitmont, M.D., is a member of the C. G. Jung Training Center of New York and maintains a private practice in New York City and Irvington, N.Y. He is the author of *The Symbolic Quest, Psyche and Substance: Essays on Homeopathy in the Light of Jungian Psychology, The Return of the Goddess: Desire, Aggression and the Evolution of Conscious-ness*, and co-author of *Dreams: A Portal to the Source*.

regrettable accident." This formulation ties the animus concept to an a priori assumption of women's natural inferiority of discrimination. At best this is patronizing, at worst outrightly insulting to women. More-- over, this formulation is not borne out by facts. While, by and large, women may be more averse to purely abstract argumentation, this does not permit us to infer an inborn natural deficiency in their ability to think clearly. This formulation confuses an archetypal dynamic with its culturally conditioned contents.

Jung defined animus and anima as archetypes of maleness and femaleness, namely primordial principles of structure and form. We must be careful, therefore, to distinguish between the archetypes them- selves and their cultural, familial, and personal contents, which are the complexes or shadow aspects which they engender. In fact, Jung expressly stated that

> Though the *contents* of anima and animus can be integrated, they themselves cannot, since they are archetypes. As such they are the foundation stones of the psychic structure, which in its totality exceeds the limits of consciousness and therefore can never become the object of direct cognition. Though the effects of anima and animus can be made conscious, they themselves are factors transcending consciousness and beyond the reach of perception and volition. (1951, par. 40)

Anatomical and hormonal dynamics are expressions of archetypal structuring. Anatomically and hormonally, both sexes partake of both female and male dynamics. It is therefore justified to postulate that, by analogy to rather than "because" of this fact, both genders are likely to be also psychologically under the influence of both male and female archetypal structuring. We describe maleness as an analogue of Yang, representing Lingam, heaven, linearity, externalization, ordering law, assertive doing, and separative partialness. Femaleness is analogous to Yin, Yoni, earth, being and wholeness, circularity and internalness, instinct, affect, and idealization. This indeed was Jung's viewpoint. We have, however, no reason to assume that every man has managed to assimilate all contents of the male archetype or every woman the con- tents of her potential femaleness. Hence both sexes will be in need of compensation and complementation by all those gender qualities of either kind that happen to have been but inadequately developed. Specifically, since the animus is a potential psychopomp, it must be presumed to compensate for an inadequate discrimination and cogni- tion of logos, whenever this should be the case, in men no less than in women, just as the anima may also compensate, as psychopomp, for an inadequate awareness of connecting needs in women or men.

In other words, as archetypal drive potentials, namely vectors to qualities that have never yet been in consciousness, animus and anima must pertain also to unrealized potentialities of one's own gender, to still missing aspects of masculinity in a man and of femininity in a woman. Not all the masculine potential of a man or the feminine potential of a woman is of necessity consciously developed and integrated. Some animus Yang elements are always likely to be undeveloped or inadequately or perversely conditioned in a particular man and likewise anima Yin elements in a woman.

Men can be as stubbornly dogmatic, unreasonably belligerent, cranky and power-driven as "animus-possessed" women; they can also be quite deficient in discrimination and will then compensate for that deficiency with that very primitive dogmatism and hunger for power which have been ascribed to the animus in women. In turn, women can be quite unrelated and hysterically overemotional and moody, as seductively unrelated and depressed as men, when their primitive anima takes over.

It is not necessary to explain this by resorting to such needlessly complicating terminology as the animus of the anima or the anima of the animus. Doing so serves only to maintain a systematization that is not even borne out by clinical facts.

Men are not necessarily more spiritual than women, nor do women have a monopoly on soul and instinct. The notion of spirituality as a predominantly male characteristic and of soul as a female property are heirlooms of nineteenth-century romanticism. They are timebound within culturally conditioned actualizations of the Yang/Yin archetypes. These culturally determined expectations and complexes are no longer valid in our time. A predominantly logos-oriented man may, in addition to his perhaps seductive anima, also be obsessed by the need to integrate a heroic animus that, while unconsciously obsessive, makes him overly combative and quarrelsome rather than objectively assertive; a philosophically inclined woman may have a compensating anima trend that induces unconsciously seductive behavior. There are many clear-thinking women who are more logos-related than many feeling- or intuition-type men who have inferior thinking functions.

In all these instances animus and anima function as archetypal trends that attempt to call forth missing aspects of a still-to-be-reached wholeness within one's own, and not only within the contrasexual, gender. Hence, the ego can be assimilated to, or overwhelmed by, the equisexual as well as the heterosexual archetype. Ordinarily, however, except perhaps in cases of homosexuality or transvestism, the mature ego tends to identify with the equisexual archetype. In this case one's self-image is determined by being a "man" or a "woman," usually stereotyped in terms of one's cultural, familial, or other bias.

A weak or damaged ego may be overwhelmed or assimilated by both the contrasexual and the equisexual archetype. Then we have the familiar states of possession. A woman's ego may be driven to act out the Great Mother Goddess or may be filled with Jehovah or Ares power. A man may be a cantankerous warrior underneath his purportedly peace-loving and conciliatory ego adaptation or act out a Great Mother or Aphroditic playboy stance.

The characterizations of anima and animus continue to be valid. But they apply to both sexes and not only to the opposite sex. Whenever an adapted instinctual or emotional response to involvement with people or things is called for but fails to occur, the anima fills the vacuum. Inadequate discrimination or failure of called-for assertiveness calls forth an animus reaction.

It follows then, that shadow figures and qualities may also appear in contrasexual and not only in equisexual form. They may represent unconscious, repressed qualities, which are projected upon and optimally depicted by a person of the opposite sex. By means of gender we cannot distinguish shadow from animus or anima quality. When a quality represented by a particular figure is psychologically clearly definable, that fact points to the personal rather than the collective unconscious and differentiates the shadow from animus or anima.

Archetypes are a priori patterns of behavior, emotive and perceptive potentials. When they appear in dreams or fantasies, they are characterized by a special magical, mythological, and numinous quality. They appear as Powers, Gods, demons, devils, anonymous and strange sinister or fascinating persons or personality types such as "the lover," "the stranger," "the child," or animals or animal-like figures that cannot be well defined in personal or rational terms. In this category, we have to classify also the so-called archetypal shadow, represented by devil or angel or any other anonymous, inferior or superior numinous figure, indistinguishable from animus or anima.

These are all collective, archetypal elements rather than personal shadow figures. Their significance cannot be approached by rational definition but only symbolically as "best possible expressions" of an unknown or unknowable content.

According to Jung, the Self, in particular, is a wholly unknowable, indescribable, undefinable entity that cannot be distinguished from the God image. Hence it is usually represented by totally impersonal numinous forms, such as mandala, light, stone, globe. These representations can be grasped, if at all, only symbolically. They bear no relationship to gender at all. They represent a wholeness pattern superseding the opposites including gender.

Since consciousness-determining figures, spiritual guides, psychopompic animus figures appear equally in the conscious as well as unconscious material of both sexes, we can no longer maintain that consciousness is a masculine Yang quality and unconsciousness a feminine Yin quality.

During the patriarchal cultures, consciousness was, indeed, shaped predominantly by masculine Yang values, while the Yin dynamics tended to be devalued, repressed and relegated to unconsciousness. During that cultural phase, masculinity therefore represented forms of collectively valued consciousness. However, in our time, feminine Yin values are reentering and restructuring the conscious collective value system. They are becoming cultural determinants and co-shapers of a new consciousness for both sexes.

In turn, archetypal actualizations that are represented as person-, group- and time-conditioned complexes of the personal unconscious or shadow are specific, rationally describable behaviors, feelings, and viewpoints. Emotionality, power drives, objectivity, or dogmatism are examples of such concrete rationally definable psychological qualities which we have tended to ascribe to animus or anima. In fact, they are archetypally engendered elements of personal complexes. I would see them as positive or negative shadow dynamics. They result in definite projections and expectations both upon the other and upon one's own sex.

As shadow they are capable of being made fully conscious. Their qualities are psychologically definable and understandable by analogy and metaphor, rather than as the best possible description of an unknown or unknowable transpersonal content.

The stingy grocer around the corner may represent a definable shadow quality, stinginess, for a woman; the uncanny mysterious dark stranger, a black magician animus for a man. An anonymous child may represent a growth potential and pertain to the animus/anima realm or, when it is felt as a divine child, to the Self. If it is a particular child, little George or Linda, it may need to be seen as a shadow element, representing a regressive or neglected quality that still needs loving care, attentive nursing, or disciplined containment.

Needless to say, what, for the sake of theoretical understanding, was described here in a neat system of classification does not necessarily present itself in such a simple fashion in reality. In actual clinical experience, shadow, animus, anima, ego, and Self representations may be rather fluent, with many overlappings that necessitate a fine sense of discrimination for what happens to be personal or transpersonal and numinous.

References

Jung, C. G. 1951. *Aion. CW*, vol. 9ii. Princeton, N.J.: Princeton University Press, 1959.

What Is the Animus and
Why Do We Care?

Caroline T. Stevens

What indeed is reality if it is not a reality in ourselves, an esse *in anima?
Living reality is the product neither of the actual, objective behaviour of
things nor of the formulated idea exclusively, but rather of the
combination of both in the living psychological process.*

C. G. Jung, "The Problems of
Types in Classical and Medieval
Thought," p. 52.

In this passage, Jung expresses his "mediating standpoint" in the
argument between realists and nominalists, between those who discover the ultimate and governing reality in the idea and those who find
it rather in the thing observed. Until I reread, quite recently, Jung's
discussion of "the type problem in classical and medieval thought," I
had placed myself quite firmly in the nominalist camp. My primary
allegiance in analytical work is indeed to the "thing observed," that is,
to the phenomena encountered in the psychological process, in our own
and others' struggles toward freedom and authenticity. And my answer

Caroline T. Stevens, Ph.D., is an analyst in private practice in Chicago and a training
analyst with the Chicago Society of Jungian Analysts. Publications include articles in the
Chiron Clinical Series, *Quadrant, The San Francisco Jung Institute Library Journal*, and
Psyche's Stories (forthcoming).

to the first question in my title was this: animus, before all else, is a word, a simple name for a most complex set of phenomena. Like all words, it has definition, and it is we who define the word, pack it with meaning. So doing, we give to the word *animus* the power to shape, where once it purported only to name.

But in asking my second question, I encountered issues best served by an emphasis on Jung's *esse in anima*, for the power of our words to shape will be felt in the souls of those so brave as to allow us entry there. The "formulated idea" of the animus must be tested against the phenomenon, or rather—and this distinction matters—against the variety of phenomena we meet in the practice of analysis with women. Here, it is image that matters, and the word is to be valued only as far as it serves the soul.

To name is to create human reality, to provide the categories that give shape to our world and orientation to our lives. This shaping power of naming and definition is recognized in stories of divine creation by and through the Word, the Christian being only one of these myths. But the power of the word, felt to be godly in its creative primacy, relies, in fact, upon the achievement of human consensus. We, some community of word-users, agree to the use and meaning of the word, agree not only to its narrow denotation of certain phenomena of experience, but (perhaps less certainly) to the aura of connotations it may develop over time. Where first such agreement may be more or less conscious, later we are likely simply to accept the naming and definition as a matter of course, "on authority."

As the community adopts and uses the word defined, so the word in its use helps to further a sense of community among its users. And, not uncommonly, consensus sufficiently achieved and experienced over time, we may begin to overlook our role in the matter, to believe that the word, assimilated to the phenomena it was chosen to name, possesses its meaning intrinsically. The Word, as defined, may then become sacred, inviolable, "archetypal" in its felt potency. It becomes very difficult to change the definition of a word which has achieved such a status, even if that definition is felt by some to be inaccurate and even pernicious in its effects. I refer to the equation of the animus with "the masculine" and the persistent identification of "the masculine principle" with Logos (as opposed to Eros), spirit (as opposed to matter), consciousness and differentiated order (as opposed to the unconscious and a threatening chaos.) As you may judge by this lengthy consideration of word and definition, I am one of those who find this usage of the word *animus*, currently quite common among us, to be undesirable.

Some of those who judge it so (usually non-Jungians) have suggested that we ought simply to quit saying "animus." Others (more likely to be members of the community) accept the generally agreed upon definition of animus and suggest instead that we alter its locus: it may appear, with anima, in the soul of a man. I still find it a useful word in the observation and experience, specifically, of women's psychological journeys, and so I don't like either of these solutions. I would like, instead, and in spite of the possible difficulty involved, to propose a shift in the commonly accepted definition of the word *animus*. The shift amounts to a simple reclamation of Jung's original vision in the matter, and I will tell you why such a move seems to me worth the effort.

Before doing so, however, I am concerned with distinguishing the word from the phenomena it has been used to name, in order both to recall us to our roles as namers and definers and to allow the phenomena to regain our full attention. Jung himself, in spite of his Platonic tendencies and extensive theoretical works, wished always to return us to the phenomena. I have always liked this observation from the Collected Works: "Reality is simply what works in a human soul and not what is assumed by certain people to work there, and about which prejudiced generalizations are wont to be made" (Jung 1921, par. 60). If we recognize animus as word, its definition quite dependent upon its users, we become more fully attentive to and respectful toward the psychological events it was chosen to name. We may then begin to wonder about our own (and Jung's) "prejudiced generalizations." Some recall of history may be in order.

Animus as word began its history among us with Jung's description and naming of certain events in the psychological lives of women. He had encountered and named "anima" a potent feminine figure in his own inner life. He then found a masculine counterpart at work in women and called it "animus." Indeed, some of his comments about this process suggest that the idea of the animus was more a matter of logical derivation than of observation. He tells us that, following his discovery of the anima in himself, he began work on an ancient problem: "Has woman a soul?" He concluded that "she could not possibly have an anima, because then there would be no check on the woman from within" (Mcguire 1989, pp. 45–46).

> Then I came to the idea that woman must have an animus, but it was not until much later that I was able to develop this further because the animus is much harder to catch at work. (Ibid.)

Ultimately, however, on the basis of his own experience and his work with patients, Jung began identifying certain characteristics and functions as belonging to anima and animus and tracing the processes by which they seemed to work in furtherance of individuation.

In 1916, Jung spoke of the anima as having "a compensatory nature" and occupying "the place between the individual and the collective unconscious." He adds that the anima is often to be met in dreams, "where it appears as a feminine being in a man, and as a man (animus) in a woman" (Jung 1916, par. 507). The attribution of a compensatory function (apparently identical in men and women except for its gendered appearance) is mentioned again in 1928, when Jung observes that "the persona, the ideal picture of a man as he should be, is inwardly compensated by feminine weakness . . . for . . . the anima . . . reacts to the persona" (1928, par. 309). And a woman possessed by the animus is in danger of losing her "adapted feminine persona" (ibid., par. 337).

Moreover, these figures present an appearance "as manifold as the limitless variety of their conscious correlate, the persona," and each is an "autonomous complex," "a psychological function that has usurped, or rather retained, a 'personality' only because this function is itself autonomous and undeveloped." Regarded correctly, animus and anima become "bridges to the unconscious," wherein lie unknown "contents" to be integrated into the conscious life. And when the unconscious processes "reflected in the anima[us]" are brought to consciousness, then these figures will be felt "simply as a function" (Jung 1928, pars. 337–339).

However, this emphasis on a function to be performed in and by both sexes is gradually overshadowed, in the writings of Jung and of his followers, by descriptions of the gender characteristics, the "content," of these "contrasexual others." Moreover, the recognition of familial and cultural influences on these characteristics, inherent in the attribution of compensatory function, is often lost. While both feminine and masculine are said to be found in each of us, the matter of their integration becomes very problematical.

> [N]o one can get round the fact that by taking up a masculine profession, studying and working like a man, woman is doing something not wholly in accord with, if not directly injurious to, her feminine *nature*. She is doing something that would scarcely be possible for a man to do. . . . Could he, for instance, be a nursemaid or run a kindergarten? (Jung 1927, par. 243, my emphasis)

Moreover, the masculine element in a woman and the feminine in a man remain inferior, always to be relegated to the "background": "If one lives out the opposite sex in oneself one is living in one's own background, and one's real individuality suffers" (ibid., par. 243).

Jung made these observations regarding the masculine in women in 1927, along with a recognition that they reflect a man's "projected feelings." However, because of her "nature," these are projections that the woman intentionally accepts. She maintains a "passive attitude with an ulterior purpose" — to capture and keep the man (Jung 1927, par. 240). The matter of masculine and feminine "nature" obtrudes more and more, along with references to masculine and feminine "instincts" and gender-specific traits to be found in the anima and the animus. By 1951, although anima and animus are still only "provisionally" identified with Eros and Logos, Jung goes on to assure us that "In women . . . Eros is an expression of their true nature, while their Logos is often only a regrettable accident" (1951, par. 29). I must wonder, who among us would wish to abandon her "true nature" in order to foster the development of regrettable characteristics?

Let us follow again the moves that have been made: we have first a dynamic function, its gendered appearance only secondarily important in its recognition and definition. Then gender gathers importance; anima and animus become "the feminine" and "the masculine." With this, observation of "the facts" of consciousness and the images of the unconscious begins to be overridden by "the ideas," by descriptions of nature and instinct, and the ascription of an archetypal origin to the meaning of animus. So Emma Jung can say that "in the animus we are dealing with a masculine principle" (not a mere appearance), and go on to ascribe to that principle, "the logos principle," the attributes of will, word, deed, and meaning (E. Jung 1957, pp. 2–3).

Originally, animus is seen as compensating for a feminine persona. Later, however, it is felt to complement or supplement a feminine "consciousness," a much broader conception and one which furthers the notion of a "natural" femininity that must be compensated by an archetypal masculinity. Clearly, feminine persona is tailored to a specific social milieu; feminine "nature" is not. Just as clearly, an animus which compensates a feminine persona may, indeed, be "manifold" across time and cultures, displaying characteristics which one's own time and place might not consider to be inherently and exclusively masculine. However, "the masculine" as archetypal is much less open to variation. Although the possibility of individual variation in animus characteristics is (barely) retained in the later formulations, the attribution of archetypal status to the animus and "nature" to conscious abilities considerably ups the ante in the game of definition. Awareness of the role of an evolving collective consciousness in the formation of persona, and therefore of the animus, is dimmed, and we find ourselves in the realm of the eternal gods.

A further complication: with an "archetypal" femininity and masculinity, we begin to be influenced by the potent configuration of gendered syzygy. In 1951, Jung took up this dimension of anima/animus and, in doing so, returned to his early recognition of these figures as "functions which filter the contents of the collective unconscious through to the conscious mind." Their contents, he finds, can be integrated, although they themselves cannot, "since they are archetypes" (Jung 1951, par. 40). And yet, he seems to find revealed in the archetypes certain eternal contents:

> Together they form a divine pair, one of whom, in accordance with his Logos nature, is characterized by pneuma and nous, rather like Hermes with his ever-shifting hues, while the other, in accordance with her Eros nature, wears the features of Aphrodite, Helen (Selene), Persephone, and Hecate. Both of them are unconscious powers, "gods" in fact, as the ancient world rightly conceived them to be. (Jung 1951, par. 41)

And so it has remained with us, as a culture and as a psychological community of Jungians. Animus has come to mean "the masculine," which continues to be associated with spirit, rational objectivity, active creativity, and leadership capacities. Dynamic function and static content are conflated in our understanding, and the aspect of gender worn by archetypal potentials assumes a central position. In effect, gender captures qualities (as with Eros and Logos above) which it had been said only to mediate. And as with the culture, collective ideas about masculinity and femininity may then take precedence over the observation of both the human propensities and possibilities of men and women and the divine appearances, the gods and goddesses, of other and more ancient myths.

Well, so what? The goal, after all, is individuation, and the path toward that end which most of us follow may well feature encounters with figures that are both gendered and the bearers of contents assigned to their gender by our culture. If we assert that both men and women carry both "masculine" and "feminine" qualities, neither to be valued over the other, then what is the harm in this dominance of the idea over the thing to be observed? Can we not imagine, may we not someday attain, androgynous wholeness? Indeed, if we assume that our culture's definitions of masculinity and femininity are unchanging, then the loading of animus and anima with cultural content may not seem to matter too much clinically—although it does compromise our theory, which will not apply where the cultural definitions are different or an individual psyche varies from the expected norm.

However, we can in fact retain this position only if we retain as well a certain blindness to the significance of social and developmental reality. One of the problems with the idea of androgyny as an image of human wholeness is that it obscures recognition of the fact that "masculine" and "feminine" qualities are *not* valued as equal in our culture, and these values are internalized by most of us, both analysts and analysands. But most significantly, the image of androgyny, too soon or too readily espoused, permits us to overlook the imbalance of power and authority which our culture and the myth that informs it have long expressed.

Although other myths may be known to us, the god of our own culture retains a central place in our conscious and unconscious lives, and the definitions he has inspired continue to shape our understanding. Since he claims to be the only god, he lends a monotheistic power to our culture's definitions and to their effect upon our psychological theory. In effect, we care about "the masculine" and "the feminine" because we have cared in a deep and pervasive way about him. And in large part, we care about an animus defined first and foremost by his gender, filled with culturally prescribed content, because we have cared about gender as the expression of this Dominant One and his "other."

The high gods and goddesses of a culture display in their attributes and activities a dominant image of creation, of our place in it, of good and evil, and of the possible and appropriate behavior of human beings. In all such personifications of the Divine, the attributes of gender are also displayed, and in them a culture understands the characteristics of human femininity and masculinity. Whether or not we actively subscribe to the religions they inhabit, we are likely to identify ourselves in the deities and in relation to the deities. Thus the image of deity, which works in us for the most part unexamined, is heavy with consequences for our psychological and social well-being; it is, as Jung put it, "the overwhelming psychic factor." In Western patriarchy, the "central archetype, the God-image" (Jung 1951, par. 170) is a creator sky-god; in Christianity, a father incarnate through his son, the Logos. Animus as archetype is drenched in this imagery, and "the feminine" is then derived and defined by its difference from and mode of relation to "the masculine." Here we do well to recall the familiar distinction between archetype and archetypal image.

As imagined by Jung, archetypes are as consistent and unchanging as human nature itself: "if they ever 'originated' their origins must have coincided at least with the beginning of the species" (1954, par. 152). Archetypes are revealed in patterns of human functioning and expressed in the products of creative fantasy, taken up and preserved in the collective expressions of fairy tale, myth, and religion. However, these revelations are not themselves the archetypes. As the archetype approaches consciousness, it clothes itself in the garments of time and place, and the image so created must then be perceived, valued, and interpreted by a conscious mind. But our consciousness, which develops at the interface of outer and inner reality, is thoroughly vulnerable to the conceits of its personal and cultural time and place. This awareness must warn against the assumption that any given archetypal image, as we apprehend it, is complete, eternal, and innate. The more powerful the archetype in its scope and significance for the understanding of human potential, the more conscious and careful must be the distinction between the eternal possibility and the historically conditioned image.

The experience of godlike power and authority in the realm of gender is given a special twist among us. We first experience these qualities in our parents, but our cultural myth and the family which expresses it require that the Mother God shall surrender her primacy to God the Father. The path of personal development is felt to recapitulate the history of consciousness, and both are imagined as a linear journey away from Mother, into a world and, at last, a heaven presided over by the Father. This understanding is both good and correct for men. It is correct, for men, because it reflects the exigencies of the development of masculine gender identity and of the hero's journey which claims that identity as its prize. It is good for men because, no matter how potent she may be, the anima can rarely be mistaken, by a man, for the Self. It is good also because, in such a world, the development of masculine gender identity in and of itself, although it denies his "weakness," his vulnerability, his right to be wrong, does not foreclose a recognition of the man's ultimate oneness with the creative source of power and authority. Therefore, creativity, an entitled will, the right to name and define and judge and generally make use of the created world fall to him as an opportunity legitimated by his sex. Struggles, of course, remain, but he is invited, in fact, urged and even required, to claim this birthright.

The case has been and in large degree remains quite different for a woman. To the degree that our cultural myth retains its primacy both in and around her, identification with the mother entangles the woman in a web of contradictions. With it, she achieves the settled feminine gender identity that enables not only social confidence but active participation in the "feminine" sphere of relationship, in the rewards of motherhood and sexual intimacy with men. But identification with mother may also foreclose a sense of the self as capable of intellectual authority and spiritual creativity. There is still no feminine archetypal image of supreme potency widely available in the culture, no divine feminine authority coequal with the masculine, through which a woman might find validation and enhancement of a feminine identity.

A man may leave the personal father to find the Great Father and a possible expansion of his personal identity. When a woman leaves her mother behind, there has been no place to go but into the Father's house, with an identity there inevitably limited and defined by her relationship to him. She becomes his wife, lover, mother, muse, nurse, and cheerleader, or she remains his daughter, and perhaps, like Athena, his right-hand "man." The linear path out and away from the mother, in the traditionally feminine life, leads only a short, circular way to the wedding and back into the home.

If the path leads into the world by way of identity with the father, it is at great price: the loss of confident grounding in the female body and of identity with a female source of life and potency. Such a woman has already recognized qualities in herself which may have caused her to think of herself as masculine, and therefore, with varying degrees of unease or pride, as an "outsider" to the company of women. She may well be relieved to discover a mode of thought affirming masculinity as a quality all women have and should develop, but, at some point, the troubling question of the integration of these qualities with her less-valued "feminine" ones will arise. Hence the emphasis, among Jungian feminists and others, on revaluing traditionally feminine qualities, affirmed as primary, "natural," and intrinsic to women, but for men at best an achievement. However, the psychological journey of a contemporary woman may not at all support these ideas about femininity. Oddly enough, the traditionally feminine qualities may be expressed in her dreams by animus figures. That is, qualities expressive of and intimately associated with the earth, with a passionate and embodied Eros, with the night and the underworld, may appear in masculine form.

I will cite my own experience here, although it is far from unique. Years ago in Zurich, while I read of masculine Logos and Spirit, panels of judges and unyielding patriarchs, my nights were accompanied by such animus figures as these: a greengrocer who invited me to contemplate the night sky; an African chieftain who objected to my "made-up" feminine persona; a revolutionary pilot who brought our plane safely to earth in a forest clearing; a construction foreman who took me on a tour of a building under renovation. I remember most fondly "Mr. Bones," a skeletal figure who offered to instruct me in the arts of love (and death?); and the night march of frog musicians, drumming and tooting through a "bourgeois" neighborhood, waking the people and calling in basso profundo voices, inviting one and all to a religious rite in celebration of sex. (Meanwhile, the "feminine" figures included a warrior queen, an abbess, and a figure I took to be the Blessed Virgin, these and other female images of primary authority in their realms, both spiritual and worldly.) In spite of all this, I continued to try to think in the terms presented in my studies and by my analyst, and then, only then, the animus grew hostile, indifferent or threatening robbery and rape. It took a while, and the later additional evidence provided by a number of female analysands, before I began more consciously to restructure my thinking to match the images, the facts presented by psyche.

In the case of the conventionally "feminine" woman, the discovery and integration of qualities named masculine will have to contend with her fear of loss, not only of feminine gender persona, but of all possibility of a friendly relationship with an ultimate authority experienced as masculine. For her, the question of the relationship between masculine and feminine in the soul may prove even more difficult to resolve. The first task must be the destruction of her refuge from full adulthood, her place in the Father's house, and the negative animus works to this end. In protest against a one-sided expression of "the feminine," excluded from honored participation in the inner community and expression in the outer world, juvenile delinquent or Mafia don, he attacks.

The more she succumbs to her fear of his attacks, resisting her rage, denying her fierce desires, striving to please, the stronger and more malicious he grows. He accuses, he blames, and then blames again for the paralysis induced by his accusations. If she strives for the perfection of performance he seems to demand, she will exhaust herself and find him waiting to sneer at her efforts, her exhaustion, her "weakness." In his most potent and insidious form, he "possesses" her, defeating entirely her efforts to enact the gracious, winning, self-sacrificial femininity, the sexually desirable femininity she believes is her only salvation. Then he will proclaim her unlovable, and she will have ample evidence in her dealings with the world that what he says is true. If his power grows unchecked, he may well drive her to her death. In this dream he appears in a triumph almost complete:

> Dream: *My father and a stronger, darker man behind him are shooting down a group of many kittens. Some of the kittens do not die, and my father gives me the gun. I have to shoot the survivors one by one until there is only one left. It is so hurt and bleeding that I think perhaps it should die, too. But I take it and tell my father I will not kill it, I'll keep it to remind me of what I have done.*

Yet the woman most demoralized by a negative animus may behave as though she loves the brute. She believes in his "high standards," she hopes against hope one day to please him, she cannot give him up. Why? Because he is her only experience of power. He retains it because in her world his power, the power of the Fathers, has been felt as the only legitimate authority. But finally and most crucially, he retains his power because the significant women in her world had little, the little they had was derived from men, and it was seldom if ever used in her behalf. For such a woman, the experience of power, the claim to authority, are the most deeply and darkly "other" of all her possibilities.

As did Jung, our culture is inclined to feel love and power to be mutually exclusive concerns, as though love were not a power in itself, as though power could not be expressed with love. Consequently, claiming the central importance of love, women are very loathe to recognize and own personal power. It seems to involve unbearable responsibilities; it makes us the target of dark suspicions. Nevertheless, it is commonly said that we are powerful indeed, especially in the lives of our men and our children. Our power, of course, is most noted when it goes awry, producing ill effects. Women are admonished about their power, warned about their power, instructed by our myth on how to use it: in a self-forgetful, self-effacing, self-surrendering way. No one seems to note the paradox. But power which is without the ease of authority, which does not flow gladly and consciously from the Self, which is not felt to be legitimate, will flow inward, draw others close and strive to hold them fast. When others flee from her, it can fuel the sneak attacks of passive aggression, erupt in hysterical rage, produce depression and despair. Power denied will not be responsibly deployed, enjoyed, or used creatively. It will be projected onto men, as saviors or abusers, and experienced within as tormentor and tyrant, with the possibly extreme effects noted above.

Plainly, the ruthlessness of such an animus compensates the helpless fragility, the denial of rage, that characterize the woman's conscious position. But no one can move immediately to befriend him. She may with luck or grace escape his power, preserve the bloody kitten, but a long, dark journey lies before the woman who says "No" to an ultimate power in animus guise and begins to claim it for herself. All that first preserves her on her journey is the seemingly fragile power of refusal, the last-ditch unwillingness to die or serve the devil, if it costs her her hands. With that commitment, after a time, comes the angel, the dove, the fairy godmother, an angry Aphrodite or the old witch-woman, and, at last, alone except for them, the growth of new, natural hands, the performance of the necessary tasks, the discovery of a power that is not animus, but Self. The true prince, you see, is not the source or the symbol of salvation, but perhaps, sometimes, the prize.

For the woman identified with a feminine persona, a course of animus development, in the sense proposed by Polly Young-Eisendrath and Florence Wiedemann (1987), is certainly required, but the progressive integration of heretofore "masculine" qualities seems always interwoven with a deepening connection to a strengthened and expanding femininity. Such development has not, in my experience, led at last to an experience of androgynous selfhood, but rather to the appropriation of qualities once named masculine, now felt to be inherent to the feminine self. Not uncommonly there is recognition of a pre- (or post-) patriarchal Great Goddess as Self figure, as the archetypal image combining all opposites, containing all potential. I believe it is fundamental to fully effective work with women that the analyst bear in herself or himself an awareness of such an archetypal possibility. In her early appearances, the feminine Self is often disguised, appearing dark and dangerous or simply "disadvantaged." Unless her central role is recognized, the path of individuation will be obscured.

Positive or negative, the animus is the servant of the Self, and he works in furtherance of individuation. As Jung first and often imagined, he compensates the gender persona, pressing toward its differentiation from gender identity, driving or encouraging the feminine ego toward an encounter with its source, the feminine Self. Do we not all discover, in fact, considerable variety in the qualities displayed by animus figures today? Many have very little apparent connection with an airy spirit, a sunny intellect. Many are anything but heroic, display no majestic command of meaning. Sometimes they are simply dull and

recalcitrant, seemingly insistent upon assuming for themselves no enabling or validating authority. Often among contemporary women, animus figures are Dionysian in behavior and bearing, earthy, sensual,
inviting (or threatening) orgiastic surrender to chaos. Yet these are all
clearly masculine figures; Dionysus, remember, was first called "effeminate" by patriarchal Greeks. What, then, does animus mean but
"other," even his gender incidental to his function in a woman's
psyche?

In the end, it seems to me, we care about the animus because we
have had long and varied relationships with many of his tribe, in both
the inner and the outer experience of our lives, and because we recognize and honor his role in the psychological development of women.
Let us then respect him as he appears, without conceptual prejudice
regarding the qualities we expect him to display or the order in which
they might appear. We might do the same then for the men in our lives
and for ourselves, becoming uncertain not about gender and its significance, nor even about our membership in one or the other, but rather
about the qualities each one may express.

At last—not sooner, no quick leaps suffice on this journey—we
just may discover that the place of gender itself is diminished. Then all
the gods and goddesses, the Great Goddess and the Great God, too,
may be seen to beckon us toward a vision like this one of the Huichol
Indians:

> We come on this journey
> To find our life
> For we are all, we are all
> We are all the children of
> A brilliant flower, many-colored flower,
> Flaming flower.
> And there is no one, no One,
> There is no one
> Who regrets what we are.

In these observations on the nature and significance of the animus, I have tried to serve a number of interrelated concerns. I would
like now to highlight two fundamental aspects of my position. First, I
am concerned that we make a conceptual space for experience, in all its
diversity. I hope for a space in which recognition and respect for the
image, the emotion, the embodied reality as they appear, are as much
as possible uncompromised by theory.

But I do not imagine we accomplish this by simply dispensing with theory. Rather, the task, for me at least, is to be clear about what I think, perhaps even more about what I have simply assumed or taken on authority about the nature of psyche in women and in men. The way that we think powerfully affects our lives and our work with others. I want a Logos of these matters, and I want it as clear and as logically elegant as possible. I also want it to have a certain flexibility, if you will, a capacity to open and bend to experience and to shift its parameters when that becomes necessary to truth.

I want a Logos informed by Eros, in fact, the servant of Eros, for I give that name to the energy that impels us into life, into manifestation, and into connection with each other. It is the experience of Eros which transforms, and it is the indispensable task of Logos to recognize and further the possibility of that experience. I believe that both Eros and Logos transcend gender; they are neither masculine nor feminine. Both may and do manifest through either gender.

Second, it seems to me that there has been and perhaps remains much effort among us to discover, define, and defend certain mutually exclusive differences between feminine and masculine — that is, between women and men — an effort which leads in our theory to the definitions by content of animus and anima. Our consequent attempt to divorce male from masculine and female from feminine is one of those moves that occurs when we try to preserve a theory. In our anima/animus theory, a cultural theory of gender difference has been wedded to a psychological theory of human wholeness. The awkwardness that we find in the anima/animus theory is due to the fundamental incompatibility of the bride and groom, of the culture with the theory of psyche.

I believe that we do not escape the confines of gender definition by denying its existence and its primary power in ourselves and in our culture. But I think it might be possible to distinguish between gender identity and gender persona. It is gender persona which is a cultural and historical phenomenon. Gender identity is more basic, embodied, and in a sense, in the beginning, empty of content. We have to be taught what gender identity means, what it implies for our lives. When we have learned this cultural lesson, we have acquired a gender persona.

Of course, we care first about gender, however defined, because we are born into one of two sexes, and the social and familial pressure creative of a gender persona is almost overwhelming. But persona, while it must draw upon archetypal possibilities, is only a selection among those possibilities, a selection designed to gain our acceptance in a specific collective. We are required to "prove" our gender by appropriate performance, rather than to discover its authentic archetypal range, and what is inappropriate to the persona is left not only to shadow, but also to anima/animus. We are strongly encouraged to identify with the gender persona and inclined to identify gender persona qualities with femininity or masculinity per se. However, the arrangements of society, which have made simplified, mutually exclusive visions of the genders easy to grasp and to bear, are shifting, and the existence of quite varied understandings of masculine and feminine capabilities and qualities is ever more difficult to ignore. When naming and definition are at odds with experience, it is time to reconsider our definitions, time, I believe, to restore the animus to the original grandeur of his compensatory function, unimpeded by attributions of specific "content."

It may be naive on my part to imagine that if we think differently, we can live differently. But at the very least, it seems to me, we can think differently if the facts seem to require it. What I am suggesting is that we give feminine back to women and masculine back to men. Then we may allow our experience of ourselves as women and as men to redefine these terms, *masculine* and *feminine*. Insofar as gender differences are real and basic, they can be trusted ultimately to announce themselves. They do not need our ego defenses, our rigid, dichotomizing, culture-bound definitions to make them or preserve them.

Does it occur to you, as it does to me, that Jungian theory and practice are founded in part upon a necessity that may not be eternal? I mean, of course, the necessity to heal a split which is a cultural creation: the split as we have known it between feminine and masculine as they have been defined. So much of our fear of ourselves and each other is the product of our repression of an otherness which, lo and behold, we are led to discover is not after all truly Other. We discover that these inclinations, these aptitudes, these weaknesses and strengths, possibilities of all kinds both light and dark, qualities we had known perhaps only in projection, belong after all to ourselves. We thought we could not fully and freely live this otherness, but we discover instead that we can and must. As women, we find we are also what we had believed was masculine; as men, we discover we are also feminine.

Then what is the use of insisting upon the old definitions of the genders? If our lives do not support the old definitions, if the gods and goddesses do not require them, then why do we?

There appears to me to be only a conventional necessity remaining, a habit of the mind. But as theoreticians of the mind, surely we should not rest our thought on habit and convention. As healers of the soul, surely we should make the maximum possible conceptual room for the manifestations of the soul. So, say I, let us suspend all attempts to define gender essence. Let anima and animus be recognized again as appearances — archetypal appearances, perhaps, but not essentially, primarily, of gender. They are appearances, rather, of archetypal human possibilities, with gender only secondary and incidental to their appearance in a given soul. Although we participate in the culture and try to heal its casualties (ourselves included), perhaps we need not repeat and reinforce it in our theory.

There is objective ground for the recognition of quite varied manifestations of gender. You may look, if you will, beyond our own myth, even beyond the Greeks, to the expressions by both masculine and feminine deities of the full range of archetypal possibility: earth and sky, lunar wisdom and solar knowledge, suffering and triumph, love and rage, above and below, life and death — all these and more, expressed now in one gender form, now in the other. Seeing in this way, we may find room and validation for each life and each vision. I can then begin to acknowledge and value the subjective ground of your vision, its force and importance in your life, and permit with less prejudice its possible relevance to mine.

My own life, my own experience in analysis and analytic work with others, has sensitized me to the limitations of traditional gender definitions. I feel I used up a lot of time and energy in overcoming them, and that really annoys me. It is time and effort that might have been more happily employed. But out of that life, that struggle to live and to know more clearly, come the thoughts I have offered here for discussion. It is important to find freer ways to live within patriarchy, but I'm not content with that. I admit I want to change it, in me and in the world.

Let me close then with this vision of syzygy. The two here are not animus and anima, but, in my view, masculine and feminine Self figures, each complete, containing all potential. It is, after all, in the Self that we may discover at last the range of our possibilities as gendered beings. This vision was inspired by my reading of Heinrich Zimmer's study of East Indian art and symbol (1972). Note then, this is my report of Zimmer's report of aspects of Indian myth.

It seems there is a god, creator and destroyer of all the worlds. Not once, but many times, the god has brought forth a universe with all its myriad forms. Many times he has danced in the flames of its awful destruction. Sometimes the god is called Siva, and his power to create is gathered in a stillness, the retention of semen, of unrevealed potential, and displayed in the erect and potent phallus. When the god ejaculates, worlds are made manifest. Those through whom the god may be revealed will do the same.

It seems there is a goddess, creator and destroyer of all the worlds. Not once, but many times, the goddess has brought forth, pouring her creative power into a universe, giving life and form to all its manifestations. Many times she has eaten it all back, devouring and destroying, only to create again. Sometimes she is called Sakti, and her power to create is revealed in her stillness, seated upon a lotus throne in the center of a golden isle, in the center of an ocean of unrevealed potential. When the goddess gives birth, the worlds of being and becoming are revealed. Those through whom the goddess is revealed may do likewise.

And sometimes Siva and Sakti sit together in passionate exchange, each in turn asking and answering questions of the other, not complementary in their dialogue, but cocreative of wisdom.

We who are their children may listen, if we will, and grow wise in our turn. Trusting ourselves and each other more, the real differences among us can emerge and be savored. They are the Two, but we are the many, and we each may discover, not The Other, one and only, but many others, with whom the dance, the dialogue of life, becomes ever more subtle, nuanced, and varied.

References

Jung, C. G. 1921. The problem of types in classical and medieval thought. In *CW* 6:8–66. Princeton, N.J.: Princeton University Press, 1921.

————. 1916. The structure of the unconscious. In *CW* 7:269–304. Princeton, N.J.: Princeton University Press, 1966.

————. 1927. Woman in Europe. In *CW* 10:113–133. Princeton, N.J.: Princeton University Press, 1970.

————. 1928. The relations between the ego and the unconscious. In *CW* 7:123–227. Princeton, N.J.: Princeton University Press, 1966.

————. 1951. The syzygy: anima and animus. In *CW* 9ii:11–22. Princeton, N.J.: Princeton University Press, 1968.

Jung, E. 1957. *Animus and the Anima*. Dallas: Spring Publications.

McGuire, W., ed. 1989. *Analytical Psychology: Notes of the Seminar Given in 1925 by C. G. Jung*. Princeton, N.J.: Princeton University Press.

Young-Eisendrath, P., and Wiedemann, F. 1987. *Female Authority: Empowering Women Through Psychotherapy*. New York: The Guilford Press.

Zimmer, H. 1972. *Myths and Symbols in Indian Art and Civilization*. Joseph Campbell, ed. Princeton, N.J.: Princeton University Press.

The Imaginal at Crossings: A Soul's View of Organizational and Individual Analysis

Pilar Montero

In the here and now, as always, the two meet. It is noon, the sun is poised at its zenith, reflecting its golden fire on the halcyon ocean beneath. The water splashes against a wide window, the glass eye through which Diotima surveys the sparkling aureola before her. A knock at the door disrupts her meditation. She eagerly opens it to the poet, Salnacious. For a spell now, they have met regularly at this time to discuss psychotherapy and the arts, and they have become true friends. He is most intrigued by the Jungian orientation and gladly engages in the ongoing dialogue with Diotima, the analyst.

SAL: Hello, Dio! Once again I marvel at your wondrous home nestled between land and sea. It seems most fitting a setting for the topic we have been uncovering. I mean the soul, of course.

DIO: Welcome, Sal. I confess I am eager to begin and have given much thought to the questions you have raised which have

Pilar Montero, Ph.D., is a Jungian analyst in private practice in San Francisco and a social systems consultant/director in group relations conferences. Upcoming publications include "The Archetypal Base of Group Experience" in [A2]The Family: Personal, Cultural and Archetypal Dimensions[A1].

led us to this theme. But first let us perch on the veranda as usual.

They sit facing the wide, watery expanse, grateful for this day.

DIO: I had a dream early this week that I and someone who looked very much like you were digging gold out of a large hole we had made in my back yard. We were very enterprising and content at our task. The dream lured me into a flurry of intellectual activity, and I have actually prepared a whole talk on the *imaginal* just for you. Today, I am compelled to elaborate the concept and apply it to an imaginary social system in transition and to our understanding of clinical work considering a case.

SAL: I am flattered and pleased. Your dream frames our meetings and awakens in me a sense of the mythological. It is as if we can spin universal meanings forever which can only be known in the still moment of the turning point, the now in us. T. S. Eliot's poetry expresses what I sense from you. He conveys our limitations and possibilities in the beautiful language he masters. For example, in "Burnt Norton," he says:

Go said the bird, for the leaves were full of children,
Hidden excitedly, containing laughter.
Go, go, go, said the bird: human kind
Cannot bear very much reality.
Time past and time future
What might have been and what has been
Point to one end, which is always present.

(Eliot, p. 186)

DIO: You have quoted from one of my favorite poems and communicate the mood and meaning of what I want to say, which is so difficult to impart linearly but so easily captured in mythology, dreams, music, and the various art forms. Jung made this point frequently as he strove to articulate a psychology with soul. For him, the soul found meaning in the embodied, so it was impossible to have soul without spirit and either of these without body. They threaded endlessly into each other through his mind-fingers as he wove a psychological tapestry, in part extracted and synthesized from numerous religions and philosophical systems the world over and across time.

I want to focus on the imaginal because that is the perspective which I think best transmits the heart of Jungian psychology. Also, because it allows us to examine a phenomenon that has plagued mankind but seems very salient this era. I refer to the extent to which people have externalized and feel victimized by the archetypal forces activated in their social environment. My sense is that, by now, it has become easier for people to flow with what feels like their inner world, despite its spooks and its misery, than to keep experiencing the dangers and pressures in institutions and the streets which can evoke unbearable emotions like impotence, helplessness, fear, and rage. This may be because we have not evolved a way to release imagination as a true path which can open and alter our vista. Then, our panorama, could be raised to the mythological level where soul and spirit rule and could be transformed by the change in the perspective and attitude.

The term *imaginal* comes from a paper by Henry Corbin called "The *Mundus Imaginalis* or the Imaginary and the Imaginal" (1971). Since then, analysts such as James Hillman, Andrew Samuels and Nathan Schwartz-Salant have used it to further our understanding of the transference and countertransference phenomena. The *mundus imaginalis* refers to a world that lies between that of the senses and the more rarified, intelligible realm of pure spirit. This sphere is the place of subtle-body phenomena and is known and traveled by means of the imaginal function which, in our circumscribed analytical work, we refer to as active imagination.

This perspective takes the connecting medium for granted. It says: people who enter into relationship are already united. It is the very air they breathe. They immediately have shared images. What is left is to make these aware. It differs from most psychologies today. For example, take Melanie Klein's concept of projective identification, which starts out with separate objects, you and me, and wants to know how the contents of one get into the other. They begin with individualized, atomized units and the question of how these can relate to each other and not to their ontological interrelatedness. The question then is how is one receptive to these images, for to be aware of an object when not perceiving out of a compartmentalized ego is to have these images already present. They are seen with the soul based on the psychoid unconscious where distinctions do not appear. That is the *mundus imaginalis*, the ether that connects all.

SAL: This sounds very much like Taoism-Zen, where subject and object are in strange sympathy to each other (which is what they call compassion). For example, you know a tree if you have an immediate, inner, spontaneous understanding of the tree. The function of their poetry is to evoke in the listener the embodied image related to the poem's content, say death, your frisky disposition, passage of time, etc. Most are about nature and embody the inner image of that aspect of nature, not to objectify it but to help your soul enter into that region. This is a conscious artistic act, and it is understood that the value of the poem is in the image it evokes in your own body-mind. For example:

The wild geese do not intend to cast their reflection.
The water has no mind to receive their image.
(Ross 1960, p.258)

This is a poem that stills you, that fills your body with a sense of tranquillity; no effort, no striving, but pure reflection. Also, there is no subject (geese) or object (water) but an interfusion of the two. The total effortless resonance of geese with water reveals the interconnectedness of the *mundus imaginalis*. In the visual arts, a good example would be Morris Graves. Do you recall his triptich painting of the crane fishing? The fish is her eye, and it triggers your own feelings when you go hunting for food, the image in your eye.

DIO: That is precisely what I mean. It is an attitude to life, akin to the one Jung described in his last stage of the *coniunctio* in *Mysterium Coniunctionis*. We psychotherapists need to be reminded that it is the soul that is forged in analysis. From the perspective of ego, we get a fragmented world, the one familiar to us twentieth-century Westerners who suffer daily the abuses our species inflicts on the earth and each other. Our hearts and thoughts have been captured by a philosophical-scientific view that largely studies parts for their own sake and splits the mind from the body to our obvious environmental detriment, though technological gain. Currently, physicists such as David Bohm, via his notions of the implicate order of the universe, the enfolding and unfolding of meaning, remind us of Jung's vision and courage when he formulated an equivalence of meaning between the psychic and the physical and supported the organic vs. the mechanistic approach. In many of his writings and very explicitly in his article on "Synchronicity, An Acausal Connecting Principle," Jung argues for the Eastern view that emphasizes wholeness and the meaningful relationship between parts and wholes in the way that the *I Ching* brings things together as if by chance. David Bohm tries to show us concretely by means of the hologram that the image of the whole is reflected in each of the parts that comprise it (Bohm 1985, p. 10). From a social systems perspective, this is similar to the way group theorists of the Tavistock tradition view groups as entities embedded in larger contexts which they mirror and for which they play a meaningful role not unlike the way their members are expressive aspects serving functions for that unit of which they are a part.

My point is that there are many perspectives. The ego's perspective splits and then tries to put the pieces together normally using some third variable. This is the approach I would associate most closely to body and to a tendency to concretize and literalize experience and to focus on the "I" and its needs and wishes. When Jungian-inspired thinkers talk of the anima and animus as gender phenomena inside individuals of the opposite sex, the orientation is most crudely at this level. In caricature, the archetype of the ego is the hero, and he views the anima as a woman to conquer and possess and the Self as an old man who has authority, can offer guidance, provides protection, and doles out punishment. In contrast to the ego's view is the vantage point of the Self. Here we have unity and the clear, pure light beyond human awareness which encompasses both the unconscious and the conscious. Jung's metaphysics state we cannot know absolute reality directly but via images and symbols. We have an *imago dei* and no direct access to any archetype per se. So we can never know the true nature of anything. This takes us directly to soul, for it is in the realm of the imaginal par excellence where we do knowing that is related and contextual. Let me quote what Jung says in his introduction to the *Tibetan Book of the Dead*:

> the creative ground of all metaphysical assertion is consciousness as the invisible, intangible manifestation of the soul. (Evans-Wentz 1960, p. xxxix)

or:

> It is the soul which, by the divine power inherent in it, makes the metaphysical assertion; it posits the distinctions between metaphysical entities. Not only is it the condition of all metaphysical reality, it is that realty. (Jung 1960, p. XXXVIII)

SAL: This sounds very Buddhist to me. Here Jung seems to be equating soul with the archetypes of the collective unconscious, which, in line with what you posit as pertinent to the *mundus imaginalis*, highlights interdependence. In Buddhist thought, everything is dependent on everything else, and the absolute and eternal coexist with the temporal and the relative.

DIO: Yes, also, it follows that it is the soul that is being taught and shaped by our life experience. We do not have to postulate the supratemporality of the soul, tempting as this may be given its consonance with religious systems everywhere, but this viewpoint does dethrone the ego as the sole center of consciousness to that of a laborer, a tool to facilitate the awareness being forged and shaped at the level of soul.

Furthermore, an important issue that gets dealt with from the perspective of the imaginal is what is inner and what is outer reality. Here what is inside or outside the individual are part of the same phenomena. We do not contain soul or spirit but rather images and thoughts come to us, in fact, locate us, and are the texture and context of our awareness.

I have been referring to soul as an imaginal matrix and the *mundulus imaginalis* as its spiritual dimension, but the function, the organ if you will, which allows for the imagining to happen needs to be mentioned. James Hillman writes very broadly, fully, and creatively about images, and in his book, *Anima: An Anatomy of a Personified Notion*, he not only pulls together what Jung has said about this notion, but describes her as a faculty for imagination. He portrays her as the bridge to the unknown and the unknowable. She leads to interiority, by which is not meant what is inside the individual but the capacity to enter an image, phenomenal or otherwise, and allow it to deliver its own meanings, affects, and intrarelationships. Thus, she mediates the embodied and the divine, the individual and the collective. Furthermore, he says she is the life behind consciousness which cannot be fully integrated but from whence it arises. And, she is the reflective partner to any pair (say, ego, animus, or wise old man) and, more generally, the moment of reflection to any aspect of nature. In fact, she is the animating vital principle in physis, the *scintillae* or divine sparks in matter which alchemists called the *anima mundi*. But she does not happen alone. Her brother consort, the animus, is always in relationship with her.

The animus is generally associated with spirit, logos, the active, the impersonal and objective, and as the mediator to the unconscious depths. Thomas Moore, in his article "Animus Mundi, or the Bull at the Center of the World," points out that by placing the animus at the core of his theory, Jung gave thought a basis in imagination. He indicates that thought itself is not a matter of consciousness or ego, but comes of its own accord and that thoughts have "an imaginal matrix, an ambiance of images, therefore, they have depth and always signify more than 'I' mean by them" (Moore 1987, p. 116). His position is consonant with the subtle body, imaginal body, vision of the *mundus imaginalis* which says that spirit locates us. In Henry Corbin's words, "spiritual reality itself is the 'where' of all things" (Corbin 1971, p. 5). From this perspective, the animus is beyond thought, and, as spirit, it is that which makes a person aware. Thomas Moore (like Corbin and Hillman) describes it as the expressive heart and opens up the notion of including character and other attributes such as will and passion which are considered expressive outpourings. Furthermore, as a spiritual force, the animus can be recognized as a creative daimon, an ancestral spirit, or, more transpersonally, as a divinity or good discerned and defined by its phenomenal face and voice.

SAL: Let me summarize some of what you are saying. It seems the realm of the imaginal is a spiritual world where a soul type of

consciousness exists which is characterized by images in contextual interdependence. This is not another world but a
capacity to see what is already present in the here and now but
with the third eye. That is, with an attitude and perspective
that is usually hard won but can be developed given a certain
spiritual discipline such as that which Jungian analysis imparts
in the course of treatment. Active imagination, which connects the person with the image, is the method Jung most
favors to move the individual through the stages of the con-
junction. These culminate in the last stage, which sounds very
much like being in the *mundus imaginalis*, the bridging
world, all the time. It seems the closer the soul is to matter,
the more its forms are multiple and colorful. That is, the more
it affiliates with the world of the senses and affects, the more
the mediating images are garbed in all the beauty and ugli-
ness the human species can experience. This in contrast to the
blinding light of the Atman or the Self, which includes the
unknowable and the conscious as unity. So you have oneness
from the vantage point of the Self and multiplicity from the
empirical, the embodied, the ego's panorama and the syzygy,
the soul-spirit vantage point, moving from one end of this
spectrum to the other, fashioning and illuminating, occasion-
ing and envisioning all the while.

DIO: Right. The syzygy is the image for the mythological brother-
-sister pair that represents in the *hieros gamos* (sacred marriage) the potential for the integration and union of any
polarity in whatever friendly or oppositional relationship to
each other they may be. And, yes, I would say that being
takes on duality as its unit, and gender as its favorite, most
profound, incarnation of any polarity, when the living is done
in the imaginal dimension of existence. Mostly people seem
blind to this realm, which used to be the everyday, animistic
perception of our primeval ancestors. Today, the drabness of a
mechanistic, persona-type world is rarely punctured for most,
but it does happen when the soul world leaps out to be seen at
times of major transitions. The images then are so intense
they awaken affects which break down basic defenses and
move individuals and social systems to a different level of
awareness despite their entrenchments in the familiar.

Joseph Henderson, Murray Stein, Daniel Levinson, Jung himself, are some of the few who have addressed and amplified the events and experiences that accompany periods of crossings in individual lives. They have affirmed that there is an archetypal base to transitions such as adult development ones which happen in the years of passage from one decade to the next. The midlife has received most attention but the phenomenon has been described in reference to initiations of all kinds including analysis, which Jung considered the only initiation process still alive and practiced in the West today (Evan-Wentz 1960, p. xi). I think it is possible to view a whole social system in motion and not just individuals. The process is as follows. It begins with the dying of the old, familiar ways. Then comes a period of time (liminal) when the deities, which inhabit the deepest layers of the psyche, are encountered and take over. Rituals that help contain and facilitate facing the death-dealing archetypes and mobilize the rebirth ones are helpful. Finally, the person or system reemerges into its daily routine but with an expanded, new attitude with which to meet it. As in initiations, the process needs to be regarded as cyclical until all heroism and tricksterism has been refined away, leaving the true adept, who learns to return to the regular order of life as soon as possible and not stay inflated at some phase of enlightenment.

A collective such as a Jung institute can be seen as an organic whole in influential reciprocity with the society in which it is embedded. It is a peculiar system in that it is characterized by transferential ties. Like-minded people come together and formally use each other as analysts, patients, teachers, and students and informally develop an extensive network of friendships, marriages, and affairs of all kinds. An imaginal body can be said to encase and leaven communication in such a place. Paradoxically, the *mundus imaginalis* is most active in settings where relationships are so incestuously intertwined that the subtle-body phenomenon is most real and, therefore, defenses are erected not to see it. The perception of this realm is blocked by the apparent threat of loss of boundaries and dissolution in it.

The functioning of the organization is greatly affected by this atmosphere and so is the analytical work carried out by its members, which does not happen in a vacuum but is influenced by the context in which it takes place. The container itself, shaped by the values, beliefs, theories, attitudes, affects, and pressures which rule us and our interactions with patients can be contaminated. Its boundaries can be threatened by events that enter it from the "outside" and which, at their most detrimental, can force the analyst to disclose his or her humanity above and beyond what the analytical cover provides to protect the patient and allow for maximum freedom to imagine and project. Yet, in all humility, we have to admit that our interconnections are so complex that even at the quietest of times we need to keep an eye on the management of our sentient ties and weave their unconscious sway into the meanings elucidated as we toil. This in itself is an illusion, for we are the stuff of sentient ties.

Let us imagine a Jungian community which, like many others, has been undergoing a major transition and, therefore, can be a striking example of the *mundus imaginalis* in action. As our story opens, there are precipitating factors propelling the events about to happen which fuel the dying that has started to become noticeable to all. Unable to disclose confidentialities and reluctant to use power which is feared as injurious to self and others, the norm has been to leave a void where authority should be heard and to lean on sentient ties to do the work. As a result, there has been a dramatic unconscious increase in size, and individuals have become alienated and unfamiliar to each other. Groups and their disruptive processes have begun to take firm hold as the new organizational unit. Because this is anathema to Jungians, who hold the primacy of the individual central, the tendency has been not to give credence to this outgrowth, to remain ignorant of group dynamics, and to despair when it has become obvious that the training program is suffused with vociferous group and intergroup activity as if groups and not individuals were being initiated. Similarly, finances have not been tended to consciously enough, and the proliferation in numbers of people and programs have depleted resources and ended the era of affluence the institution has enjoyed. Finally, it is a period of generational change. The founding fathers who knew Jung, and more generally the older generation who created and raised that society of analysts, are retiring, ill or looking aged and less involved. Sons and daughters are increasingly taking over and the place is loosing its parental order as brothers and sisters eye each other lovingly and suspiciously, try to figure out what to do, and graciously try not to compete. Formal meetings among analysts have become large group phenomena so that the typical tendency for subgroups to form and for members to feel alienated and paranoid is enhanced. People have become more fearful of soul talk and intimacy, and individual expression has been getting submerged under persona professional pronouncements.

The climate is ripe for strife and it erupts, sending the system far into the underworld. The image evoked is that of the soul of this group in the arms of Hermes, for it is Hermes who rules the experience of liminality itself, the territory where soul is most free from its attachments, able to enter the world of the dead and converse with other souls. Murray Stein eloquently describes the role of Hermes as the god of transitions and guide of souls in his book, *In Midlife*. He describes liminality as follows.

> Liminality, Hermes' home, occurs when the ego is separated from a fixed sense of who it is and has been, of where it comes from and its history, of where it is going and its future, when the ego floats through ambiguous spaces in a sense of unbounded time, through a territory of unclear boundaries and uncertain edges; when it is disidentified from the inner images that have sustained it and given it a sense of purpose. Then the unconscious is disturbed in its archetypal layers, and the Self is constellated to send messages: big dreams, vivid and powerful intuitions, fantasies and synchronistic and symbolic events. The function of these messages is to lead the ego forward, and this guidance helps it to do what it has to do, whether this is to enter liminality further or, later, to emerge out of it. (Stein 1983, p. 22)

This is a rather accurate description of the psychological state of the community when the news breaks out in a public forum, voiced by the candidate in question, that she has been having sexual relations with her analyst, and there are serious breaches of confidentiality involved. One day life is seemingly as usual and, in a flash, this piece of news breaks through the veil of deception and the system goes from tranquility to turbulence. An image of a couple that so accurately captures the deepest shadow has been incarnated and sits at the center of the institute as if the Self has vomited up a mythological pair that embodies the monstrous and hits everyone over the head with it. The institute has entered liminality as if Hermes, god of intimacy, sharing, and transference (Stein 1983, p. 131), has arrived as messenger of the Self to awaken people to the soul sacrifice that has been going on. Under secular rule, the sacred attitude has been disregarded, and it now explodes into awareness as a hideous indigestible image, and everyone gets sucked in.

SAL: Your account reminds me of the passage through death the soul transits according to the *Tibetan Book of the Dead*. The individual is dead so, in its subtle-body state as a soul, it encounters the wondrous and wrathful divinities during its passage through the *Bardos* back to life. It is warned over and over again not to take the experiences and affective states these divinities evoke as real because if so, it is lured into *Sangsara* and a new incarnation where it has to work its karma further. The aim, of course, is release from the overall cycle of life and death but it seems similar to what I hear you say about the institute. It is being pulled into a projective state by a very suggestive image of death and finds itself in the *mundus imaginalis*, its forgotten world. Its job is to see that that is where it stands in the here and now and to follow the course of the performance as a way to recapture a vision it has lost. Great playwrights such as Shakespeare repeatedly highlight the dramatic structure of existence in order to focus consciousness on the roles and scenes of our lives. For example, in *Hamlet*, Hamlet stages a play within a play to bring consciousness to his mother and his uncle, her current husband and the murderer of his father. He muses:

> . . . the play's the thing
> Wherein I'll catch the conscience of the king.
> (Shakespeare 1944, p. 204)

Or, more poignantly in *Macbeth*, after his wife's death, the grieving king delivers these famous lines:

> . . . Out, out, brief candle!
> Life's but a walking shadow, a poor player,
> That struts and frets his hour upon the stage
> And then is heard no more, It is a tale

> Told by an idiot, full of sound and fury,
> Signifying nothing.
>
> (Shakespeare 1944, p. 204)

DIO: That is precisely what I mean. The reaction to the news is a phenomenological occurrence akin to a hologram in vivo. The image of this pair is constellated in everybody and in the community right away and gets carried around, examined, dissected, related to, ejected, etc., intra- and interpsychically for months. The streets have rarely been this active with palaver between dyads and friendship groups. It is the closest to an ancient Athenian marketplace atmosphere the locality has seen, and not only gossip but constructive thoughts and feelings have been exchanged widely. In fact, one very remarkable experience has been the plurality of divergent points of view expressed even by friends who expect to think alike. The spirit world has forced a widening of consciousness by fostering the shaping and assimilation of alternative points of view to the familiar ego entrenchments. Included, of course, are the clarifications and obfuscations that have landed in and arisen from analytical and supervisory containers which have, in turn, fermented the social brew.

SAL: This is very reminiscent of the function the chorus serves in ancient Greek plays. It as if the soul speaks through the ebb and flow of individual opinion its imagistic, metaphoric, and contrapuntal register. Ironies, self-delusions, and insights are woven together, which deepens and adds multiple dimensions to the ongoing drama. The chorus personifies the divine embodied in the human secular conflicts it also witnesses (Steiner 1986, p. 232).

DIO: Yes, what we have before us is akin to a tragic drama. The tragic conflict lies between two planes of being, between two equal rights and truths, not just between two duties or duty vs. passion. This institution is undergoing a transformation not unlike the transition from matrifocal to patrifocal culture which in Athens in 500 B.C. gave rise to its great dramatic tragedies. They had become exhausted by a social system based on kinship bonds and its unending cycles of blood vengeance and were evolving a more male perspective with its impersonal, abstract conception of justice. The institute has

arrived at a turning point where the rule by friendship ties
and family feeling seem to perpetuate destructively covert
unethical behavior, and it now needs to formulate rules of
ethics and confirm the social bodies that can enforce them.
Unfortunately, it sounds good and proper but, in fact, it has
wrenched the members' souls and dislocated them from their
familiar moorings. Rules can serve as guidelines but they
readily become laws. As Jungian analysts, the spirit of our
ancestor, Jung, breathes into us a tolerance for a manner of
being seemingly unorthodox to many. In general, individuals
and the peculiar, sometimes horrid, ways of individuating
previously honored or at least tolerated and contained in the
group, can now be perceived as criminal or perverse and
punishable by the courts of the land if disclosed.

Sophocles' *Antigone* is the tragedy that for me best
captures the dilemma. There seems to be a new reign of the
victim that has entered social systems and the world in
general. Antigone was glorious in her embodiment of the
familial value confronting the necessary violence that
political-social change visits on the experienced inwardness of
being. Antigone's plight is that her choice to give her brother
Polynices proper burial is perceived as an act against the state
by her uncle Creon who now rules Thebes. She is condemned
to death by suffocation in a cave where she hangs herself
instead. However, Creon, too, suffers the death of his son and
his wife as the result of his decree. Everyone is victimized by
the social turning point and the position each upholds. Creon
represents the State where a person, like a soldier, is a role, a
function, and a number to be counted whether dead or alive.
Antigone stands for the familial where there is only one of a
kind and the individual relationship is supreme.

In our imagined institute, a projective system exists
where the Antigones of the larger group are perceived as
being on the side of elitism, privilege, inner rule versus
external authority and the old moral ways. The Creons are
composed of the disenfranchised victims of those analysts,
who are perceived as having abused their power, usually
candidates and women, and those who feel the persona of the
institute has been hurt and support the making of rules and
their clear enforcement through an established judicial
system. It needs to be made clear that the image of the

analyst–candidate violation at the center of the system is indicative of the enormous amount of splitting that is occurring. It is an atmosphere of oppositions and extremes, and it is almost impossible to speak up without being identified with a faction or clique and to be treated as such. The safest majority voice is Creon's, which leaves the Antigones silenced; sometimes by default, mistake, or in the service of justice, they can find themselves persecuted and maligned. The analyst accused of the sexual crime, who resigned right away, belongs in spirit to the Antigone camp, and it has become impossible to discuss the manifold meanings of his deed or himself as a person in any formal forum. His corpse stinks, but he cannot be buried because the situation and what it means cannot be known or handled properly while the polarization persists.

A change of perspective is called for, a look from the eye of the imaginal would help. But this requires time, patience, and a meditative stance that bows to the sacred, the opposite of the busy activity of groups behaving like autonomous, out-of-control complexes that now seem to run the show and which are, in effect, feeling and acting more impotent than empowered. The central image with which the institution has to contend is the opposite of the *hieros gamos*, the brother–sister union implying mutuality and trust. It is framed within an analytical relationship in the middle of the training program and has all the demonic force of the parent–child transference abused. It is a pair that can only fertilize by pulling everyone into the realm of shadow and death. But that is the place where souls can interact with other souls and, by doing so, can alter the creature, possibly integrate Antigone's and Creon's conflicted vantage points.

Antigone may hold some answers. I wonder about secrets. For example, did she know the nature of her parents', Oedipus and Jocasta, relationship and did this set her aside from mankind? The identified victims I have known have an irresistible need to end their alienation by speaking their verity. Innocence is irreconcilable with human action but only in action is there moral identity Victims can seem uncontained, uncaring of others, emotional and biased in their archetypal passion. But their epiphany is in the truth they herald. There is self-recognition in fury. Rationality is shed and composure cast off as the persons are consumed by the primal wildfires compelling them to seek out and wrestle with the gods. Their functions are to articulate and evoke the world of the dead. Antigone is brought near to the Dionysian with its ecstatic bent to self-destruction but Creon embodies the kind of morality that cannot come to terms with death. He wants to bar from the secular city the sacred energies of the underworld, of the chthonic, which is precisely the institute's dilemma. The analyst in question is silenced by his absence, the confidentiality of his role, and the conspiracy not to discuss him in any group setting. This death is accepted but burial refused and the Antigones in their midst feel intimidated to perform and end up more like her sister Ismenes, who, for the sake of self-preservation, went along with Creon. Victims who surface in an institute undergoing this type of transformation may clamor their pain in angry frustration but, since their issues are not penetrable in public forums, they remain unprotected despite the best intentions to do otherwise. The silence gives tacit approval to what is going on and mystifies those who participate in these groups characterized by flight-type dynamics. Beyond the danger of contamination of transferential, confidential relationships by the exposure which follows speaking up, one reason for the silence is the fact that every human being has secrets they do not want divulged. No matter how moral the people gathered, the topic alone awakens in each psyche the phantom of the illicit. The illicit is a boundary that guards the individual from merging with the group. It is the part of the "me" no one must know and as such keeps my illusion of individuality and separateness from those others and from the extraordinarily powerful energy that wants to connect and submerge one and all. This is soul pulling both ways. On the one hand, she says, "You are unique," and on the other, she affirms we are all of the same stuff and dangerously interchangeable.

Another peril lurks which Arthur Colman, who has done extensive and creative work with groups, skillfully describes in a paper called "Individuation, the Scapegoat and the Group," presented at a symposium sponsored by the C. G. Jung Institute of Chicago in 1987. He elaborates on the idea that groups are in pursuit of wholeness not unlike individuating individuals. If cohesion and unity is threatened, a group may defend itself by invoking a scapegoat dynamic. Then, not only will individuals be put in this role and split off to carry the unwanted, indigestible shadow parts of the group, but there is a danger of contagion so that those perceived as affiliated with the scapegoat are themselves soiled. Silence gives passive support to this dangerous process. At the institute, there is an ambience where the hazards of merger are as pronounced as those of differentiation. It is dangerous to discuss with imagination what goes on in sex with patients without drawing suspicion as if an offender or a potential one were at large again. Also, distrust and fear can foster a sheep mentality whereby everyone's analytical orientation and work are indistinguishably characterized by a developmental framework with true regard for the power of the narcissistic transference. It is as if the marvelous peacock tail of transferential possibilities could be reduced to the few, albeit important, feathers which represent the parent–child dimension with its themes of dominance–submission and dependence–independence. "Group-think" stands in the way of individuation because it leaves unconscious what needs to be grappled with to move the system forward. I think the way out for these groups is to stay with whatever images arise in the "here and now" and let these soul parts dialogue with the people present. This requires no disclosures and no confessions. As in analysis, it takes time, patience, and a true commitment to the imaginal and its sacred moorings to engage in active imagination and to let the dream direct the work. This is as true for groups as it is for dyads.

How else can *Antigone* be a guide through this dark phase? In the play, Tiresias enters to warn Creon of his error. His message is protective of Antigone and against the "Self-will, we know, incurs the charge of folly" (Hadas 1965, p. 104). He informs Creon that prophesies suggest he will be punished for his decree but he comes too late to save her life. Tiresias, as the wise old man with double sight, is a symbol of the Self. It is as if the young anima and he are a pair and together can unlock the dangerous conflict by bringing a new attitude. Tiresias, with his knowledge of the divine and the secular, the masculine and the feminine, is an arbiter of truth and wisdom. To me this suggests the freedom to allow for diversity instead of getting locked into any one position. There is an ego consciousness, persona consciousness, a soul consciousness, a spirit consciousness, a Self consciousness to say the least. In fact, one could say there is consciousness in potentia in all things, and there is release in being able to move flexibly within and between realms of being. It appears that as people age, the soul-spirit and Self perspectives become more pronounced but all are needed to fulfill our daily lives.

SAL: The image which has been leaping into my mind is Chinnamasta who is a goddess popular in Tantric and Tibetan Buddhism and in Hindu mythology (Kinsley 1986, p. 172). She is usually depicted as standing nude on the back of the female of a copulating couple stretched out on a lotus in a cremation ground. She has decapitated her own head with a sword and she holds it on a platter. The blood from her severed neck spurts out like an overflowing fountain and three red streams gush into her own mouth and those of two female devotees at her side. In the Hindu rendition, the two enjoying sexual intercourse are Kama and Rati, the god of sexual lust and his wife, or Krishna (Vishnu's major incarnation) and Rhada, who hold a prominent place in the pantheon of the gods. Rhada's popularity is due primarily to her impassioned devotion to Krishna, and their love affair in a devotional context is a metaphor for divine–human relationship. Krishna devotees attempt to uncover or develop the Rhada dimension within themselves. Chinnamasta is stunning as a representation of life, sex, and death as a unified interdependent system. Her nakedness suggests that openness and vulnerability are aspects of her strength. Most striking is the reversal whereby the goddess, instead of being nurtured by the blood of some sacrificed human, as is commonly depicted in the images of fierce goddesses such as Kali, feeds herself and her devotees with the vital life spouting from her body. She, in turn, is simultaneously being nourished by the life-force fecundity of the sexual act being consummated under her feet. The cutting of the head reminds me of the extraordinary pain experienced by the victims in the institute and the institute itself when it has felt victimized. I would

Figure 1. Chinnamasta. From Phillip Rawson, *The Art of Tantra* (Greenwich, Conn.: New York Graphics Society, 1973). (C.G. Jung Institute of San Francisco)

venture that the feminine is in anguish but also giving bountifully through its dying.

DIO: The force inherent in an image such as that of Chinnamasta is so great it sparks the *mundus imaginalis* into play. Immediately, I want to warn the institute not to cap the geyser of fresh blood or disperse its flow so that the goddess and the devotees are no longer nourished by it. This fountain of imaginal possibilities is the life supply which can arise from those wounded, monstrous, freakish parts that lead us to the archetypal base of life, the soul matrix, from whence new possibilities arise and old ones are reshaped. It would be tragic to seal over what has been activated with more professional persona resembling a miniaturized facsimile of the governance and adversarial judicial systems of the nation and their obvious deficits. It is an opportunity for the place to fertilize its understanding of analytical work, reassess its mission and realign its structure to match better the needs and trappings of analysts and their work. For example, a chairman and his advisory group, or a pair of leaders, or a troika, could be considered as a model for governance different from the typical president–vice president form. But more significant is the opportunity now available for people to reconnect with the sacred and give it its due place at the center and to stop treating archetypal events only as lodged inside individuals who are bad or sick and need to be punished or cured. By anchoring the forces of existence in the personal alone, it is as if the Jungian lesson that moves from the personal to the objective, because we are already both, has not been learned.

Interiority needs to be differentiated from innerness. The tendency is to think and to experience that what goes on or comes from us is ours and inside of us. The developmental approach goes hand in hand with this view because it affirms the sense of continuity and ownership of the I. It is a perspective lodged in ego consciousness and, if honored as the only one, very limiting. We need to move away from, say, mother and father to their attributes; from actions taken by individuals to the symbolic enactment of a performance in the stage of life; from "my" death to all death as a principle in action. Interiorizing frees up the imaginal, and we find

ourselves in the *mundus imaginalis*, for any image becomes
the doorway to its realm. It is like blowing up a photograph
until every boundary is diffuse or has delivered its connection
with another and the ever-finer details and emerging forms
can be examined. In physics, chaos theorists have studied the
ever-repeating patterns of magnified shapes in the beautifully
depicted Mandelbrot sets which portray these fractals as
infinitely recurring shapes within limited space (Gleick 1987,
pp. 98–118). They are reminiscent of groups because each
meaning has infinite value and all of these meanings are
bounded in one group comprised of individual psyches and
its unfolding collective energy.

The prolific image of the copulating candidate–analyst
dyad in the tabernacle is compost in yet another way. It can be
seen as a misguided ritual for renewal happening in the heart
of the training program. The impulse for sex in analysis can
be to give birth to the child of the soul, which can represent
the quest for transcendence. All people desire to give birth as
they seek immortality; it is as if their souls are pregnant and
search for the union that will deliver them. Also, the outlaw is
closer to the divine in a place where the sacred is occluded.
These must be communications to the institute, which has
served as the egg from whence this image has hatched. I hear
at least three distinct messages. The most pressing has already
been described as the need to wake up to different
consciousness and break out of the ego blinders that
organizational life fosters. Then, as a microcosm of the larger
community, it seems to warn against ignoring gigantic forces,
such as sex and groups, which autonomously proliferate and
grow beyond human control once actively incarnated and
which, once embodied as flesh and blood entities, must be
addressed. The body can be exalted to the level of the sacred
and vice versa but carefully. Lastly, it can be taken as a lesson
to all analysts, who struggle daily with the transformation
process, to beware of the inflations to which we may be prey
as we mediate the divine energies mobilized in our offices.
Jungian theory can be dangerous. The tomb is the womb and
everything tends to become everything else, itself a reflection
of the incestuous arenas, which are the natural condition of
our Jungian institutions. The analytical *modus operandi*
points our efforts to the unknown and unknowable and leaves

us grappling with the fiendish findings, hoping we are grounded enough in the imaginal to manage.

They stroll on the beach as the day wears on. The sun and moon, poised together in the sky, reflect in the wet sand like two gods kissing the center of the world. Framed in beauty, they inquire into each other's souls. She asks about the origins of his name. He responds that "Salnacious" was a parental whim and so likely to lead to banter and intrigue he has always called himself Sal. She amplifies on the meaning of *Sal*, salt, as found in Jung's writings on alchemy. *Sal*, she says, means soul. As the sparks of the *anima mundi*, the vital principle of all things, it is trapped in matter as the human soul is in the body. It is a transcendent potential that correlates with the feminine lunar side, that is, with feelings and moods. *Sal* represents such feelings as the wisdom that comes from insight and understanding and its opposite, the bitterness of disappointment and sorrow. *Luna* and *Sol*, soul and spirit, are the archetypal pair who mate in the mercurial bath as king and queen and give birth to the new consciousness.

Sal notices the wind is rising and the ocean stirring. He has mixed feelings about having his personhood archetyped and responds with a soliloquy on her name. Diotima, he states, comes from Plato's *Symposium*. She is Socrates' anima, so to speak. When it is Socrates' turn to philosophize about erotics at the feast, he deviates from the standard power, phallic sexual attitude of the Greeks of his time to a vista opened to him as a young man by this Manitean woman whose language is of the mystery religions (Downing 1989, p. 247). She speaks of love as stages of initiation which begin with the soul when pregnant, seeking its fulfillment in the beauty of another. Her vision is of mutuality and reciprocity in love. It transforms the lovers so that they recognize that beauty of the body is less desirable than that of the soul. They are opened then to recognize beauty in institutions, laws, knowledge, and wisdom itself. Finally revelation bursts forth at once in a wondrous vision of the very soul of beauty. It is the seeing of beauty itself that is ecstatic and beyond words. It happens through the inner eye of imagination and intuition. You remind me of Socrates, Sal says.

They continue their walk, now and then exchanging intimacies to the beat of the waves, but mostly in silence. In time, Dio continues her discourse on the imaginal but now with a patient in mind.

DIO: It must be obvious to you now that I am interested in the handling of archetypal forces which are experienced as coming from the outside, impersonal and enormous, and the creating

˜of containers that allow for their transformation. As analysts, we are used to following the footprints of meanings that feel inner directed to patients who take us through a panoply of dreams, fantasies, and experiences to the unknown depths. The work is difficult but facilitated by a manner that is mostly receptive. However, it happens that the unusual patient knocks on the door and the preferred and familiar style is challenged simply because it does not always work. I have been meeting with a woman three times a week since 1983 who has required of me ways of being in our sessions that can feel unorthodox and uncomfortable but necessary.

Elize is a lovely, competent, hard-working, humane woman but her connection to herself has been severely damaged so that her Self experience is one of blackness and emptiness. Little joy or nourishment have filtered into that dark place, and she exists like a transient because to go "home" is to die. This is enacted not just as an inner experience but as the reality of her life, and she is always alone at crossings and never at rest. She enters the *mundus imaginalis* but as a blind mute, and our work has been to open this dimension of existence to strengthen her soul against its abusive side.

Her imagination has been cramped since childhood by continuous, terrible, psychological violence inflicted on her by a seriously disturbed, narcissistically wounded, aggressive mother. This mother rarely stops moving and talking so she is always on stage, in sharp contrast to her authoritarian husband, who is cold, distant, and mostly absent. As my patient indicates, her parents are each a pole of the fight–flight dynamic with mother the central performer and father the onlooker who is not even a good audience since he is either hiding behind a newspaper or sleeping. She has felt relentlessly attacked by one and undefended by the other who was more likely to deliver harsh spankings to support his wife's false accusations. Humiliation, shame, self-abuse, fear of rejection, and a disconnection from her erotic nature, especially with men, have been her affective landmarks. Most pronounced, however, is the way she rapidly and easily succumbs to the dramas in her environment. All of life takes on a quality of overbearing largeness that demands her very essence and allows for no negotiation. It is not that she externalizes her inner world, but that all worlds, inner and outer, take her over and run her life. The experience is as if her mother had moved her huge frame backwards into Elize's room, taking up all the space and squashing her flat against the walls.

When I considered sharing with you my work with her, I asked for a dream and got more than I bargained for. That night I had two dreams. The first was about an intruder who entered into my house and scared me out of my wits. I must have had this kind of dream before, but she has them regularly. In fact, her few remembered dreams are so frightening and filled with attacks, dismemberments, sorrow, and rejection, it is not surprising she has had a serious sleeping problem for years. My dream made her regular psychic state utterly real to me. I lost my natural defenses against the appalling helplessness of the victim. In my second dream, I was looking at my notes on our sessions, and as I turned the pages they become larger and leaflike, floral patterns in red and green began to form a margin around each page. The more pages I turned, the more the pattern elaborated itself and began filling in the pages from the outside to the center until it seemed this beautiful, delicate, sinewy, colorful, natural design had taken over and transformed what had once been empty and dry. I was deeply moved and grateful that this could be so.

Both these dreams capture the experience of working with her that has been most instructive for me. One aspect of it is that in our sessions, our merger allows for images that pertain to her to come to me as visions. As I speak them she can connect them with her personhood and keep elaborating them in the exchange with me. Terrified as she is of the experience, her love and trust have kept her from bolting out the door, staying with the whatever it is and letting her own pictures slowly emerge. When we began working together, she told me the only drawing of which she was capable, and had done over and over again as a child, was of the typical bird on a hill. Indeed, as our relationship intensified and she attempted to draw her feelings, it was clear how blocked her imagination was, for all she could accomplish repeatedly were black lines forcefully scratched over red hearts. The absence of the capacity to imagine has left her exposed to the immeasurable depths of the psyche. This is the *tremendum*, and it requires mediation through personified images if terror is not

to set in at its vastness and voidness. But her personal representations are intolerable to her because they have been
forged in pain and abuse, so she is left bouncing between the
empirical world of people and experience, which tends to take
her over, and the bottomless pit she calls the hole in her chest.
My role is to mediate these worlds until she can take over the
job herself. I nourish her with love and understanding but
mostly I am the provider of the images she needs to establish a
nurturing self-image. Frequently I feel the imaginal flows
from me to her like Chinnamasta's fountain of blood nourishes her decapitated head and her devotees. This manner of
working is more active than that to which I am accustomed.
Typically I get a vision, say two little girls in the room, one at
my side and one in the corner, and their imaginary feelings
and actions will fill the hour. Or, commonly, she will be
frozen in her fear, trying to say how deeply she loves me but
unable to speak, and I will use images which facilitate her
expression. For example, I have said that her loving words are
like the twigs that can build the nest so that the eggs will not
fall on the floor and crack or break. This frees her to play
along, convey her emotions, and feel as connected to herself
as she is to me. She has made substantial progress. Despite
the circularity of the process, it now seems miraculous that she
can put aside the blows of voices out to destroy her very being
and begin to reel out imaginary pornographic tapes of our
ongoing sexual affair. It is not lust that primarily motivates
these images; rather, they spring from the kind of deep love,
longing, and gratitude for our relationship that has the
potential for healing if mediated by the imaginal. I feel I have
helped raise an infant who has now chanced entering adolescence, albeit to please me and ensure my caring. I realize the
negative transference, other than her fear of rejection or loss
of me, is still in the wings and there is much work ahead. But
it seems paramount that an inner sense of containment in
pleasurable, nourishing, exciting, gratifying, and inviting
imaginings be available first.

SAL: I have been reading Jeanne Achterberg's book *Imagery in
Healing, Shamanism and Modern Medicine*, and what she
describes as the shaman's way, the oldest and most widespread way of healing with the imagination, seems similar to

what you attempt to do with Elize. She says that illness is considered an intrusion from without and shamanic treatment first emphasizes augmenting the potency of the sick person. The primary problem is seen as the loss of personal power that permitted the intrusion of the external element in the first place. The shaman conducts his work in the realm of the imaginal for it is based on the supernatural and on the altered states of consciousness available to ascend skyward or descend to the underworld to obtain the healing energies. I was struck when Achterberg indicated that they move in and out of the different states of consciousness at will because it is what you have said should be required of a Jungian analyst, that is, to be able to move from one kind of consciousness to another.

DIO: Shamans have all kinds of techniques for entering and interpreting landscapes of the imagination of which we have no idea, but in principle, I agree with you. For example, one day when Elize was in anguish at the hole in her chest that would never heal, and I at my wits end not knowing how to help, I saw a spider spinning a web that connected the walls of her chest hole so that a grid was being created in a natural way. Hopefully, the grid would one day be fine enough to hold the soul food she needs to build a positive sense of herself. Since then, I know I am her spider, organically weaving with our imagination her tapestry cocoon, and it will be the finest hour when she becomes her own spider without me.

The comment you just made about shamans working on strengthening the vigor of the ill person applies to my experience with Elize in another, rather unexpected, way. I have always appreciated humor and enjoy it freely with patients and friends. But I was most surprised to find laughter become a golden road to success.

Our first years together were spent laughing contagiously at her stories about her mother's violent antics. The episodes were alarming, macabre, bizarre, and extraordinarily funny to us. She easily interlaced the laughter with tears, rage, and fear, her more usual psychic state, but it was evident our shared merriment was directing the work. In time, our derisive laughter at her parents began to include a perspective on the ways in which people and circumstance made a victim or a

fool of her at various times. By then, we were deeply involved
with each other, and it became clear to me that what she saw
was her wickedness and foolishness through my loving eyes
and would love it in herself. This extended to the world at
large, which by then was less concretized and literalized. Its
capacity to inflict pain would be experienced as more archetypally based and not just as a personal insult. At about the
fourth year of analysis, her laughter began to include things I
said or did which she could mock but still laugh heartily at
with me, so that the barbs were less obvious and less frightening to her. Her biggest fear was loosing me so she needed a
way to express hostility without harming me directly. Today,
she can put all of this into words comfortably, but we still
periodically break out laughing at some humorous quirk of
fate or human failing and feel very bonded because of it. In
fact, her appalling dreams are interlaced with some that are
best characterized by our laughter, play, and the happiness
this brings her.

SAL: You have a spirit that is very playful and reminds me of the
Indonesian Barong. I remember vividly in Bali the drama-
dance between the Barong and Rangda. For the Balinese,
the theater is a religious experience and not a profession. In
fact, as is true for their lives in general, beautifully arranged
good food, lovely music, splendid costumes, fine dancing,
and exciting drama are there to give pleasure to divine guests
as well as the villagers. Dances and play have a religious
significance, so they are constantly revived and are fantastic
to watch. Two of their main characters are Rangda and
Barong, who represent the opposing forces that hold the
natural world in balance. Rangda represents all that is hideous and malignant to man and in these rituals has a terrifying mask and dress. The Barong, on the other hand, looks
like a huge shaggy dog, tiger, lionlike creature which flops
around snapping its jaws and swishing flies with its tail. This
mystical beast represents the forces that are beneficial to
man and, as such, is the protector of mankind, the affirma-
tive, and all the favorable spirits associated with the right
kind of magic. When he and Rangda dance, he is extraordinarily playful and winsome, but there is no question of his
enormous power as these two mythical beings clash in a

desperate struggle to overcome the force of the other. It is like your healthy animus fighting the negative Mother, to use familiar Jungian terms.

DIO: It feels very good to have the Barong here. The way Elize says it is that I am the Donald Duck in her. Fortunately, we both enjoyed him as a favorite cartoon comic book character. She says he has lots of vitality, is feisty, and does well by his three nephews. She really values how playful we can be.

Laughter is rarely mentioned as one of our most effective therapeutic tools. Laughing with someone is similar to having sex because both your bodies come together despite the fact that there is no touching. It offers a huge amount of release that leads to relaxation and a sense of connectedness and well being. Furthermore, laughter not only makes you feel at one with another but is based on the shocked explosion that comes when two disparate and opposed perceptions come together at once and you can feel united with yourself and the universe. Also, in order to be able to laugh at yourself, you need to be able to love your shadow, for laughter often focuses on defects and hurts. And, it follows that in order to be so accepting of your own foibles and deficits, it takes having seen them mirrored in the eyes of someone who loves you.

When I became aware of the power of laughter years ago, I started a search for the laughing goddess. It has not been an extensive or thorough research but I never found her in mythology. Gods and goddesses laugh but none seem to have it as their primary characteristic, except, perhaps, the laughing Buddah. I think at the time I was becoming aware that I, too, had a feminine soul, and the laughing goddess was the way mine appeared to me first. I used to resent being told I had only an animus because it did not match my experience at all, and I was very glad to read in Irene Claremont de Castillejo's book, *Knowing Woman*, that in Jung's most recent writings, he foregoes making statements that brand the animus as a woman's soul. Indeed, in *Anion, The Archetypes and the Collective Unconscious* and *Two Essays on Analytical Psychology*, there is no mention of the animus in this way (Castillejo 1973, p. 170). Castillejo goes on to say that it is fictitious to insist that women fall in love with their animus at these times.

Women project the animus and come to know it as well as recognize their own feminine soul being activated (when in love, that is) once they are no longer unconsciously identified with it (Castillejo 1973, p. 172). I think this applies to my understanding of Elize's psyche since our work started. I function as the incarnation of her soul and mediate her relationship to her Self and to the empirical world until her own soul capacity strengthens. I also convey and model spiritual, logos, and experiential forces (animus) in the ways that I respond and behave. The laughter captures both and awakens her playful child occluded since childhood.

SAL: I hear you loving this woman and using your heart-mind as one of your primary therapeutic modes. Love strengthens the soul and is the road to healing. In his poem, "I carry your heart with me," e. e. cummings puts it beautifully in the last stanza:

here is the deepest secret nobody knows
(here is the root of the root and the bud of the bud
and the sky of the sky of a tree called life; which grows
higher than soul can hope or mind can hide)
and this is the wonder that's keeping the stars apart.

i carry your heart (i carry it in my heart)

(cummings 1965, p. 156)

On this note, Dio and Sal decide to share food and drink. They make a salad with flowers and dip their bread in wine. They delight in each others' eyes and review with amusement the destiny that has crossed their paths. Their ways were originally so far apart. The meal completed, they nestle side by side to gaze at the whitening moon and the falling red sun. Birds fly by with illuminated wings. The mercurial silver sea, streaked with turquoise and pink, sighs as it receives the reflecting moon and burning sun in its hold. Existence is a mystery.

References

Achterberg, J. 1985. *Imagery in Healing, Shamanism and Modern Medicine*, Boston: Shambala.
Bohm, D. 1985. *Unfolding Meaning: A Weekend of Dialogue with David Bohm*. London: Ark Paperbacks.

Castillejo, I. C. de. 1973. *Knowing Woman: A Feminine Psychology.* New York: Harper Colophon Books.

Colman, A. 1987. Individuation, the scapegoat and the group. Chicago: C. G. Jung Institute symposium.

Corbin, H. 1971. *Mundus imaginalis,* or the imaginary and the imaginal. *Spring.*

cummings, e. e. 1965. *A Selection of Poems.* New York: Harcourt Brace Jovanovich.

Downing, C. 1989. *Myths and Mysteries of Same Sex Love.* New York: Continuum.

Eliot, T. S. *Collected Poems 1909–1935.* London: Faber and Faber Limited.

Evans-Wentz, W. Y. 1960. *The Tibetan Book of the Dead.* London: Oxford University Press.

Gleick, J. 1987. *Chaos, Making a New Science.* New York: Penguin Books.

Hadas, M. ed. 1965. *Greek Drama.* New York: Bantam Books.

Hillman, J. 1985. *Anima: An Anatomy of a Personified Notion.* Dallas: Spring Publications.

Jung, C. G. 1943/1928. *Two Essays on Analytical Psychology. CW*, vol. 7. Princeton, N.J.: Princeton University Press, 1953.

Jung, C. G. 1955. *Mysterium Coniunctionis. CW*, vol. 14. Princeton, N.J. Princeton University Press, 1963.

Jung, C. G. 1951. *Aion. CW*, vol. 9ii. Princeton, N.J.: Princeton University Press, 1959.

Jung, C. G. 1952. Synchronicity, an acausal connecting principle. *CW* 8:417–531. Princeton, N.J. Princeton University Press, 1960.

Kinsley, D. 1986. *Hindu Goddesses: Visions of the Divine Feminine in the Hindu Religious Tradition.* Berkeley, Calif.: University of California Press.

Moore, T. 1987. *Animus mundi,* the bull at the center of the world. *Spring.*

Ross, N. W., ed. 1960. The World of Zen. New York: Vintage Books.

Shakespeare, W. 1944. *The Viking Portable Shakespeare.* New York: Penguin Books.

Stein, M. 1983. *In Midlife.* Dallas: Spring Publications.

Steiner, G. 1986. *Antigones.* Oxford: Clarendon Press.

The Role of Anima/Animus Structures and Archetypes in the Psychology of Narcissism and Some Borderline States

Murray Stein

During the decade of the 1980s, a significant number of Jungian authors (e.g., Asper, Corbett, Gordon, Jacoby, Kalsched, Klaif, Satinover, Schwartz-Salant) drew up comparisons between Heinz Kohut's revisions of psychoanalytic theory and comparable ideas in analytical psychology. The energy for this work was generated by the excitement around Kohut's discoveries concerning the narcissistic personality disorder and by certain obvious similarities between his concepts and Jung's.

These often elaborate exercises in comparative psychoanalytic thinking have greatly clarified the similarities and differences between Jung and Kohut, particularly regarding the meaning of the key term in both Kohutian and Jungian systems, i.e., the self. Whether the Kohutian self is comparable to the Jungian self, and if so in what precise ways this is and is not the case, has been a crucial theoretical question addressed in these studies, of which the most complete and detailed is Mario Jacoby's *Individuation and Narcissism* (1990). In general, there now seems to be agreement that the Kohutian self is not the self of

Murray Stein, Ph.D., is a member of the Chicago Society of Jungian Analysts and has a private practice in Wilmette, Ill. He is the editor of *Jungian Analysis*, co-editor of *Jung's Challenge to Contemporary Religion*, and author of *In Midlife* and *Jung's Treatment of Christianity: The Psychotherapy of a Religious Tradition*.

analytical psychology and to try to use these terms interchangeably results in more confusion than utility on both sides.

Beyond this point of theoretical clarification, the issue remains as to whether analytical psychology can be useful, either theoretically or clinically, for deeper understanding and more effective treatment of narcissistic personality disorders and borderline states. Certainly a number of Jungian authors among those cited above have thought this to be the case and have made significant contributions.

It seems to me that if there is indeed a way in which Jung's theory can be useful for shedding more light upon the structural and clinical problems presented by patients with narcissistic to borderline character disorders, the route may have to be directed through the territory of anima/animus development rather than by immediately evoking the concept of the self. It is here that closer parallels can be actually seen between the Kohutian self, the detailing of which has been of such great clinical usefulness in understanding and treating the problems presented in the narcissistic personality disorders, and the personality structures described by Jung and employed clinically in analytical psychology. On the other side, Kohut's insights can be of use to analytical psychology, particularly for understanding the development of anima/animus structures and certain pathological outcomes of their misdevelopment.

In utilizing Jung's anima/animus theory for the purpose of exploring the psychology of narcissism and borderline states, I will limit myself to two extended passages in the *Collected Works*. The first passage occurs in the "Definitions" chapter of *Psychological Types* (1921), and the second comprises the third chapter of *Aion* (1951), "The Syzygy: Anima and Animus." Between these two texts, I believe it is possible to garner enough theoretical material to link up the theory of anima/animus with some major issues of the narcissistic personality, as delineated by Kohut, and also to offer some reflections on borderline states as well as some possibilities for individuation that lie beyond narcissistic object relations.

It will be my contention that the narcissistic personality disorders and borderline states rest upon a misdevelopment of anima/animus structures.

Narcissism and the Soul

In the concluding chapter of his monumental work, *Psychological Types*, Jung provides extensive definitions of the psychological terms he has been using throughout the book. He includes an extensive passage, a small essay, on the term *soul*. Here he defines, in a rather technical way, the earliest version of the concept anima/animus. From a structural point of view, it is a single concept, although it has gendered variants. Jung deals with this concept only after first defining *persona*, however. These two terms represent complimentary psychological structures in Jung's understanding. By posing them as contrasting structures, Jung clarifies the definition of both.

Jung opens his definition of soul by speaking of the "functional complex" as a "personality" and distinguishing complexes from the ego (Jung 1921, par. 797). Everyone, he argues, has a sort of multiple personality, in that every person contains more than one personality, i.e., more than a single attitude, in the psyche. A man's personality at his place of work—typically it is businesslike, aggressive, decisive, etc.—is often different from his domestic personality, which may be compliant, passive, and easy-going.

What this reveals, Jung argues, is that we possess—or are possessed by—a variety of "functional complexes," each of which can be thought of as a personality (Jung 1921, par. 798). The ego is in turn colored by these functional complexes, or personalities, through "identification" (ibid.). When the executive at work adopts his typical commanding tone, for example, his ego is actually identifying with a functional complex of a certain (usually highly collective) sort and enacting its attitude. This is not necessarily his "true," or his only, personality (ibid.).

The functional complexes with which an ego identifies in order to deal with the outer social environment make up the persona structure. The persona may itself be quite multisided and plural, not always the same in every environment. Jung is impressed by how chameleonlike the human person is, changing situationally to adapt to the needs and expectations of a surrounding milieu. Personality, then, and to some extent even character are highly milieu-sensitive.

It is quite easy to grasp and to use the concept of the persona. It is a mask, or a set of masks, worn to adapt situationally. It is harder, though, to grasp the complimentary concept of the anima/animus. This is the functional complex that faces the inner world. Like the persona, it often contains a typical and collective attitude. And it is usually—Jung appeals here not to theory but to experience—quite different from and complimentary to the persona. If the persona complexes are hard, aggressive, businesslike, then the anima complexes are typically soft, sentimental, and emotional.

It is crucial to recognize that Jung does not at this point link anima/animus structures to gender, at least not as the *essential* definition of this functional complex. The anima/animus complex is simply the face turned inward, the attitude taken toward one's own subjective reactions, dreams, impulses, instincts, fantasies, etc. The anima/animus complex is the means for adapting to inner states of mind. If one is soft and open and tender with oneself, this is the face of the anima/animus; if one is hard, aggressive, attacking, then this is the anima/animus's face. And the complimentary face will be turned outward.

I have casually suggested using an ungendered, neutral term like *anime* to refer to this psychological structure. Of course, anima and animus are usually strongly gender-linked in the minds of those who read, study, and employ Jung's writings, for the good reason that Jung himself usually speaks of these structures in that way. When he discusses the anima and leaves abstraction for experience and psychic image, he nearly invariably refers to its feminine features. And, conversely, with the animus he refers to the masculine element in a woman's personality. Jung's account of how he first came to speak of the anima in this way is instructive.

In his *Analytical Psychology: Notes of the Seminar* (1989), he confesses that his first realization of the anima in himself occurred during his work on Miss Miller's fantasies, which eventually resulted in his seminal book *Wandlungen and Symbols der Libido* [*Psychology of the Unconscious*] (1912). It was while he was writing this book that he first became fascinated with mythology and mythological thinking. This kind of thinking, which he found so pronounced in the Miller materials, actually began to overtake him too, he says, and as a scientist he was horrified:

> As a form of thinking I held it to be altogether impure, a sort of incestuous intercourse, thoroughly immoral from an intellectual standpoint. Permitting fantasy in myself had the same effect on me as would be produced on a man if he came into his workshop and found all the tools flying about doing things independently of his will. It shocked me, in other words, to think of the possibility of a fantasy life in my own mind . . . and so great was my resistance to it, that I could only admit the fact in myself through the process of projecting my material into Miss Miller's. . . . I had to realize then that in Miss Miller I was analyzing my own fantasy function . . . and thus in this book the question of the inferior function and the anima comes up.   (Jung 1989, pp. 27–28)

This association among a man's inner fantasy life (usually inferior compared to his more conscious and rational functioning), the image of woman, and the inferior function would remain constant throughout

Jung's writings on the anima. The place of the feminine in this set, however, is arbitrary and more accidental than essential. I believe one can use the terms *anima* and *animus* to refer to the mind's fantasy function without linking them to gender and still retain their conceptual value for analytical psychology. It was only by historical accident that anima became linked with the feminine in the first place.

In *Psychological Types* (1921), written in the decade following that analysis of Miss Miller's fantasies, Jung points out that the ego can identify with anima/animus complexes as well as with persona complexes. When it does, the ego becomes, as it commonly said, anima (or animus) possessed. For the ego, there is a Scylla and Charybdis problem here: on the one side lies persona identification, on the other anima/animus possession. Either way, the ego loses its neutrality and freedom to the values and styles embedded in the functional complex. Only the relatively conscious person tries, Odysseus-like, to chart a course between them.

When the ego tends toward persona identification, Jung points out, the anima/animus complexes are projected onto a suitable external object, typically a person of the other sex and certainly someone who embodies in his/her character style the strongest features of the anima/animus complexes. This seems to be the usual state of affairs, developmentally speaking. A person relates first to mother and father, to the family, and then to the peer group. The functional complexes that get built up to carry out this adaptation (the persona) are based principally on the models offered. A little girl will relate adaptively to her mother, and then will relate to others *like* her mother. One says casually that she "takes after her mother," more technically that she has introjected her mother and identified with this introject. What has actually happened, according to Jung's theory, is that a functional complex has been created out of the interaction between the daughter's latent personality and the mother-object, and that the ego tends to identify with this complex when relating to others. This is especially the case when the mother is seen to be successful in *her* adaptations. If mother is admired for the way she handles herself in the world, then daughter sees this as a promising strategy for doing the same thing. Kohut speaks of the transmuting internalization of idealized objects, while Jung spoke of complex formation and identification. Other theorists might speak here of imitation, of "modeling," or of learning.

For men, it is the father who typically plays the role of persona model. Through the interaction between the little boy's unconscious and his father's character, he builds up a functional complex with which he can identify in relating and adapting to the world. The father's imago (an inner psychic image) thus helps the son to "bridge to the world" by way of this functional complex, a persona, through the son's identification with it.

The anima/animus functional complexes come into being alongside this persona development and seem to be somewhat dependent upon what happens there. While the persona "is strongly influenced by environmental conditions," Jung writes, "the anima is shaped by the unconscious and its qualities" (Jung 1921, par. 806). But, when the external environment is "primitive," he continues, the persona will necessarily also reflect this, and "the anima similarly takes on the archaic features of the unconscious" (ibid.). These processes of persona and anima/animus formation are seen, therefore, as correlated: what happens in the one sector has a strong effect on what happens in the other. The anima/animus complexes reflect something of the outer environment even if only by compensating for the one-sidedness of persona complexes. They are, however, principally shaped by the unconscious and its qualities. The anima/animus complexes are, in a manner of speaking, the individual's unconscious answer to the environment — to the mother on the daughter's part, to the father on the son's, to the predominant family attitude, and even to society and contemporary culture as a whole.

As indicated, the usual picture of a personality's development shows the ego identifying increasingly with the persona complexes, which reflect the environment and are shaped by important figures in it, like mother and father and other significant people. Meanwhile, the anima/animus complexes remain distant and other, on the whole *not* being identified with in the sense of forming a person's conscious identity. Typically they are projected onto suitable others. This projection creates intense bonds of soul-mating, the other person representing the inward-turned "other." Later in life, a person may gradually become conscious of the anima/animus complexes as inner attitudes and cease projecting them somewhat. This is the expected course of maturation and individuation.

Jung mentions another possibility, however. This occurs when the ego does *not* identify primarily with the persona complexes but rather with the anima/animus complexes:

> If the soul-image is projected, the result is an absolute affective tie to the object. If it is not projected, a relatively unadapted state develops, which Freud has described as *narcissism*. . . . If the soul-

image is not projected, a thoroughly morbid relation to the unconscious gradually develops. The subject is increasingly overwhelmed by unconscious contents, which his inadequate relations to the object makes him powerless to assimilate or put to any kind of use, so that the whole subject–object relation only deteriorates further.

(Jung 1921, pars. 810–811)

Here Jung uses the term *narcissism* in Freud's sense, as he says. This usage is rare in Jung's *Collected Works*, occurring only some half-dozen times all told. Occasionally Jung uses the term to refer to a disparaging way of thinking about introversion.

In the kind of narcissism being considered here, Jung sees development going awry because of an ego's lack of identification with the persona complexes. The individual's ego does not want to identify with the persona complexes that are available. This means, practically speaking, that the complexes associated with the same-sex parent are more negative than positive, these valences indicating simply the ego's attraction or aversion to them. Of a son, one would way that he does not, or cannot, identify with his father. With a daughter, this would be true of her relation to her mother. The persona complexes formed around the interaction with these figures do not attract the ego sufficiently to form a positive identification. There is a gap. The girl may admire and even idolize her mother, but she cannot identify with her because the persona complex needed to do so has not formed or because the one that has formed is repellant. The boy may look up to his father but from a distance and from a position of inferiority and fear; his persona complexes do not draw his ego into a bond of identification.

If we ask why this is the case, we need to look deeply into the intricacies of development in infancy and early childhood. The object (i.e., the mother for a girl, the father for a boy) around which the persona complex forms may communicate a subtle, or blatant, rejection of the infant or young child. This element of rejection gets built into the complex in such a way that the ego cannot get close to it without feeling rejection, low self-esteem, or criticism. If this parental object is envious or rivalrous, then hatred is built into the complex and creates self-hate. The persona complex hates the ego, so to speak. It is a negative image from the ego's point of view. Thus, bad outer objects become bad inner ones. The function of therapy for this person is to cure this by providing a caring and empathic new object around which to form a new persona complex that *can* be identified with.

However this pathological early development takes place, it throws the ego into a state of social alienation and isolation, such that the result is a profound lack of adaptation to the outer world and a state of absorption in the inner world.

It might seem that the unconscious would, under these circumstances, compensate the bad persona complex with a positive and attractive anima/animus complex. To some extent, this is what happens, but it turns into a seduction and becomes an escape from the world. The anima acts as a siren, the animus as a demon lover. When this incestuous (i.e., self-involved) development takes place, the ego withdraws into the secluded inner world, hides increasingly from the outer world and from its demands, and the psychological state that Jung calls "morbid" comes about. This is a schizoid withdrawal, as classically described by Fairbairn (1952). Unfortunately, the anima/animus complexes, when unhitched this much from the outer world, deepen into their archaic and highly charged, intensely conflicted archetypal polarities. Beside the seductive, sirenlike anima lurks the death-dealing witch; beside the ghostly lover animus stands the dark magician. Typically, the people who enter into this psychological condition become fascinated with magic, esoteric religion, and occultism. They are highly vulnerable to archetypal influences and symbols and easily fall victim to persons who employ such to gain power and to manipulate. Others simply retreat into a world of their own personal fantasies and obsessions, becoming confused and delusional in their identifications with these inner figures.

The anima/animus functional complexes do not, it seems, become structured particularly well, in the sense of providing protection and suitable adaption to the inner world of unconscious forces and figures, if the persona complexes are poorly or negatively structured or are defective. This is most likely due to the practical reason that if one parent is defective, the other probably is as well. The persona complexes are usually structured in and through the interaction between the subject's personality and the same-sex parent. Girls use their mothers to bridge to the world, and boys their fathers. This forms the functional complex that the ego can use to deal with the outer, social world. In parallel, the anima/animus functional complexes are formed and structured typically through the interaction between the subject's personality and the other-sex parent. Sons use their mothers, daughters their fathers, to face inward and deal with the inner world, to meet its demands and face its pressures from instincts and archetypes. If the anima/animus complexes are inadequate, the person's ego will be insufficiently adapted to the unconscious and will tend to be over-whelmed by the unconscious.

In cases where only one parent is available for both persona and anima/animus constellation and structuring, or where one parent is so inadequate as to be useless for this purpose, there is likely to be confu-sion of identification and consequently of identity. Persona and anima/animus structures will be similar and used for purposes of adaptation to both the outer and inner worlds. A man will come across socially as effeminate, a woman as masculine, and each may feel ashamed and self-conscious about this. Similarly, this person may have a difficult time facing inward if the single parent was of the same sex. Such is a typical picture of the narcissistic personality disorder: a sense of shame and low self-esteem combined with inner shallowness.

If the problem deepens further, we come upon the borderline personality disorder. Consider the person, not an uncommon candidate for psychotherapy, who has had a more or less distant same-sex parent with whom he or she could not easily identify. This means that the persona ends up being inadequate, defective, or generally unavailable. This person also has a negative other-sex parental complex, due to a domineering and controlling attitude in that parent, and this means that the anima/animus structures are defective and cannot be relied upon to face up to inner life and the unconscious. Here we see that we have a person who is poorly adapted to the outer world and extremely vulnerable to onslaughts from the unconscious. It is not that this person has *identified* with the anima/animus complexes — this would yield the picture of extreme introversion or schizoid withdrawal — but he or she has *neither* persona *nor* anima/animus structures to identify with and rely on. This, it seems to me, lies in the background of the borderline personality — there is an ego that is fragile in the outer world and excessively vulnerable to being taken over by the unconscious, by affect, ideation, imagination, from within. This person may appear to be creative but is also extremely vulnerable to the world without and the world within. Sanity and madness are intertwined like muscle and fat in this personality.

A Case

Godfrey is the oldest of seven children. Born to a young woman slightly more educated and cultured than her handsome but unambi-tious husband, Godfrey was only two when his next sibling came along, and then in rapid succession five more appeared. The house was small and quickly overcrowded. Godfrey's father was a traveling salesman and out of the house most of the time on his routes. His mother was overwhelmed with all the children and looked to Godfrey, the oldest, to help with the others. Early on, he realized that he would not much enjoy the other neighborhood children, especially the rough and rowdy boys. Godfrey was sensitive and artistic, not especially athletic. He often longed for solitude, for order, for beautiful things. There was little money to go around, and the father was not available both because he was gone much of the time and also because he was narcissistic and favored his own hobbies and interests over his son. So Godfrey grew up more or less by himself, despite a crowd of family members.

In adolescence, Godfrey suffered from acute social unease and developed severe skin problems. He did not feel accepted by his peers and tended to be a loner. Somewhat effeminate in his mannerisms, perhaps due to the influence of his mother on his persona complexes, he discovered in adolescence quite a large interest in sex, drugs, and clothes. In college, he was courted by an older male student whom he admired, and he yielded to a homosexual relationship. At the same time, he had a girlfriend and eventually he married her. Homosexual and heterosexual themes run through his history from that point on.

Godfrey came to see me when he was in his mid-thirties, had several young children, and suffered from severe mood swings, depression, and a feeling of inner emptiness. He tended to be anxious in groups and had occasional nightmares. He was quite successful in his career but dreaded interpersonal interactions and tended to need long periods of time alone. His preferred form of sexual activity was masturbation with homosexual fantasies. He had once attempted suicide ten years earlier, using drugs, and had narrowly escaped death. Presently he did not abuse drugs except for an occasional hit of marijuana. His career was in the arts, and he was highly gifted and creative when his anxieties and moods allowed him to be productive. He was suffering from acute abandonment anxiety when we began because his wife had threatened him with divorce after one of their frequent arguments.

Analysis quickly revealed the structural problems. The absence of a father figure resulted in inadequate persona complexes, hence his extreme anxiety in social situations, especially with men. His fear was that they would laugh at him and consider him inadequate as a man. He could not speak with them on their level. With women, he felt more comfortable but he did not usually like them or respect them. The anima complexes were colored by his negative mother complex.

His mother had been intrusive and domineering, and she had been too close to her son for his comfort. The anima, therefore, as she appeared in dreams, was usually threatening. Godfrey lived in terror of his inner life—his moods were extremely unpredictable and extreme, veering from euphoria to painful depression. The slightest emotional event in his world could trigger massive inner upheavals and panic attacks; his imagination came up with fiendish Satanic figures, and his dreams contained similar images. His conflicted relations with the outside world were matched by his conflicted relations with the inner world. He tended to berate himself on all counts, and he felt he could not trust himself in any way.

The point I want to make with this brief description of Godfrey has to do with the anima problem. His anima complexes were structured in such a way that they did not protect him from his own unconscious material. This was most probably due to the lack of an empathic mother and the failure of her mirroring. This inner structural defect in the anima left Godfrey severely at risk with respect to his inner states and emotional reactions, highly charged as they were with affect, and left him vulnerable as well to inner attacks and sudden loss of self-esteem. This is a narcissistic character disorder with some borderline features.

An incident illustrates how this psychic structure is experienced. At one point in the analysis, Godfrey had begun to admire an older man, who happened to be a teacher. On one occasion, Godfrey had been invited to lunch by this man, but at the last moment, the teacher had cancelled the lunch with what seemed to be a poor excuse. Godfrey took it in stride at first, but by the time he saw me for analysis a few hours later he was in an inexplicable funk. We traced his black mood to that event. In the days following, this mood actually deepened to the extreme and lasted for about two weeks. Dreams reflected this injury to his self-esteem, and all of our analytic work during this period was taken up examining this incident. No amount of insight or empathy on my part, or understanding on his, had much effect on his mood and feelings. This sort of extreme sensitivity to a slight from an idealized other is one hallmark of narcissistic vulnerability, of course, and indicates a strong transference to the man in question, but the deeper problem is the failure of the inner structures, of the anima, to preserve the ego from inner attacks from the unconscious. The whole sense of self-worth is blasted, and there is no inner resiliency.

Godfrey had a sort of pasted-together exterior shell that functioned as a persona, while suffering extreme vulnerability to attacks from within. Only after nearly two years of analysis did this begin to ameliorate. Then we saw, for the first time, a helpful, *praising*, masculine dream figure who shows him the way on his quest into the depths. His persona complexes, meanwhile, were being slowly modified and formed around his interaction with me, and his relations with the outer world improved both in effectiveness and in reduction of anxiety. There was also some evidence in dreams of the constellation of a more positive and helpful anima figure.

From clinical examples such as this, it is evident that in cases of narcissistic to borderline character disorders there are inadequate developments in both the persona and the anima/animus sets of functional complexes.

Anima/Animus as the Projection-Making Factor

There is another and more subtle kind of narcissistic problem, one in which there seems to be a normal and good enough development in both persona and anima/animus functional complexes. This type of problem has to do with a developmental issue that is usually only encountered in adulthood and often in the second half of life. The challenge here has to do with becoming conscious of the anima/animus complexes and the psyche's projection of them. This kind of narcissism — not the obviously pathological kind discussed above (the Freudian kind, in Jung's words), but a subtle and insidious narcissism — results in object relations that are highly determined by projection of the anima/animus complexes.

In *Psychological Types*, Jung points out that normally a person's ego becomes identified with the persona complexes and the anima/animus attitudes are found only in projection onto others: "In all cases where there is an identity with the persona, and the soul accordingly is unconscious, the soul-image is transferred to a real person. This person is the object of intense love or equally intense hate (or fear)" (1921, par. 808). (An implication of this, incidentally, is that when the ego is *not* identified with the persona complexes, the person also does not project the anima/animus complexes. That this person does not fall in love, or hate, is a diagnostic which helps differentiate between primary and secondary narcissism. The primary narcissist cannot fall in love; the secondary narcissist falls in love regularly and compulsively.)

There is a feature of the narcissistic personality that has to do with the *projection* of the anima/animus functional complexes and with the object relations consequent to this dynamic. Kohut speaks of "selfobjects" in this connection. A selfobject is an object so interlaced with projected psychic material that it stands more for an inner content than for itself, and so the ego's relation to it is to a piece of its own unconscious psyche. When we conceive of an individuation process—a maturational process—as moving past this type of object relating, we are in the area of an *opus contra naturam*, for to relate *affectively* to the world-as-projection-created seems to be the more or less natural human state of affairs, insofar as it is natural to remain unconscious, particularly of the projections of the anima/animus complexes.

By the 1940s, when Jung was writing *Aion*, which includes the chapter entitled "The Syzygy: Anima and Animus," he had extended his understanding of anima/animus projection from the magical love relationship to include a much wider range of object relations, indeed perhaps in the case of a narcissistic personality the entire gamut:

> It is often tragic to see how blatantly a man bungles his own life and the lives of others yet remains totally incapable of seeing how much the whole tragedy originates in himself, and how he continually feeds it and keeps it going. Not *conscious* of course—for consciously he is engaged in bewailing and cursing a fruitless world that recedes further and further into the distance. Rather it is an unconscious factor which spins the illusions that veil his world. And what is being spun is a cocoon, which in the end will completely envelop him.   (Jung 1951, par. 18)

Women, Jung adds, are similarly subject to this cocoon-spinning activity (of the animus): "The woman, like the man, becomes wrapped in a veil of illusions by her demon-familiar, and, as the daughter who alone understands her father (that is, is eternally right in everything), she is translated to the land of sheep, where she is put to graze by the shepherd of her soul, the animus" (1951, par. 32). Anima and animus are parallel structures and dynamic, archetypal factors in men and women, and in both sexes they are responsible for spinning illusions, creating projections, and disturbing the ego's object relations.

For Jung, as for Melanie Klein (1959) in her later theorizing, projection and introjection begin in earliest infancy. An internal picture of the world is built up by a combination of these processes. For Jung, the personal mother is the first carrier of the son's anima projection and the father is the first carrier for the daughter's animus projection (1951, par. 28). These figures (i.e., mother and father) are, of course, also introjected, and so the anima/animus complexes develop their particular lineaments and features. But behind these anima/

animus complexes, which are used by the ego to relate to and govern the expression of the unconscious and of instincts in daily life, there lie the archetypes of anima and animus. And the archetype extends far beyond the personal mother/father figures and continues to function as projection-maker throughout later life. It is this factor that is, in Jung's view, responsible for turning objects into selfobjects.

A Case

A clinical example illustrates the kind of problem that appears in a man when there is strong ego identification with the persona functional complexes, almost total unconsciousness of the anima functional complexes and archetype, and consequent narcissistic object relations.

Jason, in his early forties, was "sent into therapy" by his wife with the ultimatum: either learn to relate to me or learn to live without me. He himself did not understand her problem, only knowing that she was extremely unhappy and serious about divorce. He was happy and successful in his profession, came into therapy well-dressed and groomed, and had a charming and pleasant demeanor.

Since it was his wife who had the complaint, I asked to see her for a session to hear her side of the story. She told me that her spouse had pursued her ardently in courtship and had insisted on marriage. She had been ambivalent and would have preferred to wait, but his intense pressure was too much for her, and she made a premature decision to marry him. She quickly regretted this, but went ahead with the wedding anyway, not wanting to rock the boat once launched. During courtship and the early years of marriage, her husband was, she said, passionately sexual, but this diminished and after a few years became almost nonexistent, largely by his choice. He remained extremely jealous of her, however, and would often check on her whereabouts during the day. There was never any doubt of his loyalty to her, and she never had the sense that he wanted another woman or wanted to change anything about their relationship. He was most content when she stayed home and was there for him on weekends. When they were together, however, he rarely spoke or listened to her, and this was the major problem. She had the feeling that he was completely unaware of who she was or what she thought or felt. He was not interested in her actually, although he wanted her to be around all the time. When they did have sex now, he closed his eyes and seemed to be in his own world. He was totally preoccupied with his own thoughts, which focused on work and his hobbies. He made unilateral decisions about expenditures but resented her doing the same. She felt completely controlled by him and unseen. All of their friends found him charming and few could understand her problem with him. Only the ones who knew him more intimately could see what she saw.

As his story was revealed in therapy, it turned out that he was the oldest child in a tightly structured, traditional, patriarchal family. His mother served his father, who was largely silent at home and preoccupied. As a boy, he admired his father but had no personal relationship with him, and he grew up to much like him in appearance and demeanor. Many people commented on this. After his father's death, he continued to have a close but largely nonverbal and unconscious relationship with his mother.

When he met the woman he was to marry, he fell in love with her instantly. To have her was his greatest desire, and he could not believe his luck when she responded positively to him. He viewed their marriage as basically a success and was completely content with it and with her, except for her bitter complaints, which he could not understand and which made him increasingly uncomfortable. He felt devoted to his family and wanted nothing to change in it. His work gave him great satisfaction, and he was making steady progress up the corporate ladder. His bosses and coworkers all liked him. He could not understand what he was doing here with me. Perhaps his wife was the one who needed help! But he was willing to come. He would do anything to save the marriage.

This is the picture of a man in the anima cocoon. His eros has reached out, claimed a soul-mate, and now is trying to preserve her in amber. He is unreflective, "objective," without interest in self-knowledge, and has never considered his own inner processes. He accepts the world as it is, and it is as he sees it. Jung would say he had identified with his persona complex and was projecting his unconscious anima into the world. The real world, meanwhile, is receding from him. Witness his wife.

Object Relations Beyond Narcissism

Jung acknowledges the difficulty of making the anima/animus factors conscious: "whereas the shadow can be seen through and recognized fairly easily, the anima and animus are much further away from consciousness and in normal circumstances are seldom if ever realized" (1951, par. 19). This type of narcissism would seem to be the normal human psychological state, and only in abnormal circumstances would one be forced or drawn to an analysis of the very foundational concepts and attitudes and perceptions by which consciousness operates and from which the psyche has made up a world.

Fortunately, therapy usually begins with such abnormal circumstances. Persons come to therapy in crisis, in inner and outer upheaval, and their deepest and dearest assumptions about life, about themselves, and about their grasp on reality are exposed for conscious examination. When the psyche is opened up in this way and a person is painfully suspended in psychological liminality, the necessary readiness for a thoroughgoing analysis is available. Until then, transformation of consciousness and release of the occluded or ensnared self cannot take place.

Jung claims (1951, par. 42) that when the anima/animus factors are made conscious, through crisis and confrontation and analytic introspection with a suitable "other," a "triad" emerges: there is the ego (the subject), the other (the object), and the "transcendent" element (the anima/animus). Object relations have therefore been radically altered: no longer is the other an anima/animus projection carrier, a selfobject. Rather, a conscious distinction can now be made between the soul-image (as inner other, transcendent, i.e., belonging to the unconscious) and the actual other. The relation to the other, now freed from projection, can take entirely new forms. There is a new kind of freedom in this for both ego and other, to be themselves more fully vis-à-vis the other, with no need to enact the projection of anima or animus.

Winnicott, in a late paper entitled "The Use of an Object and Relating Through Identifications" (1969), writes about this as the difference between projection-based "object relating" and projection-free "object use." In the latter, the subject is much freer to be creative with the object because it is now known that thought and fantasy cannot destroy the other, as it can be if related to through identifications. For Winnicott, the passage from the one type of object relation to the other is not automatic and "natural" (as it is also not for Jung, where making the anima/animus conscious is an extremely rare and difficult *opus contra naturam*), but is achieved through the experience that destructive fantasy and expression do not kill the other or drive him or her away. I believe Jung would also subscribe to this, although he does not emphasize this explicitly. Both would agree that through patient and caring analytic work, this result may be achieved and that this is also the way to the experience of the (true) self.

References

Asper, K., 1987. *Verlassenheit und Selbstentfremdung*. Olten: Walter.

Corbett, L. 1989. Kohut and Jung: a comparison of theory and therapy. In *Self Psychology, Comparisons and Contrasts*, Detrick and Detrick, eds. Hillsdale, N.J.: Analytic Press, pp. 23–47.

Corbett, L. and Kugler, P. 1989. The self in Jung and Kohut. *Dimensions of Self Experience: Progress in Self Psychology, Vol. 5*, A. Goldberg, ed. Hillsdale, NJ: Analytic Press, pp. 189–208.

Fairbairn, W. R. D. 1952. *Psycho-analytic Studies of the Personality*. London: Tavistock.

Gordon, R. 1980. Narcissism and the self. *Journal of the Analytical Psychology* 25:247–264.

Jacoby, M. 1981. Reflections on Heinz Kohut's concepts of narcissism. *Journal of Analytical Psychology* 26:107–110.

———. 1990. *Individuation and Narcissism: The Psychology of the Self in Jung and Kohut*. London: Routledge.

Jung, C. G. 1912. *Wandlungen und Symbole der Libido*. Vienna: Franz Deuticke.

———. 1951. *Aion: Researches into the Phenomenology of the Self. CW*, vol. 9ii. Princeton, N.J.: Princeton University Press, 1959.

———. 1972. *Psychological Types. CW*, vol. 6. Princeton, N.J.: Princeton University Press, 1971.

———. 1989. *Analytical Psychology: Notes on the Seminar Given in 1925*. Princeton, N.J.: Princeton University Press.

Kalsched, D. 1980. Narcissism and the search for interiority. *Quadrant* 13(2):46–74.

Klaif, C. 1987. Emerging concepts of the self: clinical considerations. In *Archetypal Processes in Psychotherapy*, Schwartz-Salant and Stein, eds. Wilmette, Ill.: Chiron Publications, pp. 75–92.

Klein, M. 1959. Our adult world and its roots in infancy. In *Envy and Gratitude*. New York: Dell, 1975, pp. 247–263.

Kohut, M. 1977. *The Restoration of the Self*. New York: International Universities Press.

Satinover, J. 1980. Puer Aeternus: the narcissistic relation to the Self. *Quadrant* 13(2):75–108.

———. 1984. Jung's contribution to the dilemma of narcissism. *Journal of the American Psychoanalytic Association* 34(2):401–438.

Schwartz-Salant, N. 1982. *Narcissism and Character Transformation*. Toronto: Inner City Books.

Winnicott, D. W. 1969. The use of an object and relating through identifications. In *Playing and Reality*. New York: Basic Books, 1971, pp. 86–94.

Anima, Animus, and Selfobject Theory

Lionel Corbett and Cathy Rives

Anima / Animus as Psychological Functions

Narcissistic character disorder as understood by modern psychoanalytic authors is phenomenologically identical to Jung's description of the anima-possessed man and the animus-possessed woman (Corbett and Rives 1991). The former is said to possess traits such as irritability, moodiness, jealousy, vanity, and bitchiness (Jung 1954a, par. 144) while the later is described as obstinate, dogmatic, argumentative, and opinionated (Jung 1950a, par. 223). However, according to classical Jungian theory, the only way to describe a woman with characteristics of the negative animus, is by describing such features as components of shadow or complex. It seems odd to call the same phenomena by different names in men and women, especially when their developmental roots can be shown to be identical — the result of selfobject failure (Kohut 1971), whose quality and effects are not different in either gender. The term *selfobject* is used by Kohut to describe another person who is experienced intrapsychically as necessary for maintaining the cohesion or integrity of the self. Within self-psychology, failure of

Lionel Corbett is a Jungian analyst in private practice in Santa Fe and Clinical Associate Professor, Department of Psychiatry, University of New Mexico.

Cathy Rives is a psychiatrist in private practice in Santa Fe and clinical Assistant professor, Department of Psychiatry, University of New Mexico, and an analyst-in-training at the C. G. Jung Institute of Chicago.

the parental selfobject function is responsible for characterological difficulties such as those attributed by Jung to anima/animus pathology.

Jung (1928, par. 339) suggests that anima/animus are psychological functions that behave like autonomous subpersonalities when they
are unconscious, undeveloped, and unintegrated. Kohut (1971) also
conceives of narcissistic character disorder as characterized by the presence of vertically split-off, often autonomous, sectors of the personality, poorly integrated into the individual's fragile self-structure, which
produce moodiness or grandiosity as attributed by Jung to anima/
animus pathology. We propose to show that this overlap in description
is not coincidence, but is due to the fact that under certain circumstances, the intrapsychic functions of anima/animus and the selfobject
are identical, so that their disturbances are synonymous. It is our further contention that Jung's (1946) discovery of the importance of the
coniunctio in the transference actually illustrates the archetypal basis of
the selfobject experience later described personalistically by Kohut
(1971). The Rosarium pictures depict a shared psychic field, or stages in
the development of a self via merger with another — exactly the concept
of the selfobject, which means that one has the experience of wholeness
while emotionally held together by another person. The pictures indicate various vicissitudes in the development of the selfobject bond,
until the emergence of the "Rebis" (Jung 1946, par. 525), or lesser
coniunctio, which indicates a solid selfobject transference.

To focus on the common etiology and phenomenology of narcissistic difficulty in both men and women, while removing differential
terminology, assists in removing a sexist bias from the terms anima/
animus. The classical concepts have attracted confusion and controversy
among feminists and Jungian writers alike, because Jung ascribed particular characteristics to only one gender. For instance, many people
take exception to the typical cliché that masculinity is necessarily and
essentially assertive, while receptivity is a feminine trait. Such bias is
the unfortunate result of a patriarchy that dictated such norms. Furthermore, certain of Jung's opinions suggest that women are less capable of independent action and objectivity than men (Jung 1927, par.
243), and there are other similarly objectionable attitudes to be found
in his writing. In spite of these difficulties, we believe that the terms
anima and animus do, in fact, describe essential intrapsychic functions
whose nature can be clarified in a manner that will free them from both
culturally contaminated gender issues and a tendency to devalue
women. This requires that these concepts be completely freed from

their rigid, historical association with contrasexuality and instead examined in terms of fundamental intrapsychic processes.

Anima / Animus as Soul and Spirit

Considerable confusion has arisen from the number of different ways in which Jung used the terms *anima* and *animus*. They may refer to the intrapsychic contrasexual (Jung 1928, par. 297), the bridge to the unconscious (Jung 1957, para. 62), the unconscious itself (Jung 1940, par. 107), eros and logos (Jung 1957, par. 60), feeling and thinking (Jung 1921, par. 640), the inferior function (Jung 1944, par. 145), or soul and spirit (Jung 1954b, par. 55). Anima has also been used to mean the archetype of life itself (Jung 1954b, par. 66). In view of all these usages, it seems arbitrary to insist that we use the term in only one sense—but to try to retain a very fluid definition with multiple meanings perpetrates some impossible inconsistencies. Accordingly, we choose to focus selectively on Jung's definitions of anima as soul and animus as spirit, because this follows Jung's own etymological understanding (Jung 1934, par. 664). His initial and quite consistent use of the terms involves relationship to the unconscious, in contrast to the persona which relates to the outer world (Jung 1921, par. 803). We suggest that this bridging function best defines anima/animus, but also that this function no longer need be equated with contrasexuality. Same-sex dream figures may guide us to the unconscious, such as the appearance of the chthonic masculine in the dream of a modern man who has lost touch with it. Such a figure is a soul figure whatever its gender, while spirit or organizing figures may also be of either gender and are not limited to male figures in women's dreams—the spirit may perfectly well take a feminine form. This suggestion separates the gender of the figure from its intrapsychic function. It is important to emphasize that the *function* of mediation to the unconscious must not be confused with its *content*, or the resultant projection, image, or fantasy. In Jung's writing, function and content are so conflated that the anima became exclusively feminine. We believe that Jung overgeneralized when he described the bridging factor as necessarily contrasexual. For him personally, it was always personified as feminine—for example, Salome. And when we remember the numinosity of Jung's mother in his childhood, and how uncanny she seemed, it is understandable that the nonrational became connected to the feminine. But such is not universally the case.

If instead we choose to continue to use the terms *anima* and *animus* to refer to the intrapsychic contrasexual, which would be equally valid as an arbitrary usage, we then cannot also use them to refer exclusively to soul and spirit functions, since in today's clinical practice these are not necessarily carried out by contrasexual figures. Obviously, there is intrapsychic contrasexuality, but it would impossibly overstretch its significance to insist that it always carries our all of the functions in Jung's list.

All of this is clearly a plea for degenderizing the terms *anima* and *animus* in order to free us from their culture-bound associations. We may then recognize that both men and women experience intrapsychic soul figures which bridge to the unconscious and spirit figures which order and provide discrimination and meaning. But gender does not need to enter into these processes, and when these figures are in fact gendered, for instance, in a dream, this simply indicates the way they operate within human personality concerned — not necessarily generally. The function of relation to the unconscious is powerful and must contain and connect with those characteristics and qualities most repressed by the individual and his or her culture. In Jung's time, because contrasexuality was so rigidly defined, it is understandable that it became *the* bridge to the unknown, but that is no longer necessary. We are now allowed to claim behaviors and qualities previously restricted to the opposite sex. For instance, there is no need to label a man's capacity to nurture as his "inner feminine," or a woman's assertiveness as her "masculinity" — these can be reclaimed, to allow authentic masculine nurturing or feminine assertiveness. Then the whole question of the nature of contrasexuality can be reopened, free at least of the conscious baggage of the patriarchy. But a fuller discussion of this question will be postponed until we have explored some details of the process by which anima and animus create a relationship between individual awareness and the objective psyche. Meanwhile, it is important to emphasize that the function of relation to the unconscious is a genderless, archetypal potential, but the way we experience it is shaped by our contact with gendered beings.

Soul and Spirit as Processes

Our suggested metaphor for understanding these terms is that of a film moving through a projector which casts an image into consciousness. Spirit refers to the film, which carries a holographic code composed of fundamental, ordering or archetypal patterns. The actual nature of the film and its information is unknowable; only the resulting image can be known. The projection, decoding, and image-making mechanism, which is soul, converts the pattern of the film into a perceivable image. The screen that captures or reflects the image is the body, which includes the brain; the audience is the "ego." Anima/animus coupling thus leads to the creation and projection of intrapsychic imagery, which allows consciousness to perceive the unconscious and to be self-reflexive. Anima (soul) creates the subjective experience of being alive by virtue of its capacity to give image to archetypal potentials (spirit) in forms that can be made conscious—it is a bridge or transducer of energy from one form to another.

The process of embodiment of spirit is also mediated by the interaction of spirit with soul; anima as *ligamentum corporis et spiritus* (Jung 1950b, par. 553) links spirit with body in the form of both image and affect. The affective component of the complex is the channel of entry of the archetype into the body, where affects are felt as the effect of the archetype. This is the somatic end of the soul's process, which simultaneously produces associated intrapsychic imagery. The *soul* is a term for the realm of contact between personal and transpersonal; more properly, it is a process—soul receives the experience of spirit and transforms it into embodied psychic life. Spirit, or animus, is therefore the principle that provides meaning, discrimination, value, and order—or sometimes disorder—in order to superimpose new structures. It may become manifest in either masculine or feminine form, but this attribution of gender occurs within human consciousness. As Hillman (1985) puts it, soul brings spirit into personal experience. Clearly, soul and spirit are found within both men and women; within our usage, each sex possesses both anima and animus. This simply restates Jung's notion of the intrapsychic syzygy as an archetypal pattern common to all (Jung 1951, par. 41).

The Embodiment of Soul: Anima as Mirror of the Self

Hillman (1985, pp. 86–87) has clarified the manner in which the anima is related to psyche's capacity for self-reflection. He begins with Jung's (1937, par. 242) idea that psyche is the result of reflection and, through reflection, "life and its soul are abstracted from Nature and endowed with a separate existence" (Jung 1948, par. 235). According to Hillman (1985), anima both performs this abstraction through reflection and also personifies the result in a reflected form, so that nature can become conscious of itself. That is, consciousness arises from reflection, and anima produces the images which allow this process.

Here we are able to link the notion of anima with Kohut's (1971) emphasis on the importance of mirroring in the development of a cohesive self. The function of the anima is to mirror and attune. When a parent sees and acknowledges (reflects) the child's joyful, subjective experience of the Self, the Self is able to embody as soul. Parental affirmation of the child's experience is essential for this to occur. A piece of the child's consciousness is structured when its perception is consensually validated (reflected) by a loving figure. To some extent, children learn who they are in the course of relationship to others, by virtue of others' accurate perception of them. Whatever aspects of a child's archetypal potential (spirit) are mirrored can then be built into a personal self structure. Empathic attunement to the child, especially to his or her affects, is critical for this to occur (Basch 1983). Affect—which is embodied experience—is the crucial factor by virtue of its connection to archetype and complex. Affect must be mediated and contained by means of the parent's attunement so that it is not over-whelming to the child.

Thus it takes soul to allow the experience of soul. The child's soul, allowing a felt sense of authentic essence and subjectivity, is mirrored by the soul of the parent. Children are gradually able to reflect on themselves accurately—that is, know themselves—if they have received adequate reflection by their selfobjects. Eventually, this capacity is internalized and allows a relationship to the images of dreams and fantasy which reflect the Self. The mirroring selfobject function thus becomes an anima or soul experience.

In this way, mirroring allows incarnation of the potentials of the Self into the self. Depending on the responsiveness of the selfobject milieu, different aspects of the Self incarnate preferentially, with posi-tive or negative feeling tones. Some of this depends on the parent's own needs, anima pathology, and typology, leading to a particular fit between parent and child. The self that results will be a partial incarna-tion of the Self, with certain deficits, which are unincarnated or conflic-tual areas of the personality. These are also associated with negatively toned complexes and are the nuclei of later selfobject needs. For instance, those qualities which the family associates with the contrasex-ual, or which they will not allow the child to express at all, are not mirrored. Instead, they are repressed or split off to form the contents of shadow, complexes, or problematic anima/animus in the classical sense. Thus, in a girl, aggression, if not allowed normal expression, might be identified with nonego, often male, figures in dreams or in projection onto outer people.

To summarize the process, soul mirrors spirit, which, as it becomes embodied, is felt as the experience of soul. Soul therefore refers to both the function of mirroring and its result; it bridges to the unconscious by allowing the self to experience what it is otherwise unable to experience. Anima figures in dreams and fantasy are the hypostatization of this process, and there is no reason for them to be exclusively feminine.

Animus: The Principle of Order and Meaning

Idealization means the perception of another person, or a belief or system of thought, as a source of order, value, and meaning. According to Jung, spirit or animus conveys just this internal capacity, for instance, producing philosophical or religious (logos) ideas (Jung 1951, par. 33). Jung equates spirit with ruling principles and ideals (Jung 1926, par. 633) and suggests that spirit gives meaning to life (ibid., par. 648). Idealized figures are seen as the source or carrier of spirit — when an archetype is projected, as in an archetypal transference, the other is endowed with larger-than-life qualities. The idea that the child projects the Self onto the parent is synonymous with Kohut's idealized parent imago. The child needs to project onto the parents in this way because of the archetype's overwhelming affective intensity. The experience of the Self, or of the negative dimension of the archetypal parent, is potentially disorganizing, terrifying, or overstimulating, so that the child needs soothing and containing in order to structuralize these affects into complexes adequately, which allows the personality to become cohesive and coherent. Complexes allow the personalization of spirit into character structure.

As the parent is able to carry such idealized projections, the idealized selfobject is gradually internalized, allowing self-structures to be built which are an internal source of self-soothing, values, and ideals. These also allow the individual to integrate and order archetypal experience, for instance, as this occurs in dream or fantasy or is experienced as an outer event. The selfobject function then becomes an internal capacity to experience spirit. Without it, if the deficit is severe, the self is constantly vulnerable to fragmentation and chaos, or, if milder, the person cannot relate comfortably to the inner world.

In summary, the selfobject is an intrapsychic phenomenon linking us to our unconscious need for another to feel whole. This links it to the function of relationship to the unconscious, carried by anima/animus. The selfobject makes up for an unconscious deficit, whose effects are

the same as those attributed to problematic anima/animus functioning. In both cases, there exists a defective conscious–unconscious relationship, or self-Self axis, which requires mediation—we use the term
selfobject when this is carried out by an outer person, but the selfobject
is simply a name for the personal carrier of anima/animus projections.
Jung understood well such need for another person and approaches the
selfobject concept in this passage: "The unrelated human being lacks
wholeness, for he can achieve wholeness only through the soul, and the
soul cannot exist without its other side, which is found in a 'you' "
(ibid.). This is a good description of the selfobject.

Masculinity, Femininity, and Otherness

Although we feel that it is no longer possible to equate soul and
spirit with femininity and masculinity, the development and integration of contrasexual imagery and experience obviously remains an
important psychological function. However, it is not synonymous with
that of relation to the unconscious since, at times, this may have nothing to do with contrasexuality and indeed may have to do with "ipsesex-
uality" (we suggest this word in this context as a more exact antonym
than *homosexuality*). Contrasexuality is an aspect of archetypal otherness, closely related to, or a component of, the shadow. It is a personal
repository of qualities that people of a certain gender are not supposed
to manifest, within a particular family or culture, and which are accordingly repressed or split off. To integrate this material into consciousness
is a movement toward wholeness. But anima and animus bring into life
any unconscious potential, not just contrasexuality, although this is a
part of their function.

Masculinity, Femininity, and Gender

So far, we have begged the question about the nature of masculinity or femininity themselves. But it is easier to define what is unique in
the case of archetypes such as the child or mother than in the case of
gender factors, because of the archetypes wide range of variation due to
cultural influences. To grasp what is specific about the otherness of the
opposite gender requires that we define in what ways masculine and
feminine psychologies *intrinsically* differ—a task that, so far, defies
definitive description. It is widely believed that anatomy is destiny—
the structure of the body reflects archetypal differences in the psyche,
leading to the usual body metaphors, such as the feminine as containing, etc. But Haddon (1988) has pointed out that these metaphors do

not always support our stereotypes. For instance, testicular masculinity is nurturing and containing, while uterine femininity can be very thrusting. The body is not simply one way or the other and neither are our psychological characteristics. Further, with regard to most organ systems, we are more alike than different. Certainly the possession of a particular organ such as a penis or breast confers or allows experience which is not otherwise possible. But there is no reason to overgeneralize the metaphorical significance of such experiences to the point that the capacity to nurture or to be assertive at the psychological level belongs exclusively to one gender. Neither need there be specifically masculine or feminine forms of feeling or thinking; when a man is feeling, he is being masculine however he feels, as long as he is being authentic, and the same is true for a woman's thinking.

The body is exclusive in certain ways, but the psyche does not seem to follow suit, which puzzles us if we try to be nondualist. At first, it seems that with regard to archetypal masculinity or femininity the "blue" or psychological end of the spectrum is more flexible than the "red" or somatic end, unless there are, in fact, psychological or spiritual qualities that are not only *uniquely* masculine or feminine but also, like the body, not culture-bound. These would be hard to find.

We suggest that the reason for this apparent dilemma is that masculinity and femininity, as we know them, are actually two poles of a more fundamental archetype, that of gender. Gender runs through everything from language to reproduction, and its manifestations are extremely polymorphic. Like all archetypes, it is a potential whose content is filled in by local and cultural conditions—hence the enormous plasticity we see in what is defined as masculine or feminine. It is pointless to ask what is "essentially" one or the other, since the feminine and masculine are not the archetype itself but its manifestation. Masculinity and femininity are variable contents of a more fundamental reality. Like all archetypes, archetypal gender is not differentiated until it is within a human body or psyche, and it is only then that it appears as masculine or feminine. Gender expresses itself in the body as anatomy and psychologically by means of whatever the culture or the individual psyche defines as masculine or feminine. The archetype as spirit or organizing principle is found in the body as the form-determining principle governing sexual characteristics; the spirit of gender acts via the chromosomes, and these cannot be affected by culture. But psychologically, the situation is more complicated; gender manifestations are very plastic because the spirit can also act via the culture, allowing tremendous fluidity. Thus it may be that, in the last analysis, with maximum consciousness, the only differences between men and women are those related to the body and the particular psychological functions associated with it.

References

Basch, M. F. 1983. Empathic understanding: a review of the concept and some theoretical considerations. *Journal of the American Psychoanalytic Association* 31:101–26.

Corbett, L. and Rives, C. 1991. The fisherman and his wife: the anima in the narcissistic character. In *Psyche's Stories*, M. Stein and L. Corbett eds. Wilmete, Ill.: Chiron Publications.

Haddon, G. P. 1988. *Body Metaphors*. New York: Crossroads.

Hillman, J. 1985. *Anima: The Anatomy of a Personified Notion*. Dallas: Spring Publications.

Jung, C. G. 1921. *Psychological Types*. *CW*, vol. 6. Princeton, N.J.: Princeton University Press, 1971.

———. 1926. Spirit and life. In *CW* 8:319–337. Princeton, N.J.: Princeton University Press, 1970.

———. 1927. Woman in Europe. In *CW* 10:113–133. Princeton, N.J.: Princeton University Press, 1970.

———. 1928. The relations between the ego and the unconscious. In *CW* 7:123–304. Princeton, N.J.: Princeton University Press, 1966.

———. 1934. Basic postulates of analytical psychology. In *CW* 8:338–357. Princeton, N.J.: Princeton University Press, 1969.

———. 1937. Psychological factors determining human behaviour. In *CW* 8:114–126. Princeton, N.J.: Princeton University Press, 1969.

———. 1940. Psychology and religion. In *CW* 11:1–105. Princeton, N.J.: Princeton University Press, 1969.

———. 1944. *Psychology and Alchemy*. *CW*, vol. 12. Princeton, N.J.: Princeton University Press, 1968.

———. 1946. The psychology of the transference. In *CW* 16:163–338. Princeton, N.J.: Princeton University Press, 1966.

———. 1948. A psychological approach to the dogma of the trinity. In *CW* 11:107–198. Princeton, N.J.: Princeton University Press, 1969.

———. 1950a. Concerning rebirth. In *CW* 9i:113–150. Princeton, N.J.: Princeton University Press, 1968.

———. 1950b. A study in the process of individuation. In *CW* 9i:290–354. Princeton, N.J.: Princeton University Press, 1968.

———. 1951. *Aion*. *CW*, vol. 9ii. Princeton, N.J.: Princeton University Press, 1969.

———. 1954a. Concerning the archetypes, with special reference to the anima concept. In *CW* 9i:54–72. Princeton, N.J.: Princeton University Press, 1968.

———. 1954b. Archetypes of the collective unconscious. In *CW* 9i:3–41. Princeton, N.J.: Princeton University Press, 1968.

———. 1957. Commentary on "The Secret of the Golden Flower." In *CW* 13:1–56. Princeton, N.J.: Princeton University Press, 1967.

Kohut. 1971. *The Analysis of the Self*. New York: International Universities Press.

The Anima in Film

John Beebe

I

The anima in film is much like the anima anywhere else:[1] a confusing, deceptive presence with the capacity to engender inner transformation. Perhaps the only advantage a film-goer has (in common with the individual who can remember dreams) is that the archetype is *visible* as well as effective. For that reason, I have frequently turned to movies to understand better the typical role of the anima, and my hunger, as a clinician, to get a clearer sense of the functioning of this unconscious feminine presence has not gone unsatisfied. What I will offer here is a guide for exploring the anima through film, as well as an indication of some things film has helped me to discover about the anima's function in relation to other archetypes of the psyche, most particularly the persona.

I do not think it is appropriate to call every woman in film an anima figure, although the luminous representation has the important characteristic of turning a human being into an image that can be manipulated to aesthetic effect by a supraordinate creative personality, the film director. The director's role in making a film is already, therefore, not unlike that of the Self in creating dreams. The Self seeks to

---

John Beebe is a Jungian analyst in private practice in San Francisco. A graduate of Harvard College, the University of Chicago Medical School, and the C. G. Jung Institute of San Francisco, he is the editor of *Aspects of the Masculine*, *The San Francisco Jung Institute Library Journal*, and co-editor of *The Journal of Analytical Psychology*.

261

achieve the goals of the total psyche by affective stimulation of the ego through images that are no longer simple representations but feeling-toned complexes of unconscious life made to simulate conscious reality so that consciousness will take heed of them and hear out the important "home truths" they are there to convey. Of these feeling-toned complexes that mediate, in the regulation of psychic balance, between Self and ego, none has such a memorable effect as the anima (which is why so many women are not content with Jung's insistence that their mediating figure appears as a male, the animus). In a movie, the importance of the female image in stimulating emotionally relevant fantasy is obvious. One has only to point out the heavy emphasis the motion-picture medium has always placed upon its leading actresses.

Not every leading female character in a film is an anima figure, but often there are unmistakable signs that an unconscious, rather than conscious, figure is intended. It may be useful at the outset to specify some of these signs:

1. Unusual radiance (e.g., Garbo, Monroe). Often the most amusing and gripping aspect of a movie is to watch ordinary actors or actresses (e.g., Melvyn Douglas and Ina Claire in *Ninotchka*) contend with a more mind-blowing presence — a star personality who seems to draw life from a source beyond the mundane (e.g., Garbo in the same film). This inner radiance is one sign of the anima — and it is why actresses asked to portray the anima so often are spoken of a stars and are chosen more for their uncanny presence, whether or not they are particularly good at naturalistic characterization.

2. A desire to make emotional connection as the main concern of the character. One of the ways to distinguish an actual woman is her need to be able to say "no," as part of the assertion of her own identity and being.[2] (Part of the comedy of Katharine Hepburn is that she can usually *only* say no; so that when she finally says "yes," we know it stands as an affirmation of an independent woman's actual being.) By contrast, the anima figure wants to be loved, or occasionally to be hated, in either case living for connection, as is consistent with her general role as representative of the status of the man's unconscious eros and particularly his relationship to himself. (Ingrid Bergman, in *Notorious*, keeps asking Cary Grant, verbally and nonverbally, whether he loves her. We feel her hunger for

connection and anticipate that he will come alive only if he says
yes. His affect is frozen by cynicism and can only be redeemed
by his acceptance of her need for connection.)

3. Having come from some, quite other, place into the midst of a
   reality more familiar to us than the character's own place of
   origin. (Audrey Hepburn, in *Roman Holiday*, is a princess
   visiting Rome who decides to escape briefly into the life a
   commoner might be able to enjoy on a first trip to that city.)

4. The character is the feminine mirror of traits we have already
   witnessed in the attitude or behavior of another, usually male,
   character. (Marlene Dietrich as a seductive carbaret singer
   performing before her audience in *The Blue Angel* displays the
   cold authoritarianism of the gymnasium professor of English,
   Emil Jannings, who manipulates the students' fear of him in
   the opening scene of the movie. Jannings pacing back and
   forth in front of his class and resting against his desk as he holds
   forth are mirrored in Dietrich's controlling stride and aggressive
   seated posture in front of *her* audience.)

5. The character has some unusual capacity for life, in vivid
   contrast to other characters in the film. (The one young woman
   in the office of stony bureaucrats in *Ikiru* is able to laugh at
   almost anything. When she meets her boss, Watanabe, just at
   the point that he has learned that he has advanced stomach
   cancer and is uninterested in eating anything, she has an
   unusual appetite for food and greedily devours all that he buys
   her.)

6. The character offers a piece of advice, frequently couched in
   the form of an almost unacceptable rebuke, which has the
   effect of changing another character's relation to a personal
   reality. (The young woman in *Ikiru* scorns Watanabe's
   depressed confession that he has wasted his life living for his
   son. Shortly after, still in her presence, Watanabe is suddenly
   enlightened to his life task, which will be to use the *rest* of his
   life living for children, this time by expediting the building of
   a playground that his own office, along with the other agencies
   of the city bureaucracy, has been stalling indefinitely with red
   tape. He finds his destiny and fulfillment in his own nature as

a man who is meant to dedicate his life to the happiness of others, exactly within the pattern he established after his wife's death years before, of living for his son's development rather than to further himself. The anima figure rescues his authentic relationship to himself, which requires a tragic acceptance of this pattern *as* his individuation and his path to self-transcendence.)

7. The character exerts a protective and often therapeutic effect on someone else. (The young widow in *Tender Mercies* helps Robert Duvall overcome the alcoholism that has threatened his career.)

8. Less positively, the character leads another character to recognize a problem in personality which is insoluble. (In Nicholas Ray's *In a Lonely Place*, the antisocial screenwriter played by Humphrey Bogart meets an anima figure played—with a face to match the cool mask of his own—by Gloria Grahame, who cannot overcome her mounting doubts about him enough to accept him as a husband. Her failure to overcome her ambivalence is a precise indicator of the extent of the damage that exists in his relationship to himself.)

9. The loss of this character is associated with the loss of purposeful aliveness itself. (The premise of *L'Avventura* is the disappearance of Anna, who has been accompanied to an island by her lover, a middle-aged architect with whom she has been having an unhappy affair. We never get to know Anna well enough to understand the basis of her unhappiness, because she disappears so early in the film, but we soon discover that the man who is left behind is in a state of archetypal *ennui*, a moral collapse characterized by an aimlessly cruel sexual pursuit of one of Anna's friends and a spoiling envy of the creativity of a younger man who can still take pleasure in making a drawing of an Italian building.)

II

Simply recognizing a character in a film as an anima figure does not exhaust the meaningfulness of what an analytic approach to cinema can unlock. The true interest of this approach comes when, through it, the dynamics of a cinematic experience of the anima are revealed and one can see how the figure herself changes in relation to the character whose life she affects. In film, as in no other medium, we can actually see the behavior of the archetype; in life, we know her far more indirectly, as moods, impulses, symptoms, and as a shape-shifting fleeting personage in our dreams — if, indeed, we can remember them. In film, we can see the anima figure over time, in a more or less stable guise, at her strange task of mediating the fate of a protagonist. We are permitted to watch as the anima relates to the other complexes of a psyche.

A way to understand a film psychologically is to take its various characters as signifying *complexes*, parts of a single personality whose internal object relations are undergoing change.[3] These object relations are represented by the interactions of the characters, who usually include a figure representing the anima. Because the relation of the anima to other complexes is of particular interest to a therapist, I have often recommended to therapists that they use the movies they view in their leisure time to train themselves in visualizing the internal relationships involved. In addition to enhancing their enjoyment of films, those who have followed my advice have often found that their sensitivity, within analytic work, to dream and associative material is greatly improved. This exercise, following in the Jungian tradition of having analysts-in-training engage in the interpretation of fairy tales, has the advantage that the material studied for archetypal comparison to clinical material is drawn from the same culture as our patients. It also draws a therapist deeper into what is essentially a new ritual context for the immersion into visionary archetypal experience.

Filmmaking, at least in the hands of its acknowledged masters, is a form of active imagination drawing its imagery from the anxieties generated by current concerns, and filmwatching has become a contemporary ritual that is only apparently a leisure.[4] Going to movies has achieved, in this country, almost the status of a religious activity. As a teacher, I have found that seminars built around the showing of a movie rich in imaginal material have been more successful in getting students to enter into a dialogue with images than my similar efforts to work with materials drawn from a more remote culture form, and I think this is because the viewing of films is numinous for us. Few myths impact contemporary Americans the way the films of Spielberg, Coppola, and Lynch do.

I would like to examine here the work of a somewhat less immediately familiar triad of American directors, out of a potential pool of dozens of similar rank who have worked within our mainstream Hollywood tradition of using commercially established stars, cinematographers, and scripts to create works of art that are as meaningful as they are entertaining. The directors that I have chosen are undisputed *auteurs* who have particularly concerned themselves with the anima.[5] Both in their obsessive devotion to certain female stars and in the seductiveness of their ability to make good scripts built around movie formulas come alive enough to seem real, George Cukor, Alfred Hitchcock, and Peter Bogdanovich belong to the culture of anima, so much, in fact, that it sometimes feels as if the anima chose these directors to make her presence visible to us in our time.

In what follows, I will address films by these directors—*A Star is Born*, *Vertigo*, and *Mask*—that express the extreme of their inspiration by the anima archetype, films that I would call masterpieces of the anima. In each of these films, the neurosis of the *auteur*, or at least that of his creative personality, is painfully evident.[6]

Each takes as its starting point a major malfunction of a hero's persona which threatens permanently to impair this male character's ability to work or find love. Each of these films, as is characteristic of movies about the anima, engages this wounded character with an anima figure who is symbolic of a deeper aspect of his suffering and who attempts to move his psyche beyond it. However, in these films, she fails. None of the films lead to an enduring, happy connection with the anima or to genuine transformation. The function of the anima here is significantly more tragic than therapeutic: her presence serves to deepen our sense of the hero's suffering, and to make us, and him, accept it as his fate.

These films were released in America between 1953 and 1985, but they share the distinction of finding special favor with critics and audiences grown sophisticated enough to appreciate their imaginal power at a particularly self-reflective moment in the history of filmwatching, 1983 to 1985, when the sense of a lull in the general level of current American films combined with the widespread availability of American movie classics on videocassette led a mass audience to undertake what until then only cinema buffs had been able to pursue, a basic reexamination of the entire corpus of the American cinema. This kind of reflection on an aesthetic tradition is itself an anima activity, one that the archetype will insist upon at times when its further evolution in life or in art seems blocked by an excessive insistence upon persona values. The period just before and just after Reagan was elected to his second term was such a time, when a one-sided interest on what the hero "can do" was in evidence. It is not unfitting that, at this point in our history, the great American war-horses of anima disappointment, *A Star Is Born*

and *Vertigo*, films about what the hero could *not* do, would be re-
released in their restored or rediscovered widescreen formats and that
they would generate in theaters the kind of interest that is usually
reserved for new films. It is more surprising that Peter Bogdanovich,
whose early career had involved him in the role of American film
appreciator celebrating our *auteurs* of the hero archetype, Ford and
Hawks and Welles, would be able to break through with *Mask*, a great
new American film putting forward so solidly the anima theme of the
hero's failure. Bogdanovich's film is in the tradition of the hard-boiled
sentimentality and macabre kitsch of his earlier masters, who could
satirize heroic aspirations, but it is less macho in its assertion that an
ideal relationship to the anima on the hero's terms in not an American
possibility and more gracious in its acceptance of the necessity for the
defeat of the hero.

A Star Is Born

George Cukor's *A Star Is Born* draws explicit life from the assumption that its audience will be steeped in Hollywood culture. It begins
with the crackling of carbon arc lights coming alive to illuminate the
skies of Hollywood for a premiere; much later in the film, we will hear
Judy Garland's electric voice cry out "lights!" as she begins to panto-
mime a production number she has been rehearsing for the cameras.
The story is about the birth of the star portrayed by Garland, but in
Cukor's handling the real theme is the culture of film turning a search-
light upon itself. Judy Garland, as a band singer pulled into a new
career in the movie business, becomes the image of a bewildered creative consciousness assimilating the many ironies of filmmaking itself.
These ironies are presented as pitfalls of the studio system, but it is clear
that the resonance is to the introverted problems of the creative process
as well. Filmmaking is, above all, what Andrew Sarris has called "a very
strenuous form of contemplation" (1968, p. 37), and in many films a
leading actress becomes the personification of the director's meditative
stance toward the materials of story, acting, photography, and music.

In *A Star Is Born*, Garland becomes the anima image of Cukor's
approach to creativity. The person she is here could not have been the
prototype for any actual woman initiating a career: she is far too reac-
tive to the man in her life and to Hollywood itself. Moreover, she is not
particularly good at shaping herself even to these expectations. As a
come-back vehicle for Judy Garland, the movie was a disaster, despite
its excellent critical reputation and its part in securing her niche as

cinema legend, but as a depiction of the middle-aged commercial Hollywood artist's anima, the demonic energy, the androgyny, the slightly worn and worried look, and the now puffy, now beautiful head of Garland, and even the grandiosity and tiresome intensity of this fascinating but self-destructive star, work to the director's advantage. Making everything too much is a hallmark of the anima, and Garland indelibly conveys the intensity of the Hollywood *auteur* in imposing meaning on a commercial film. The frightening aspect of this dark film musical — and not just its plot, but the murky tones of its technicolor qualify it as a true color *noir* film — is the way the anima of the film-making totally overtakes the persona, so that reasonable proportions give way to overproduction and melodrama. This is the subtext of Vicki Lester (Garland) supplanting Normal Maine, the Barrymore-ish star who discovered her. By the time of Maine's suicide, Vicki Lester is able to present herself accurately to her public as "Mrs. Normal Maine."

Throughout Moss Hart's script, a grandiose Hollywood possibility is followed by a grim Hollywood reality (for instance: "the wedding to end all weddings" ends up getting held in a county jail, to avoid the press), but Hart's jokes at the expense of the Hollywood persona have for Cukor the larger meaning that the persona is losing control to another archetype. The songs of the score — most particularly "The Man That Got Away" — reemphasize the loss of masculine identity (pro-tested for most of the movie by James Mason as the doomed Norman Maine) in favor of the archetypal emotionality represented by Garland. In the end, the movie's command of voice and dialogue and gesture (as ably defended by Mason's performance) give way to an overwhelming presence, mood, and intensity, as personified by Garland, whose unconscious energy is more interesting than her conscious skill at char-acter portrayal. Yet Mason and Garland are in vivid relationship to each other. To watch Garland lust after James Mason's control and precision, and Mason appreciate and envy Garland's magnetism, is to participate in a mystery at the core of cinema experience, the interplay between movie star and actor expressing a reciprocal tension between anima and persona. Cukor's appreciation of the neurotic dynamics of this relation-ship in the work of cinema artists in what makes this movie great, especially in its mad moments, like the one where Norman Maine walks into the midst of his wife's Academy Award acceptance speech to make a drunken pitch for a job and ends up smacking her in the face with the back of the hand he stretches out to make a point.

A Star Is Born is not the only movie where a director works out of the tension between a command of style that is losing ground and a capacity for creative expression that is still vibrant (Federico Fellini's *Ginger and Fred* has exactly this theme), but I think it is by far the greatest one, raising this peculiar problem to the status of creative tragedy. In *A Star Is Born*, Cukor delivers one of the seminal lessons of cinema: even though movies are nothing without stars that can act, stars are finally more important than actors to the emotional effect of a screen experience. This is a truth that the actual Academy Awards loves to obscure, with its frequent honoring of thespians like F. Murray Abraham, Geraldine Page, and Jessica Tandy, and its slighting of authentic movie stars, like Chaplin and Garbo and Garland, and of *auteur* directors, like Hitchcock and Spielberg, who understand how to turn actors into images. (Look at *The Prince and the Showgirl* and watch what happens when Laurence Olivier is pitted against Marilyn Monroe.) What Monroe and Garbo and Garland understand with their star acting (which, despite their occasional ambitions, was never of the Broadway or London variety) is that film, unlike the stage, is not a medium of actors, but of actors' *images*. The actors are not up there on the screen, their images are; and this translation of person into image is crucially important psychologically, because it moves film past the personal and into the archetypal realm of psychological experience.

When, in the first decade of this century, Griffith adapted the new "trick photography" effect of the close-up and projected gigantic "severed heads" of actors upon the screen, cinema became a medium for our direct engagement with archetypes. A cinematic close-up is analogous to an aria in opera, a moment when a timeless dimension of human experience can be caught and contemplated (Balázs 1985). But once the archetypes are summoned, they take on their own life. The magical moment in *A Star Is Born* where Garland (entertaining Mason) looks out at us and says, "Now here comes a big fat close-up!" framing her face with her own panning hands, is extraordinary not just because it reveals the role of the anima in creating the close-up, but because the anima wrests control of her own image away from the director. It is in the nature itself of the anima to use a medium to create images of herself and to concern herself with the style of these images. This relationship between the anima and the image of herself that she creates is corollary to the intense interaction between anima and persona.

Perhaps the most telling example of this dynamic comes as a silent monologue played out on Judy Garland's face, as the band singer is being readied for her first screen test. While the make-up men recite possibilities for dealing with the lack of statement in her visage, Garland, staring into a make-up mirror, tries on the arched look of "the

Dietrich eyebrow" and puffs her lips to get the fullness of "the Craw-
ford mouth." Then, for a fleeting moment, she stares in despair at her
own trapped and suddenly shapeless face, the personification of an
anima without an image, wondering if she will ever find one.

Vertigo

That this anxiety lies at the core of the anima archetype is made
even clearer by Alfred Hitchcock's *Vertigo*, where an unknown, and
perhaps unknowable, woman, working to convince a detective that she
really does not know who she is, becomes trapped by the fiction she has
created. The movie turns on the slightly malicious question, "Who is
Kim Novak?" a question which becomes more frightening, and unan-
swerable, once the secret of her dual identity within the film is
revealed. The initial sequences, for all their beauty in summoning up
the enchantment of the anima archetype, belong to a familiar-enough
theme in psychology and art — the man as victim of seduction. The fall
of James Stewart's character Scottie into "acute melancholia complicated by a guilt complex" is what he deserves from biting into this
familiar apple. Indeed, the cumulative kitsch elements of the
romance — the staginess of the exposition of the preposterous plot; the
tourist's view of San Francisco's prettiness in the long, languishing
silent sequence; the poor quality of the "museum painting" of the
nineteenth-century woman Kim Novak is supposed to be obsessed by;
the monotonous unreality Novak brings to the reading of her lines; and
the ponderous earnestness of James Stewart as he becomes her victim —
all have a wearying effect, much like the depression of coaddiction. But
when the trickster beneath all this gnawing at the bone of hopeless love
is exposed to us, and both characters know that it was all a trick, the
film develops a wildness in which anything could happen. Stewart's
solution — to precipitate the total loss the archetype in the fever pitch of
his disillusionment — is a truly shocking finale, forcing the audience to
the conclusion that the premises of romantic love have themselves
disappeared. If *Vertigo* has, as Royal S. Brown (1986) argues, the form
of an Orphic tragedy, a story of the romantic artist's need to gaze
murderously upon the illusion-based love at the center of his creative
impulse, then the irretrievably lost Eurydice within this poet's film is
the anima herself as we have known and used her to support the image
of ideal romantic love. At the film's end, a bell tolls for the loss of the
archetype.

The film's extraordinary poignancy turns upon Kim Novak's

uncanny ability to make us care what happens to her, despite the palpable deceptiveness of her many guises. She is presented initially as Madeleine Elster, the elegant wife of a San Francisco shipbuilder, and is supposed to be hysterically possessed by the ghost of her great-grandmother, Carlotta Valdez, a woman who committed suicide after her rich and powerful husband discarded her and took her baby away. Later we learn that Novak is really Judy Barton, a San Francisco shop girl from Salina, Kansas, who had been coached to impersonate Madeleine by Madeleine's husband so that he, too, could dispose of his wife. James Stewart plays a detective, Scottie Ferguson, used by Madeleine's husband to verify the cover story for the wife's murder. He is to follow Novak around San Francisco, and he falls in love with the deception she creates as the pseudo-Madeleine. This Madeleine is a classic 1950s woman, who confines her body within a gray tailored suit, her hair close around her head like a man's, except for the elegant feminine knot behind the head. Her image is the extreme of compliance to the demands patriarchy makes upon the feminine, to be voluptuous and pleasing within a masculine mold. Like a fourth-century B.C. marble bust of Aphrodite, Novak-as-Madeleine is a personification of the goddess as patriarchal anima, asleep to her other feminine possibilities and almost Apollonian in the balance of her contours.

Later, when she appears, in shocking contrast, as Judy, Novak is painted in a hard Dionysian style, like a vulgar theater mask. She is incapable of getting Stewart's Scottie to find any taste for this more florid, and angry, assertion of femininity. Instead, Scottie forces her to recreate the Apollonian image for him by redoing her make-up, her hair, her clothes, and even her nails in the image of the former, illusory Madeleine. We realize to our horror that, for all the cruelty and male chauvinism of his project, this is the only style through which Novak's soft femininity can express itself. We pity her the more because we love her this way, recognizing that we, too, are fatally attracted by the patriarchal anima style. There can be no happy outcome, but the fall from grace of this presentation of the feminine at the end of the picture is nevertheless an occasion for pity and dread. The film leaves us mourning, with Stewart, for this unworkable anima image — and with the repulsed sense that we have seen the archetypal background of all our own failures at love.

This cynicism is a sign of the appearance of the senex archetype once the anima disappears.[7] We can read *Vertigo* as the initiation of a vulnerable man into the psychological senescence produced when the anima is irretrievably lost. Jung has given this classic description:

> After the middle of life . . . permanent loss of the anima means a diminution of vitality, of flexibility, and of human kindness. The result, as a rule, is premature rigidity, crustiness, stereotypy, fanatical one-sidedness, obstinacy, pedantry, or else resignation, weariness, sloppiness, irresponsibility, and finally a childish *ramollissement* [softening of personality] with a tendency to alcohol. (Jung 1954, par. 147)

Vertigo defines the process by which the anima is sacrificed in a man destined to assume the senex character, making clear the role the anima plays in her own withdrawal from the psychological scene. The anima that seduces a man into permanent disillusionment with the feminine is under the spell of a malignant father complex, so that her energy is infected by the demands of the complex and ceases to serve the total personality. This is the *shadow* of the process that therapists more usually imagine the anima to be catalyzing for a man in midlife, which is normally the discovery of the value of his aliveness to him. In the dark variant depicted here, the anima is a tragic accomplice to a form of negative initiation, by which the man is denied an inner life in favor a hollow victory over his emotions.

There are two sequences in this movie which are organized around the unexpected, and uncanny, experience of Madeleine/Judy staring indirectly into the camera.[8] In both cases, Novak's face is frozen with the unhappiness of her unfree condition, disclosing to us her tragic foreknowledge of the role she will be forced to play in Scottie's psychological demise. The first of these direct gazes occurs in the car just before she and Scottie reach the mission at San Juan Bautista where she will meet her accomplice, Gavin Elster. This gaze is transposed to the livery stable of the mission, where she sits in a old carriage rather than the car. She keeps staring for a long time, then begins to move to join Elster, who is set to throw his real wife's dead body from the top of the tower and make it look like her own suicide.

The second of these direct gazes at the camera occurs when Judy sits in her hotel room, her face a mask of tragedy, and recalls what actually happened when she did reach the top of the bell tower ahead of Scottie. As before, the actress's gaze prefigures further actions that will lead to the completion of the project—which Elster set in motion and which Hitchcock, as director, will finally use her to complete—to destroy any basis Scottie, or the filmwatcher, may have for believing that a healthy connection to the feminine is possible.

Scottie's vulnerability to such control by a cynical complex is the vertigo of the film's title, visualized as an acrophobia that affects the way he sees the base of the bell tower's stairwell when he looks down.[9] Its square geometric shape is a Self-symbol that recedes further away from him as he contemplates its enlarging possibility: we are looking at a man's terror in the face of the depths of his own being. It is this terror that the father complex represented by Elster can successfully manipulate: since the anima promises connection to the Self, the complex moves the anima to convince the man that he must discard her for her own survival and mastery of his fear.

Mask

If the anima in A Star Is Born overtakes a failing persona, and is lost in Vertigo to a hollow persona, Mask suggests the healing of a wounded persona by an anima neither too strong not too weak to do her real job of protecting the personality. Like A Star Is Born and Vertigo, Mask is set in California, but twenty-five years later, in the matriarchal, counterculture California that had grown up to one side of the freeway, and the film is only superficially about a tragedy within patriarchy. Part of the fun of the film is to watch the resilience of a personality that could never get by if it played according to the patriarchal rules set for persona and anima behavior that the films from the 1950s delineate. The hero, Rocky Dennis, collects Brooklyn Dodgers cards from 1955, and some of his mother's biker friends tell him that that seems like yesterday, but clearly we have entered another system of values. His mother, Rusty Dennis, is a beautiful queen of the counterculture, permanently estranged from her critical Jewish father, and, as played with perfect ease and authority by Cher, who looks like a dark Aphrodite in this movie, she can oppose her own authority to anything that patriarchy can dish out to stand in her son's way. The film opens on a day when she has to take him to be enrolled in a new junior high school, and it will be a problem, because he was born with craniodiaphyseal dysplasia, a rare condition that causes him to deposit calcium in his skull at an abnormal rate. His face looks like a Halloween mask, or more precisely, the long, bent facial shield of a Mycenean warrior. His mother's defiance of doctors (who told her he would be retarded, blind, and deaf) and of school principals who don't think he can fit in (he gets along well with the other kids and is in the top 5% of his class) has become legendary, and her verve in defying their authority makes almost anything seem possible. When his head aches (they've been told that because of the pressure on his spinal cord he may have only a few months to live), Cher can get him to talk himself out of it; when she puts her hands against his head, the pain goes away. He is, in turn, her conscience and her moral support, forcing her to look at her serious drug habit and urging her on to a stable relationship with one of the nicer bikers.

This is the naive condition of the mother complex in the junior high school period when it is most hopeful, humorous, and aspiring, when a son and mother living without a father can truly be two against the world. The boy, who is, in fact, hopelessly unadapted to the patriarchal world, gets by as a charming and poignant exception to the usual patriarchal expectations, and, for a time, it is possible for him to make a successful adaptation, as Rocky does. In a brilliant sequence that takes the movie down to the level of the myth involved, Rocky wins his class over with his retelling of the Trojan War. This choice is not accidental; like Achilles, who calls weeping to his mother for help when his girl is taken from him, Rocky is a mother's hero. He will not be able to outgrow fixation at the awkward developmental stage he epitomizes for everybody else.

Girls are a particular problem for Rocky; they admire him, but he cannot attract them. His mother brings a prostitute home for him, but that is no solution, because Rocky needs to find out if he is lovable on his own. As this sequence makes clear, the anima is an archetype that the mother complex cannot deliver to a man; she must be found outside the mother's sphere of authority and as a consequence of his own initiative.

Pushing himself away from his mother with the excuse that she won't do anything about her excessive use of drugs, Rocky accepts a summer job as a counselor's aid at a camp for the blind, where he meets a beautiful blind girl his own age. Her name is Diana Adams, and with his interest in mythology and the milky radiance Laura Dern brings to the part, Rocky is quick to associate her to the White Goddess whose name she bears.[10] When she asks him what he looks like, he tells her that he looks like the Greek god Adonis and then the truth about the condition deforming his face. She runs her hand over his features and tells him he "looks pretty good" to her. They fall in love, but she is a daughter of careful, protective, upper middle class parents from a southern California suburb, and when they come to pick her up, her father takes a pained look at Rocky and whisks her away in the family station wagon. Rocky tries to telephone Diana but her mother intercepts his messages. It is evident that he will never be able to make a permanent connection with any patriarchal anima figure.

Bogdanovich appears to tell this true story naively, as if it were a docudrama enlivened only by the extraordinary naturalness of his direction, which gives the film the look of life. Yet everywhere, seamlessly introduced into the smooth cinematic narration, is his sense of the archetypal background of this strange but charming matriarchal constellation. In one scene, Rocky, teaching the blind girl how to associate to visual adjectives, gives her some cotton balls to feel and tells her, "This is billowy." The movie reverses this process, giving us images that bring us as close as a visual medium can to the texture of a mother complex, a secret sacred marriage between mother and son that finally excludes all other loves. Like Laura Dern, we are given a first-hand grasp of the soft intractability of Rocky's mother complex.

In this set-up, the anima's contribution is an acceptance of the insolubility of the problem. Rocky goes to find Diana once more and learns that she is being sent away to school. His headaches are getting worse, and he will have to go back home to die. Caught between the feelings of her own parents and the powerful sway of Rocky's irresistible fate, Diana can only console Rocky with her acceptance of him and of his limited access to her. Beautiful as she is, she must return him to the still more beautiful goddess who is his mother and to the archetypal pattern of the son-lover who dies young. This brief connection with the anima is enough, however, to enable him to accept his fate. Rocky is able to move on within his myth and to objectify it for us, so that when he dies and his mother becomes the grieving goddess, we experience the completion of his pattern and the sense that there has been an individuation.

The film itself does not step outside the frame of reference of the mother complex; it is not afraid to be sentimental or defiant. Yet Bogdanovich somehow achieves objectivity by letting us see the entirety of Rocky's situation, in both its personal and its mythological aspects. I suspect that this rounding out is an effect of the anima. Within the mother complex that cannot be overcome, the anima can sometimes find opportunities lacking in a patriarchal pattern of development for establishing the wholeness of the arrested personality.

Both *A Star Is Born* and *Vertigo* are patriarchal in their premises and narcissistic in their pathology. They can be understood by the nature of their affective tone, as well as through the archetypes they present. *A Star Is Born* is hypomanic; *Vertigo* is depressed. *Mask*, although similarly concerned with persona wounding and anima vulnerability, is neither. Its even feeling-tone reveals a surprising resilience in the regulation of self-esteem, which seems a gift of the character's freedom from patriarchal expectations. In *Mask*, neither the persona nor the anima has very much to lose. Without a fantasy of patriarchal success, there is no expectation of ideal apotheosis for either pole of the adapting self and, therefore, no liability to titanic disappointment. Instead of tragedy, there is pathos in anima disappointment and a humorous humility in the face of the persona's shortcomings. Within this matriarchal pattern, the anima can play only a limited role in extending the range or the health of a personality, but she can satisfy other needs of the psyche, for self-acceptance, integrity, and love.

III

It remains for us to ask what it does for a cinema *auteur* to reflect his anima problem so directly on the screen. It is clear that these films concern themselves with fatal constellations and reject the hope of heroic healing. One likes, nevertheless, to imagine that these directors healed themselves, or at least resolved tensions in their creative personalities, with these films. I have observed, following Jung, that it is therapeutic simply to visualize the anima with such clarity. Jung often expressed the opinion that the way for a man to analyze his anima is to get to know her better. In this process, as these films make clear, a man will come to experience not only her style and her nature, but her autonomy as a factor that stands behind his ego in shaping his destiny. This independence, which promises an endless creative capacity for self-renewal, is sharply restricted by the nature of the other personality complexes with which the anima must contend. The film medium allows the director to articulate the limits of his anima's freedom in shaping his creative life. We who are interested in psychological creativity may understand from the urgency with which these cinema masters have attended to the fate of the anima that the anima's vicissitudes refer to an imagination struggling to keep its capacity for psychological connection to itself alive and that this desirable outcome is by no means a guaranteed inevitability.

Notes

1. The most succinct general description of the ways the anima manifests herself can be found in Hillman (1975, pp. 42–44). A critical examination of the concept of the anima in analytical psychology is given in Hillman (1985).
2. I am indebted to the Jungian analyst Beverley Zabriskie for first making this distinction for me.
3. This is the basic principle, as well, of Jungian dream interpretation (see Jung 1906).

4. See my recorded seminar, "Film as Active Imagination," C. G. Jung Institute of San Francisco, October 10–11, 1981.

5. See Sarris (1968) for a discussion of rank and *auteur* in regard to Hollywood directors.

6. It is best to resist the temptation to draw conclusions about the personal psychology of a director from his films, but "personal filmmaking" does open up the psychology of the creative personality to everyone's inspection.

7. Hitchcock supplies an exact personification of the senex archetype in the figure of the coroner who presides over the jury called to determine the cause of Madeleine's death after the first bell-tower episode. The coroner's tone in delivering the verdict of suicide insinuates that Scottie is at fault, which becomes the attitude Scottie assumes toward himself in his subsequent depression.

8. A particularly lucid account of the first of these moments can be found in Rothman (1988), who invokes Stanley Cavell's "melodrama of the unknown woman."

9. Lesley Brill, in his careful analysis of the camera's movement in *Vertigo* (1988, pp. 202–206), points out that a geometric spiral is implied in this figure.

10. Robert Graves's use of this term for Diana/Artemis is well known (1960, pp. 85–86). Peter Bogdanovich revealed to Barbara Grizzuti Harrison that he was reading Robert Graves's *The White Goddess* in 1981, just after his lover, Dorothy Stratten, was killed (Harrison 1990).

REFERENCES

Balázs, B. 1985. The close up. In *Film Theory and Criticism*, 3rd ed., G. Mast and M. Cohen, eds. New York: Oxford University Press, pp. 255–264.

Brill, L. 1988. *The Hitchcock Romance: Love and Irony in Hitchcock's Films*. Princeton, N.J.: Princeton University Press.

Brown, R. S. 1986. *Vertigo* as Orphic tragedy. *Film/Literature Quarterly* 14(1):32–43.

Graves, R. 1960. *The Greek Myths*. New York: Viking Penguin.

Harrison, B. G. 1990. Peter Bogdanovich comes back from the dead. *Esquire* 114(2):146–156.

Hillman, J. 1975. *Re-Visioning Psychology*. New York: Harper and Row.

_____. 1985. *Anima: An Anatomy of a Personified Notion*. Dallas: Spring Publications.

Jung, C. G. 1906. Association, dream, and hysterical symptom. In *CW* 2:353–407. Princeton, N. J.: Princeton University Press, 1973.

_____. 1954. Concerning the archetypes, with special reference to the anima concept. *CW* 91:54–72. Princeton, N.J.: Princeton University Press, 1959.

Rothman, W. 1988. Vertigo: the unknown woman in Hitchcock. In *The "I" of the Camera*. Cambridge: Cambridge University Press, pp. 142–173.

Sarris, A. 1968. *The American Cinema*. New York: Dutton.

Book Reviews

To Be a Woman: The Birth of the Conscious Feminine
Connie Zweig, ed. Los Angeles: Jeremy P. Tarcher, Inc., 1990. 279 pages. $12.95

Reviewed by Bea Reed

This book was inspired by a dream, and who can resist such a dream, complete with careful attention to the color of the wallpaper, a grisly twist, and no simple interpretation? In images, it tells the story of the editor's complicated relationship with her mother and the sacrifice of the father. Interestingly, as a hidden motif in the construction of the book, there are far fewer male contributors and all the male authors who were asked to write about the anima refused. The father is indeed in eclipse.

The introduction by Connie Zweig to the various sections and articles is infused with her creative search and a generosity of spirit. She spends a few pages in the prologue recounting her own story and development in her family of both masculine and feminine traits. She also takes on the vexatious question of what the Feminine is, offering some of her own ideas such as contemplative and nurturing versus active and invasive for the Masculine. Some thoughts of Marion Woodman are also included, such as preference for process over product, journey over goal, body and receptivity. But the whole process of distinguishing between Masculine and Feminine is beset with difficulty, partially because almost all our gender-related terms are far from value free. It helps somewhat to substitute terms from a

Bea Reed, M.A., is a graduate of the C. G. Jung Institute in Zürich, Switzerland, and has a private practice in East Lansing and Grand Rapids, Michigan.

non-Western language, such as Yin and Yang, and some of the authors have done this. Another difficulty is that many of us lose sight of the level at which we are discussing differences, beginning with an archetypal sense of the Masculine and Feminine and slipping unnoticed to the level of men and women or mother and father and finally writing as though women alone carry the archetype of the Feminine and vice versa.

The book is divided into six parts, retracing our common evolution, remothering ourselves, refathering ourselves, resacralizing the female body, rewaking the divine feminine, and renewing the world. The topic of this work is extremely timely and its range is extraordinary. The various contributions range from academic formulations of the questions surrounding gender to reformulations of somewhat shopworn Jungian insights, from very personal stories regarding gender formation to poetical images in active imagination. The drawback in this type of presentation is that no one audience is assumed. Some of the articles are probably a bit technical without some background in Jungian psychology and others are too elementary. The different levels of presentation tend to be disconcerting rather than enriching, as no doubt the editor intended. Having settled down to really thinking about a new model of gender discrimination such as Haddon's four-fold Yang and Yin masculinity and Yang and Yin femininity, one stumbles a bit over, "Amid the nodding roses sits a slender girl in blue, the book of Isaiah on her knee. Under her foot the serpent's head is bruised. The moon beneath her reflects the light above. Dawn entwines her hair" (Speeth on the Madonna, p. 111). Can one mind-set deal well with both these approaches?

Overall the book is a little like a dinner party. In an attempt to put paid to all one's social obligations, one invites a few too many people and is left with the notion that the guests one cared about the least rather monopolized the conversation. Two articles which were particularly thought-provoking were the above-mentioned Haddon, "The Personal and Cultural Emergence of Yang-Femininity," and Robert M. Stein, "From the Liberation of Women to the Liberation of the Feminine." Stein begins his article with a discussion of the roles women have played in our time, and how these roles have become oppressive and unfulfilling. Using Greek mythology, he outlines the main expressions for the feminine, the mother as nurturance, the love goddess as erotic attractor, and the Artemisian aspect of independence and freedom. As a good psychoanalyst, he points out that projecting these qualities, and the complementary ones for masculinity, keeps both sexes in a state of dependence. We all need access to both as inner lived experience. He feels that women in the West have been oppressed not so much by men as by an overdevelopment of the masculine perspective which values reason, objectivity, detachment, noninvolvement, and denigration of feeling. Although Stein may impress some as a little glib about women's needs in the outer world (equal pay, etc.), he couldn't be more correct when he states, "The Feminine in both men and women is suffering" (p. 44); "If we neglect and denigrate the soft, open, receptive feminine aspects of ourselves, our lives become progressively more rigid, empty, sterile, inert and filled with meaningless action" (p. 47).

Haddon uses a four-fold model of gender discrimination postulating a Yang masculinity with its physical correlate of the penis and a Yin masculinity with its correlate being the testicles. The Yang femininity is imaged in the exertive womb and Yin femininity in the the containing womb. These energies are to be found in various amounts and levels of development in both men and women. She also extends the metaphor to include the chromosomal level and develops the theory that the Matriarchal, Patriarchal, and Emergent Ages can be seen to be characterized by participation, differentiation, and egalitarianism, respectively. Perhaps the physical correlates may seem a bit forced at moments, Yin masculinity and testicles, for instance, but thinking about these images does lead one to ponder what may be an even deeper level of difficulty in treating the subject of gender.

At the gross physical level, where we tend to assume quite clear separation of the sexes, there is overlap and ambiguity. Because of certain genetic abnormalities, there are individuals in the world who are neither clearly chromosomally female (XX) or chromosomally male (XY). Individuals with Turner's syndrome (XO) are recognizably female but have certain physiological characteristics which mark them as special. Klinefelder syndrome individuals (XXY) are masculine in their basic physiology but develop breasts and some female secondary sexual characteristics. And then there are conditions such as testicular feminization in which the individual is born XY but lacks the receptor sites for masculine hormones and thus develops outwardly into a woman without the ability to conceive or bear children. Does it not seem possible that, at the psychological level also, our attempts to see complete separation between the sexes is doomed? What we may have here is one archetype, not two, an archetype of gender which runs from one pole of the feminine to the opposite pole of the masculine. Some of our most egregious errors in thinking and writing in this area come from an overt or convert postulation of two archetypes.

Nonetheless, this book has something in it for everyone interested in the issues of the feminine, and to a lesser degree the masculine, and not too much of any one approach — and therein lies its greatest virtue and worst failing.

Intimate Friends, Dangerous Rivals: The Turbulent Relationship between Freud and Jung
Duane Schutz. Los Angeles: Jeremy P. Tarcher, Inc., 1990. 247 pages. $18.95

Reviewed by Jeffrey Satinover.

The conflicted relationship between Freud and Jung exerts a powerful fascination over anyone who delves into it. This fascination echoes, if faintly, the fascination for the other that gripped each of the two founding fathers of the modern religious of psyche.

What is the mystery of this relationship and the source of its power? The answer must shed light not only on the importance of Jung and Freud idiosyncratically to each other, but universally to us as well. The relationship must, in other

---

Jeffrey Burke Satinover, M.D., a Jungian analyst trained in Zürich, is president of the C. G. Jung Foundation of New York and executive director of the Sterling Institute for Neuropsychiatry and Behavioral Medicine in Stamford, Connecticut.

GENDER AND SOUL IN PSYCHOTHERAPY

words, have enacted some great recurring drama, or dramas, into which we, like the spectators of all great drama, are drawn, whence we discover—ourselves, or God.

As a Jungian theory of man has become increasingly more successful in the marketplace of ideas, and as neuroscience has begun to challenge (Freudian) psychoanalysis as the dominant intellectual model for psychiatry, a number of historians and analysts, both Jungian and Freudian, have turned to reexamine the relationship between Freud and Jung. Most have done so with the sense that the personal conflict between the two giants amplified their differences and thus led each, and their followers, to a greater degree of blindness to the value of the other's vision than would otherwise have been the case.

And yet most students of the conflict between Freud and Jung have also concluded, although not necessarily for quite the same reasons, that a fatal rift between the two men was inevitable, precisely because of the mysterious dynamic that forged the relationship in the first place.

The Jung/Freud literature produces three *leitmotifs* in explanation of the ambivalent fascination that underlay the relationship. The major motifs are sometimes adduced alone, sometimes in combination, and sometimes including some additional minor motifs. The three major ones are:

1. Oedipal: Freud and Jung are classical oedipal enemies—King and Prince, Patriarch and Heir, Father and Son. The major issue between them is hence power, with both men being both extraordinarily gifted (due to chance) and extraordinarily ambitious (due to the peculiar relationship each had with his mother). A corollary motif in this scenario is the role of latent homosexuality in each man.

2. Religious: Freud and Jung enact a classic attraction and repulsion of Jew and Christian. Freud, the Jew—and as a Jew—is the older, weaker, more intellectual, mature, world-weary, rational, skeptical, and pessimistic of the two; Jung, the Christian, is younger, stronger, more imaginative, callow, enthusiastic, romantic, mystical, and optimistic.

3. Spiritual: Freud and Jung restate, and dispute, in terms and concepts appropriate to the late nineteenth–early twentieth century, the age-old question: Does man have a "soul," that is, some dimension to his existence beyond the material, which nonetheless plays a role in his quotidian existence and which must therefore be included in a complete accounting of human nature and behavior?

 Jung says, "Yes." Freud says, "No." Furthermore, says Freud to Jung, "You only say, 'Yes,' because it's the answer you so desperately want, a sign of your youth." To which Jung says, "You only say 'No,' because you are old and bitter, and have failed to find what you, too, desperately want. Furthermore, by saying 'No,' you destroy any chance of finding it."

Although I haven't seen it explicitly detailed, the literature is replete with hints that these three explanations may not be at all unrelated—on the contrary, they may be but somewhat different facets of a dynamic that has formed and driven Western civilization from the start, hence, the enormous ongoing fascination for us of this one relationship.

Unfortunately, *Intimate Friends, Dangerous Rivals* is an annotated condensation of this drama. The author provides a roughly accurate chronology of most of the major events in the protagonists' relationship. He fails to reference a number of important works on the subject by Jungians (Liliane Frey-Rohn's *From Freud to Jung*, for example) and, even though Freudian references outnumber Jungian by three to one, he misses the most important of the psychoanalytic contributors: Gedo, Winnicott, Glover, and Eissler.

As the book's title suggests, the author opts for Oedipus as the single overarching explanation of the mystery. Other than those for whom, indeed, unresolved and unacknowledged oedipal conflicts drive their current self-examination (and to be fair, I'm sure there are plenty), Jungian readers are apt to find this tedious. Even dyed-in-the wool Freudians have been experimenting of late with alternative, or at least additional, theories of motivation.

The book's value is a rough-and-ready guide for someone embarking on a thorough investigation of the relationship between Freud and Jung. Read this first and get a bird's eye view of the lay of the land. Don't be guided by the bibliography, however, as you set out on your actual journey: you'll miss too much. Use a Boolean search including both Jung and Freud at your local university library's social science database.

Goethe's Faust: Notes for a Jungian Commentary
Edward Edinger. Toronto: Inner City Books, 1990. 112 pages. $13.00

Reviewed by Josip Pasic.

With publication of Edinger's book *Goethe's Faust*, subtitled "Notes for a Jungian Commentary," one could exclaim: finally somebody wrote on a piece of literature that makes a greater appeal to the human condition than any other work of art. Jung himself was haunted by the work from his youth to the end of his life; yet he never wrote an "official" psychological commentary on it, unless it was when he wrote of his Personality #1 and Personality #2 in his posthumous opus *Memories, Dreams, Reflections*. They have an obvious similarity with Goethe's characters of Faust and Mephistopheles, thus it is possible that in some indirect way he wrote the long overdue, psychological commentary on Goethe's work.

In order to understand the intricate interrelatedness between Goethe's Faust, Jungian psychology, and Edinger's commentary, we will start with the last.

As explained by Edinger, Goethe's *Faust* is a tale of classical Jungian individuation process. The individuation process, as a dialectical interaction of the opposing forces consciousness and unconsciousness, geared itself toward the arrival of a state of wholeness and oneness with life, coinciding with Faust's striving for more and more knowledge in order to be liberated from all the bondages to reach union with life.

Josip Pasic, M.D., is a Jungian analyst and faculty member of the C. G. Jung Institute of Chicago. He conducts a private practice in Chicago and Evanston, Ill.

To explicate somewhat more specifically Edinger's premise, one could say that in Part One, Faust, as the representative of human consciousness, strives to confront the unconscious as it is projected onto the world around him; and in Part Two, Faust confronts the unconscious by actually descending into the unconscious. Not unlike an old alchemical manuscript, the chapters of Edinger's commentary take the reader through the wealth of the mytho-poetic material in an attempt to capture the psychological meaning of the Faust story, of Jung's story, of our story.

It is rather obvious from Edinger's commentary that Faust and Mephisto are seen as two arch-psychological opposites (complements) among other innumerable opposites which are drawn into the dialectical play by Mephisto and Faust.

To do full justice to Goethe's Faust, I could not help seeing this basic premise to be correct; yet I had the persistant conviction of something essential being omitted. This sense of incompleteness revealed itself in the complexity of a question — "While Mephistopheles and Faust were dialectical counterparts on a certain level, could it be that on a more essential level they were not counterparts at all?"

What if Mephisto only placates, deliberately playing into the Faustian dialectical attitude of living through the movement of opposites, only to enable Faust eventually to see for himself its utter futility! It cannot be emphasized enough that the purpose of these questions is not to minimize Edinger's premise but rather expand its scope. In order to better understand the expanded premise — that Goethe's Faust is and is not a dialectical, developmental process — one must explore the very nature of human consciousness. That Edinger's work is a psychological commentary is altogether another reason for seeing Faust and Mephisto as well as all others, even if only episodal characters, as aspects of that consciousness.

Consciousness, throughout this review, is meant to be the totality of consciousness. It is rather obvious that Faust is the aspect of consciousness that insists on assuring the *very* propagation of itself. Faust's striving in consciousness is presented as longing for more and more knowledge and stands for psychological development, psychological becoming. Could it be that Mephisto is the aspect of consciousness that insists essentially on negation, destruction, and corrosion of itself, only superficially seen as Faust's counterpart, his shadow promoting dialectical unfoldment of consciousness?

It is interesting to suspect that consciousness, in general, as a network of psychological knowing, has built into itself both of these attitudes (or mechanisms), one insisting on building more and more "order," the other tending to corrode that order. While the first builds order through accumulation of more and more psychological knowing, hoping to achieve more and more psychological security, the other, triggered at certain points of progression of that "orderliness" of consciousness, is a fundamentally different tendency, a tendency to dissolve orderliness, creating disturbance, a feeling of insecurity.

Edinger's entire commentary is a rich example of that aspect of consciousness which insists on its progression through the striving for a *coniunctio* with the various images of the unconscious in order to achieve orderliness. The ego, as the center of that consciousness metaphorically represented by Faust, strives to unite with the unconscious as the various shadow figures such as Mephisto and Earth Spirit, a string of feminine images known in Jungian psychology as the four stages of anima, as well as with innumerable other images emulating mythical personages of classical Greece and the Orient.

Is it possible that orderliness rendered by gaining more and more consciousness on the account of the so-called unconsciousness is not at all an orderliness but rather a quasi-orderliness, invented through the inevitable projection of the accumulated conscious and unconscious knowledge?

Can one furthermore say that this man-made orderliness always carries a quality of discontent, never being quite true orderliness?

If Mephisto were only a "dynamic factor" (p. 18) in Faust's tendency to individuate, as claimed by Edinger, then there would be no way out of this persistent discontent. But is it possible that Mephisto is also essentially the urge to entropy in our consciousness, a tendency to dissolve the whole developmental process toward seeming orderliness, the sheer negation of it in order to come upon the void? By this is not meant the void of life, which is a nihilistic position, but rather a void of that quasi-orderliness necessary for true natural orderliness of life to break out. Orderliness, since not invented by our consciousness nor made by anybody, by being simply true, does not urge more and more orderliness and therefore does not trigger the familiar agitation of the developmental process.

Goethe, as well as Edinger, was of the deep conviction that life was a series of uninterrupted metamorphoses of the universe, the Faustian individuation process being an aspect of it.

But later on in his life, all of these hopes placed in the developmental abilities of consciousness with all its monads and forms (archetypes) as factors of metamorphoses seemed vain. If he looked back, be it to the actual history of humanity or to psychological history as inner development, all that picturesque and confused abyss we so confidently hold onto, trust, and draw from—the past—he would repeat Mephistopheles' words:

> Past! A stupid word, Why past? Past and simply not, exactly the same thing. What use to us is eternal creative effort—if not merely to obliterate what has been created? It is past. What meaning has this statement? It is the same as if the thing had never been, and yet it runs around in a circle as if it existed. I should prefer the eternally empty. (Bennett 1986, p. 37)

These words of Mephistopheles are an answer to the Lemurs' mythical undertakers' exclamation upon Faust's sudden death: "It is past," or, in other translations, "It is all over," "All is over," "It is finished." In order to understand these seminal words poignantly pointing at the essence of Goethe's Faust as well as to understand that aspect of Mephisto not dealt with in commentary, it is of utmost importance to focus on their accurate meaning as well as bring them closer to our psychological vocabulary.

When the Lemurs say, "It is all over," "It is past," they are referring to the ending of Faust's life. Why is the Lemurs' simple, logical statement—that with one's death one's life is over—met with Mephisto's vehement reaction of negation? What may be simple for us readers, as well as for the Lemurs, may not be so simple for a far more complex and thoughtful character like Mephisto. Mephisto's final utterance may be the single most significant one in the entire work. When he speaks of "past" with its "eternally creative effort," he speaks of human consciousness. Human consciousness as knowledge, as network of abstractions essentially based on memories of the personal as well as the collective nature—all that being psychological time—obstructs and obliterates the living life, the creation which nobody created and which is not of time.

As long as consciousness, be it as past or as past stretched into the present or even as an extension of itself, further misrepresentating itself as a future creating an illusion of psychological time, persists, it will, instead of coming upon that authentic life, obstruct it, elude it.

The statement that Faust's life is over is a farce because his entanglement in the problems of consciousness is the equivalent of not living.

In order not to see Mephisto's/Goethe's statement as nihilistic or cynical, one ought to explore it further by asking a fundamental question: What does it mean to be conscious, and what is its modus operandi? The meaning and its modus operandi are closely related to the most essential quality of consciousness, namely, its being limited and liminal in its very nature.

By the very virtue of this limitation, the mere presence of consciousness produces three fundamental phenomena, or one may say, three most basic archetypal situations. They are isolation, projection, and division. Isolation, as a consequence of the liminality of consciousness, produces a sense of loneliness and anguish; the same limiting quality of the consciousness is bound to project itself, creating illusion and misperception; and by being divisive, conflict and strife is created.

Innumerable variations of these three basic phenomena are responsible for all psychological problems. If we further understand that not only consciousness is bound to produce these three phenomena, but that the unconsciousness is equally bound to produce them, then we can see the utter futility of the individuation process. Can one say then, contrary to the Edinger's premise, that Goethe's *Faust* is *not* a tale neither for it nor against it, but rather a tale about the inevitability of undergoing the process of individuation in order for its basic fallacy to be revealed? But we, together with Faust, often do not know that as a fact. For Faust, as well as for us, the blinding factor preventing us from seeing the fallacy of a developmental psychological attitude hides in a deeply rooted conviction that consciousness is fundamentally different from the unconscious.

The notion of the difference between consciousness and the unconscious turns upon the further belief that consciousness, with its inevitable attitude of onesidedness, is more or less seen as a problem and unconsciousness, being supposedly fundamentally different from consciousness, is seen as a creative solution.

If these deeply rooted convictions did not exist, could the dialectical process based on the problem/solution as conscious/unconscious movement even be possible? Mephisto seems to be the only one to see the full scope of the ground responsible for the psychological problem. He clearly thrives on the insight that the totality of human consciousness is the problem. He is the only one to see the arbitrary error of the division into consciousness and seemingly fundamentally different unconscious. The unconscious, not unlike consciousness generating inevitably the problems of isolation, projection, and division, can no more solve these same problems than blood can wash blood. Like a Zen master rather than a Christian devil, Mephisto, in a roundabout way, is asking, Can psyche as the totality of human consciousness ever heal itself? His answer is a riddle, a mystery amplified by a mystery not unlike a Zen koan demanding nothing less than self-discovery. Mephisto demands the same rigor from Faust as he does from the readers and from himself—the necessity of the psychological void for the insight into the riddle to take place. Only in that void, in the utter stillness of the noise of our busy consciousness, does the truth of the riddle reveal itself as the most obvious fact: consciousness, the fragmenting agency, can never produce wholeness. The state of wholeness in our lives, so longed for by Faust, can only happen in the undoing of the intricate network of knowing. That *negation*, the total absence of psychological knowing, enables the flowering of life in its nameless yet ever-present way. The original meaning of the Greek word *psyche*, meaning "breath," is emulated in that negation; the genuine sense of psyche is as "no-thing" instead of the accustomed sense of "some-thing."

Speaking and acting out of that void, the psyche in its true sense is an action, not a reaction, is an "acting now," not a reaction which is a misrepresented action distorted through the layers of personal and collective conditioning we call human consciousness.

To look at *Faust* from a cultural, archetypal perspective, one may say the dynamic progression of the character Faust is an example of a progression of a typical hero myth. Mephistopheles, an infinitely more complex phenomenon, as well as being a certain definitive character, participates as a dynamizing factor, as goader and prodder in the hero-myth affairs of the Faustian journey. To this extent, we can agree with Edinger that Goethe's whole masterpiece is nothing more than a brilliantly elaborated literary example of the hero myth. When taking into account the most essential quality of Mephisto, namely his fundamental thriving on void (void resulting out of the insight into the whole fallacy of the psychological progression of the hero-myth movement), one may say that Mephisto's unfoldment is as well an unfoldment of a hero myth, yet a hero myth that grew aware of its own fallaciousness. In that insight, collapse takes place, assured by one's own pyre, set by oneself, dissolving oneself without any regret in flames, leaving as little as ashes. In that void, a divine phoenix is born, nothing less than a pristine life unfettered and untethered by any conditions of psychic determinism—this announcing Mephisto's story, a story a la phoenix, Mephisto's myth par excellance.

The only good reason for Mephisto, epitome of void and negation of personality, to acquire a particular personality carefully appropriated to the circumstances of time and people, Faust in particular, was to communicate with Faust. For Faust, essentially definitive personality could only establish a relationship with Mephisto as long as Mephisto himself was a personality. When Mephisto spoke from his true essence, namely the void, Faust could not relate to him.

Mephisto's appropriation of a certain personality was, then, only a necessary evil. Only when an equal to Faust, only when appearing as a particular personality, could Mephisto be listened to. Hoping that eventually an understanding into the very nature of the personality as an obstructive psychological factor would take place, ultimately resulting in its negation—the psychological void—Mephisto became a particular character.

Well known to all of us is the sense of being persistently caught in the psychological developmental process which never ends, which only modifies psychological problems, thus assuring their chronic persistency. It is Mephisto's negation of that whole dialectical movement of consciousness, instead of the entanglement in it, that is so crucial and most enlightening for total understanding of Goethe's *Faust*, and this was not dealt with in Edinger's commentary.

Equivalent to the Mephistophelian attitude is Jung's well-known treatment of Personality #2, which is actually not a personality at all, but rather a negation of Personality #1, the personality that thrives on self-known identities, definitions, and boundaries. A passage from *Memories, Dreams, Reflections* depicts the pure phenomenology of Personality #2, a negation of any trace of personality enabling a pure presence of life: "At times I feel as if I am spread out over the landscape and inside things, and am myself living in every tree, in the splashing of the waves, in the clouds, and in the animals that come and go, in the procession of the seasons" (Jung 1965, p. 225).

It is from the psychological void Jung called Personality #2 that he spoke when he claimed that ego is not a real thing, and "I don't believe such a center (as the self) exists," and "individuation is not that you become an ego, you would then be an individualist. An individualist is a person who did not succeed in individuation—this person is a distilled egotist. Individuation is becoming that which is not the ego . . . What you are not . . . you feel as if you were a stranger" (Serrano 1959, p. 50; Jung 1975, p. 3).

So familiar to Goethe as well as to Jung was that true unconscious, ensuing from undoing of the known, the consciousness, the a priori ground of human conditioning that has been established through the millenia. Mephisto persistently insisted upon that unknowing, and Faust resisted it with all his might. Of that true unconscious, fundamentally different from what we usually call, in the field of psychology, "unconscious," Jung wrote also, "The concept of the unconscious posits nothing; it designates only my unknowing" (Adler and Jaffé 1973, p. 44).

At the end of this brief review, could we accept, instead of an *either-or* exclusivistic position, meaning Goethe's *Faust* is a story of the individuation process or it is not a story of the individuation process, the more inclusivistic and so participatory position of *either and or*, meaning it is and it is not a story of the individuation process.

To make even more clear the new perspective added to Edinger's interpretation of the work, can one dare paraphrase the above-mentioned koanlike riddle of Mephisto's/Goethe's statement with the risk of Sphinx turning us into stone? Upon Faust's death, when everything, so it seemed to the Lemurs, was over, Mephisto, by calling the Lemurs' statement stupid, finally revealed the whole truth of the so-called Faustian way. The truth being, how can Faust's life, meaning living in a true sense, be over if it did not even happen? For something to be over, to end, to die, it must first of all happen, actually exist.

Both Goethe and Jung in their later years saw the fundamental difference between the necessity of being individual and the process of coming upon it, namely the individuation process. That state of undividedness and supposed process by which one is to come upon it are not only different but actually a contradiction in terms. The individuation process as a movement of consciousness, as a basically limited and inevitably divisive phenomenon, can only breed division and fragmentation. The state of wholeness, undividedness, can obviously then not happen through any psychological process of the consciousness. It can only happen when the movement of the totality of consciousness stops.

When Goethe subtitles his masterpiece a tragedy, he was referring to this clash between the consciousness, that psychological knowledge everlastingly fragmenting, divisive, the wrong tool with which to come upon wholeness and the presence of wholeness. The ending of that consciousness, the void, is the wholeness that does not need any tool.

References

Adler, G., and Jaffé, A., ed. 1973. *C. G. Jung Letters, Vol. 1:1906–1950*. Princeton, N.J.: Princeton University Press.

Bennett, B. 1986. *Goethe's Theory of Poetry*. Ithaca, N.Y.: Cornell University Press.

Jung, C. G. 1965. *Memories, Dreams, Reflections*. New York: Vintage Books.

———. 1975. Psychological commentary on Kundalini yoga. *Spring*.

Serrano, M. 1959. *C. G. Jung and Herman Hesse: A Record of Two Friendships*. Garden City, N.Y.: Doubleday.

The Living Psyche: A Jungian Analysis in Pictures
Edward Edinger. Wilmette, Ill.: Chiron, 1990. 213 pages. $19.95

Reviewed by Diane Martin.

I found this newest book by Edward Edinger, champion and chief lineage carrier of the classical Jungian method, to be representative of what I consider both the best and most problematic from that approach. In keeping with Jung's role as a scientific empiricist, this book stands as a document—of visual representation of psychic processes, of the diagnostic capacity in imagery, and of the providing power of the dream to transit the ego into the felt numinous fields of archetypal reality.

This book clearly demonstrates the primacy of an initiatory understanding of image to any in-depth grasp of the work of the psyche toward self-regulation and healing. It delineates key processes such as 1) ascent/descent cycling, 2) differentiation of the anima out of the Great Mother, 3) gestaltic appropriation of the archetypal field by the historical complex, 4) structural enhancements due to sufficient shadow work. These are all psychic processes that do not lend themselves to verbal explanation.

There is further value in this book as a teaching vehicle for trainees, students of Jung and carriers of modern culture. We need accessible, well-formatted books such as this (dream painting on one side of the page, dreamer's description and analyst's comment on the other) in order to communicate our Way, its method of art and discipline, and its unique contribution. Jung's place in twentieth-century science and culture is not where it should be and that fact presents us with an ongoing teaching responsibility. Jung himself, of course, took with utmost seriousness the task of amalgamating distillations from ancient wisdom systems and modern psychoanalysis into an individual and collective healing mode. His sense of cure was based on the ego's continual education about and direct entering into the unconscious.

Even though it was Freud who first labeled dreams as constituting the "royal road to the unconscious," modern Freudians in their current phase of privileging

---

Diane Martin, Ph.D., is a clinical psychologist and Jungian analyst who conducts a private practice in Milwaukee and Chicago. She is also a teacher of Zen Buddhism.

certain interests and diminishing others, seem to have relegated the dream to a position of minor concern and discourse. More than ever, Jungians thus become primary "keepers of the mysteries" of the world of the dream. We see dreams simultaneously as conduits to the wisdom of the unconscious and as the mediating region in which the necessary self-healing work of returning repressed contents to consciousness occurs.

As Jungians, our living work is to constellate in order to secure a permanent structural realignment. This restructured ego-Self alignment constitutes the religious function of the psyche. Therefore our work is primarily carried through the descriptive, compensatory, and synthesizing functions of the symbolic mode. This book stands simultaneously as a scientific document, a statement of creed and method, and a presentation of ritualistic coherence. My own personhood and professional working style—a basic orientation to and from the image and dream, a positive religious complex, and profound gratitude to Jung—all contribute to a general resonance and respect for Edinger's latest book and message.

When I turn from this position of appreciative awareness to other modes of perception, however, I find that I have serious questions to address to this book. Specifically, it is the historian, the general (as opposed to sect-contained) psychoanalyst, and the feminist theologian in me that have concerns. To begin with, I do not consider this a state-of-the-art book. Rather I consider it a lineage homage book. As such it contains its own set of internal contradictions and complexes that are part of the Jungian tradition. In terms of state-of-the-art, I find this book sorely lacking in transference/countertransference awareness and input. One could argue that this was not the subject matter of the book nor its stated intent; but it has become (nearly one hundred years after the inception of the psychoanalytic field) considered constituent to any analytic approach to include this all-important dimension.

I consider Edinger himself to be carrying an unresolved identification with an idealized Jung. Continually while reading his interpretations, I get the feeling that the "living psyche" processes of the analysand are being usurped and appropriated in order to serve as a springboard to free associate to Jung's own process. In the course of the book is built up a not-so-hidden-assumption of a correspondence between dreamer's symbol, analyst's interpretation, and Jung's thought and between sources and Christ as godhead. In my opinion, this results in a three-way, unresolved, unanalyzed father/son confabulation between son analysand and father analyst, son analyst and father Jung, and son Christ and father God.

The theological underpinnings of the book are apparent from the beginning. The first presenting dream is of Christ's severed head on the stage of the Metropolitan Opera. Edinger interprets this image as showing that the patient was unconsciously participating in Jung's all-important concern with the decline of Christianity. I, on the other hand, would have noted analytically that here was Christ's head without a body! Resonating to Hillman, I would say: stay more within the image itself. It is, of course, commonplace or epidemic for followers of a Way to reify backwards in time from contemporary data to the particulars of the founder of the sect's individuation milestones.

Edinger goes on throughout the book to repeat his (and Jung's) preference for a "corpus astrale" type of theology of a general, phallocentric kind. It is assumed, for example, that the natural instincts and the body are the expectable, sacrificial payment for entry into the life of the spirit. This collective fantasy has controlled the life of organized religions worldwide for millenia, but this historical fact constitutes no absolute. I consider Nature to be spiritual in its own right and subscribe to a spirituality that has no such hydraulic as leverage into spiritual participation or transformation.

I also was troubled as a Jungian by what I considered the selective inattention to issues of the "feminine" in the book. Sorely absent were meaningful comments on sexuality, human relations, community, and what would be considered "descent to the goddess" types of attitudinal containment. To cite one example: in the final, supposedly resolved dream that is presented, the dreamer images as the collective an ocean liner that he associates to both the *Titanic* and the Ship of Fools—and Edinger leaves this unanalyzed. This is resolved conflictual material? Again we have the conventional and stereotypic image of the lone hero in his self-contained boat heading out into the dark night. In the classical sense, I consider this material to be caught in personal complex, one-sided and ego navigating—certainly not an alchemical ending to an analysis.

We share with Freudians a corpus of belief in the ever-present and necessary work of liberation from first half of life psychology, i.e., the uroboric repetition compulsion of complexes, parent/child, imago-saturated ego identifications, and the general self-healing work of returning repressed unconscious contents to consciousness. As Jungians, we relate to the unconscious as a repository of consciousness and source of wisdom acting primarily through a liberated symbolic function.

In an age which has reduced dreams to REM sleep derivatives, day residues, coping strategies, and stimuli bombardment regulators, it is of utmost import that we stand with Edinger as carriers of understanding of the primacy of dreams in human life and their capacity to transcend developmentally the triple time trajectory of past, present, and future. For this reason, it is of particular importance not to bracket the dream but to include it in an interpenetrative understanding of other key psychic processes. This view brings up certain issues for us as Jungians.

In our preference for registries of timelessness do we avoid immersion in content issues and formative contexts of our contemporary historical period? As analysts do we know ourselves as knowing subjects and attempt to protect our analysands from the force-fields of our eroticized attachments and dissociative aversions? Have we struggled enough with our own collective transference to Jung?

Jung's definitive framework of humans as hermeneutic image-makers and image-receivers ties in with his metapsychological concerns both for the issues of wholeness and the responsibilities of co-creation. It is in the spirit of those concerns that this review is written.

Jung, Jungians and Homosexuality
Robert H. Hopcke. Boston: Shambala, 1989. 208 pages. $19.95

Reviewed by Jonathan J. Goldberg.

Hopcke's title clearly demonstrates the scope of the first two-thirds of the book: a critical review of what the literature of analytical psychology has had to say on the subject of homosexuality, primarily in the male. The last third of the book represents an attempt on the author's part to offer a theoretical approach to the question of sexual object choice. His orderly presentation of the references to homosexuality by Jung and his followers offers a worthwhile summary, although the structure and tone regrettably retain too much of the thesis jargon out of which the book grew. The first part can certainly be recommended as a convenient guide for researchers. The section of his work devoted to his own theory has at least the merit of raising important questions.

Unfortunately, the book has a pervasive flaw. I do not wish to be overly critical of this central shortcoming. The youthful enthusiasm of the writer (he finished the writing while still in his twenties) is part of the book's appeal, and there is material here for a larger work. Yet his failure to differentiate statistical from archetypal thinking causes him to vacillate between the concrete and symbolic poles, finally not standing anywhere. At its worst, when he argues as if archetypal changes can be derived from sources like Kinsey's rating scales of sexual habits, his perspective becomes mere wordplay.

Let me illustrate. Early in Chapter 1, Hopcke says, drawing on Kinsey's research:

if over a third of the American male population has engaged in homosexual behavior as adults, one is hardly justified in seeing such prevalent behavior as abnormal—sexually, statistically, or psychologically. (p. 4)

He continues:

The net effect of both Kinsey's studies and the *APA*'s removal of any form of homosexuality as a mental disorder is to depathologize homosexuality once and for all and therefore irrevocably change psychological thinking on the nature of this form of human sexual behavior. (p. 5)

The problem in paralleling "sexually, statistically, and psychologically" is that the third is qualitatively different from the first two. Obviously, from the perspective of a statistically based norm, nothing that occurs frequently can be viewed as deviant. Psychologically, however, where normalcy is conceived of in relation to a developmental or structural model of the psyche, statistical data are beside the point. When we evaluate psychologically, we do so by considering how close some-

---

Jonathan Goldberg is a graduate of the C. G. Jung Foundation of New York and conducts a private practice in New York City.

© 1992 by Chiron Publications.

one comes to a given level of development, with a specific thinker's theory defining the norm. Similarly, the argument that a reclassification by the *APA* "depathologizes homosexuality once and for all" is simply ridiculous. By this reasoning, there could have been no war against the Jews, since in many countries Jews had been assimilated to full citizenship. Hopcke attempts to bypass the truth that social norms change constantly, and that what the activism of the civil and minority rights movement produced in the 1960s and 1970s could be radically altered in a future political climate. Or is he naive enough not to consider the uproar that would have accompanied the *APA* reclassification had AIDS struck fifteen years earlier—assuming that a move to reclassify would even have had credence under those conditions?

Later, he concludes:

> A truly useful theory of sexual orientation would go beyond the various forms of sexual orientation and provide an archetypally based way of understanding the full range and psychological import of the Kinsey scale. . . . Second, a Jungian theory would need to be firmly tied to Jung's most far-reaching discovery, the archetypes of the collective unconscious. (p. 130)

Again, Hopcke vainly tries to combine under one heading two entirely separate ideas. The quantitative behavioral aspect of the former deals with what people literally do; the latter is concerned with the teleological aim of behavior conceived within an individuation pattern. To treat the numbers on a rating scale as psychologically relevant is to discount the archetypal rather than include it. He could be no more misguided if he were weighing apples alongside mountains, thinking the mountains were oranges.

These errors in juxtaposing dissimilars are too extreme to come from oversight. They stem, I think, from Hopcke's own bias, according to which he views favorably any material that acknowledges the normalcy of homosexuality, celebrates concretely lived homosexuality, and sees the patterns of wholeness within the homosexual path, while he ridicules any contrary position as antiquated and misguided. He writes as a gay activist, purporting to use a scholar's objectivity. He would have done well to own this approach, making it conscious to the reader and perhaps also to himself. By failing to do so, he alternately sounds arbitrary, capricious, or doctrinaire in his positions.

Had Hopcke been concerned to open discussion of sexual orientation with the archetypes as ground, he would have had to proceed differently. Even the word *homosexuality* used to describe a sexual orientation is, according to the *OED*, only a hundred years old. Similarly, the idea that the orientation of desire is central to a person's identity—as seen by himself and by others—is a distinctly modern notion that would have been incomprehensible, for example, to the ancient Greeks.

The reason that sexual activity and the experience of sexual desire alter in diverse social and historical contexts has to do with widely varying presuppositions as to the purpose of sexuality. *We* may take for granted that—in addition to its reproductive function—sexual expression is about personal fulfillment and counts among our most deeply private experiences. This is why, for example, we view ourselves within a *Weltanschauung* where choice of sexual lifestyle becomes analogous to religious and political preference. The sacredness of the freedom to go to bed with whomever you want is to be defended in a manner analogous to one's right to choose a place of worship: the multiplicity of individual choices left to unfold unfettered furthers the vitality of the collective.

Viewing the freedom to live one's private life as one wishes as a supreme value implies a society like our own, which bifurcates the private and public spheres. It is certainly cause for celebration that at least segments of our culture have become fully able to validate the lives of people who happen also to be homosexual; however, the party takes place in the fields of sociology and morals, not in the territory of depth psychology.

Depth psychological and cross-cultural studies of sexuality converge where the teleology of sexual behavior is at issue. The ancient Greeks appear to have had little interest in who went to bed with whom but an almost obsessive concern with who did the penetrating. The focus derives from their understanding that the key to full citizenship included the ability to dominate those of lesser rank, which for adult males meant women, slaves, and boys. Sex, for them, was a metaphor of status, much as for us status is a determiner of what is likely to be available to you sexually. Sex can have no goal beyond itself in our culture because our culture has no aim beyond providing the opportunity for personal satisfaction as broadly as possible.

In his conclusion (pp. 187ff), Hopcke does recognize archetypal complexity where mythological images are concerned, leading the reader to hope that his first book may have a more substantial sequel. Even a casual observer of homosexual men will note distinct patterns of desire, which remain constant in essence and persistent over time: the man who is only attracted to younger or older men; the man compulsively in search of the erect phallus of the largest size; the man who wants to be with his double; the light man drawn to the dark or the dark to the light; the man who would enact dominance or being dominated; the man who can do anything with anyone sexually *once* (as long as the other is a pure fantasy object)—all these patterns have their mythological parallels. A study of these parallels would show a great deal about the life of certain archetypal images in the contemporary world.

Should Hopcke proceed to further exploration of myth in modern dress— freed of the task which he has here undertaken of discrediting orthodox heterosexist Jungian assumptions—he would have to grapple with issues of developmental psychology. Jung, Neumann, Layard, Jacobi, and other contributors in this field approach homosexuality as they do through their presuppositions about stages of personal development. Does Hopcke subscribe to the model of shadow integration and anima development at the heart of classical Jungian thought? Is anima development furthered by monogamy or is it equally compatible with traditional patterns of gay male promiscuity? What stories of the gods and heroes are we to turn to for enlightenment?

In summary, *Jung, Jungians and Homosexuality* is a book full of Jungian language and concepts but its value is sociological rather than psychological, polemical rather than theoretical, descriptive rather than archetypal. It is the work of a therapist, counselor, and skillful recorder of the current scene, not that of a seasoned analyst.

Sunset at Ghost Ranch

Bruce Noble

A meadowlark trills the death of this day.
From atop her pole she surveys the dying domain
commenting upon the doings of bird life
and how it feels to watch its end.
There is no note of sadness on her lips
held tightly against last throaty breaths
calling daughters to transcendent perches
hearing Hindu murmurs, gifts of motherly love
from part to part, giving up preciousness
for the sake of passing the everlasting mantle
of womanhood.
Hear this our prayer,
now,
and at the last breath of day.

June 3, 1990

SPRING 51–1991

A Journal of Archetype and Culture

Edited by Charles Boer, Ross Miller, and James Hillman

Order Your Copy of This Issue Now

Spring Publications • P.O. Box 222069 • Dallas, TX 75222

Enclose payment: $12.50 per copy, plus (in U.S.A.) $2.25 shipping for first book, $.50 each additional book; (Canada) $2.50 first book, $.75 each additional; (all other countries) $3.00 first book, $.75 each copy thereafter. Please write for library, institution, and resale terms.

Harvest

Editor: *Joel Ryce-Menuhin*
Deputy Editor: *Renos Papadopoulos*

Harvest has wide-ranging interests - all enriched by Jungian thought and ideas. Harvest No. 37 for 1991, to appear in September, will include the following papers

BOOK REVIEWS *edited by Renos Papadopoulos*. Some of the books reviewed:

ISSN No. 0266 - 4771

ORDER FORM

Price with postage & packing £12.50 sterling, $25 USA. Also limited number of past issues, from No.30 for 1984 onwards, obtainable from Harvest Administration, 37 York Street Chambers, 68-72 York Street, London W1H 1DE Tel: 071-724 5661

NAME..

ADDRESS..

....

....

Please make cheques payable to APC (Harvest)